HAN
The story

# HAND OF STEEL

## The story of the Commandos

RUPERT BUTLER

THE SHERIDAN
BOOK COMPANY

This edition published in 1994 by
The Sheridan Book Company

First published by Hamlyn Paperbacks 1980

Arrow edition 1986
Random House, 20 Vauxhall Bridge Road, London SW1V 2SA



Printed and bound in Great Britain by
Cox & Wyman Ltd, Reading, Berkshire

ISBN 1–85501–559–5

# ACKNOWLEDGEMENTS

In preparing this book I owe a very special debt to Mr Henry Brown MBE of the Wartime Commandos' Old Comrades Association who supplied much useful material, answered countless questions and read the final manuscript. It was due to Mr Brown that I was able to meet many Commandos and record their experiences. These former wearers of the green beret were Ken Phillott, Charles Mellows, William Bradley, Harry Roberts, Joe Molloy, Richard Bradley MM, Bill Nash, Jake Ure, John Smale, Tim Regan, Jack Scantlebury MM, Geoffrey Wilson and Bill Cochrane. A particular word of thanks is due to Lieutenant-Colonel Stuart Chant-Sempill, OBE, MC (formerly Stuart Chant) who not only gave me a rich account of St Nazaire but checked the relevant passages for accuracy. Material from a broadcast on the first Lofoten raid held by the Department of Sound Records at the Imperial War Museum is reproduced by kind permission of the BBC. Other acknowledgements are due to Mr Sidney Salomon of the Ranger Battalions Association World War II and his members Alex Szima, Lou Lisko and James Altieri. The latter allowed me to draw on material from his book *The Spearheaders* (Bobbs-Merrill, 1960). Ranger material was also supplied by Terence Macartney-Filgate of the Canadian Broadcasting Corporation. Valuable research and assistance have been given by the Imperial War Museum, William Fowler, James Ladd and Bruce Quarrie.

'There comes from time to time a hand of steel
which plucks the German sentries from their posts.'

*Winston Churchill, 1942*

# 1

In his snug office on the Casquet lighthouse west of Alderney in the Channel Islands, Chief Mate Munte was finishing the same routine paperwork that he had carried out daily since his Nazi masters had seized the islands in July 1940.

The former stoker in the German navy was content with his lot. The Channel Islands were considered something of a soft number and the last two years had passed pleasantly enough. But on this particular night, the silence was broken by the click of a door opening softly. Munte swung round in his chair and immediately felt his bowels turn to water. The two men who were leaning against the door had blackened faces. They were wearing crumpled khaki uniforms and a stream of water was coursing down their trousers and forming a small pool on the floor. But Munte's attention was riveted on the two pistols levelled at him by his sinister visitors.

The whole scene suddenly blurred into grey nothingness as he pitched forward in a dead faint.

One of the men stepped towards Munte; the palm of his hand crashed into the German's face. When he saw the colour flooding back, he and his companion seized the prisoner and frogmarched him out of the lighthouse to a small boat which was bobbing in turbulent waters.

Munte noticed that six of his colleagues had been taken in the same way: the wireless operator and the lighthouse guards. Clad in their pyjamas, they looked decidedly sheepish.

The journey in the boat took six storm-tossed hours, during which Munte lay wishing that he could die. By four in the morning, all the Germans were profoundly thankful to be in warm clothes and prisoners of war in England.

These men had been prised from their seemingly comfortable billet by the steel hand of the British Commandos.

Successful raids such as these increased as the grim years wore on in those countries under the Nazi heel. But the role of the Commandos was far more sophisticated than merely snatching away lighthouse keepers.

By 1942, the year that the war ended for Chief Mate Munte, there was a general feeling that the Germans were trapped hopelessly in Russia.

But it had been a very different story in the summer of 1940.

In under two months, the unthinkable had become reality; the German Panzers had knifed through Denmark, Norway, Holland and Belgium. In Paris, confidential documents were being burnt in the gardens of the British Embassy. Hitler held the Channel ports and his armies, like a coiled spring, threatened the British south coast.

On the top floor study of a seventeenth-century house in London's Stratton Street, a man sat far into the night brooding over a pile of papers. Lieutenant-Colonel Dudley Clarke, a professional soldier of more than twenty years' experience, currently Military Assistant to the Chief of the General Staff, recalled the recent words of Winston Churchill on the withdrawal of troops from Dunkirk '... out of the jaws of death and shame, to their native land and to the tasks which lie immediately ahead.'

As rhetoric, Clarke reflected, it was irreproachable. But the facts were grim nonetheless. The men who decamped from the beaches of Dunkirk had neither arms nor ammunition. For weeks, perhaps months, they would be a total loss as fighting troops. There would be inevitable despondency, destroying public and service morale alike.

Clarke was a soldier with a strong sense of history, and as he crouched at his desk he began searching for precedents.

Had things ever looked so black for the nation before? Clarke remembered reading how beleagured Spain in the Peninsula War had tried to improve a hopeless situation through guerrilla warfare – the first of the modern resistance movements. But it was what he had heard of the Boer War which really gripped Clarke's imagination.

He had been born in the Transvaal just before war broke out. His father was one of the young men who rode out to meet Dr Jameson, who had been intent on overthrowing the Boer government of Paul Kruger. By the end of 1900, the Boer army was defeated and the whole of South Africa conquered. Peace seemed assured; but the enemy was stubborn. For two years, the fighting went on. Loosely organized bands of horsemen – the Boer Commandos – proved of considerable nuisance value to a quarter of a million British troops.

*Commandos* ... Clarke seized a single sheet of Stratton Street writing paper and scribbled far into the night.

It may have been understandable tiredness, but next morning Clarke sensed a leaden despondency hanging over his office. Even more alarming, it seemed to have spread to the normally unflappable General Dill. The Chief of the Imperial General Staff had been talking to some of the Dunkirk survivors; the psychological consequences of their eviction had profoundly depressed him.

'We've simply got to find a way to get the offensive spirit back into the army,' he declared. Right on cue, Dudley Clarke produced the notes from the night before and the CIGS began visibly to brighten.

What Clarke outlined was the formation of specially trained troops of much higher mobility than the enemy. The aim would be to concentrate at the best point of attack quicker than the defenders could mass – and then to disengage and run for it before the enemy could bring up superior strength. In this sort of lightning war, wasteful casualties could be avoided and a force at a high peak of freshness would always be ready for the next day's scrap.

Clarke pointed out : 'The Boers had relied upon seasoned local horses and their independence of supply columns and baggage trains. That had meant mobility. Well, the British had the sea, traditional element of the race, and there at least they should have mobility superior to any German.'

Independence? Imagine specially trained British troops shorn of heavy equipment and echelons of supply, stripped for quick action, ready to live off the land for the short time that an action lasted.

Dill moved fast. Within twenty-four hours, Winston Churchill and the Cabinet were listening to a crisp, literate digest of Dudley Clarke's scribbles.

An *independent* sort of army? There were murmurs of dissent and incredulity. But none of these mattered compared to the pronouncements of the bulky figure at the head of the table. The Prime Minister rumbled: 'A decision will be made in two days.'

And it was – accompanied by a positive avalanche of memoranda, all of it headed Prime Minister and all of it full of pointed questions fired like deadly salvoes at Dill and Clarke.

On 18 June 1940, Churchill was writing: 'What are the ideas of the C-in-C Home Forces about "Storm Troops" or "Leopards" drawn from existing units, ready to spring at the throat of any small landings or descents?' The question did not require an answer; the Prime Minister had already made up his mind that the 'Storm Troops' would exist come what may. Blandly ignoring the doubts – and there were many – Churchill sailed on: 'These officers and men should be armed with the latest equipment, tommy guns, grenades etc., and should be given great facilities in motor-cycles and armoured cars.'

An official War Office handbook later went into more detail:

'The primary mission of the Commandos is to carry out raids and for that purpose they are to be specially and vigorously trained. Raiding parties may vary in size from a small reconnaissance group to a complete Commando troop or even a large force, and every raid will aim to destroy enemy installations and to obtain information.'

The document then went on to define what were seen at that time as 'secondary missions'. These were:

'1) to act as an élite or shock-assault brigade to seize and hold a bridgehead for covering a landing in force and 2) to provide specially trained covering forces for any operation ...'

In fact, such 'secondary missions' eventually formed an integral part of Commando operations as a whole. But that lay in the future.

Churchillian rhetoric grew progressively more purple. The Commando ideal seized the vivid imagination of the Prime Minister, who was soon relishing 'a trail of German corpses' being left along the entire Nazi-occupied European coastline.

This was echoed by the War Office, whose handbook was admirably concise: 'The idea that no type of operation is unusual is inculcated into the men. At a moment's notice, they should be able to ride bicycles or motor cycles, drive cars and trucks of unfamiliar types; ride horses and camels; and travel in aircraft, ships and boats of any sort, all depending on the nature of the operation, the availability of means of transport, and the terrain in various theatres of war.'

Faced with organizational difficulties, however, those who had the job of bringing the Commando blueprint to reality found themselves forced to make modifications. Some of these brought forth impatient grumblings from the Prime Minister, who harangued the service chiefs into action, not simply against the Germans, but also the civilian bureaucrats who plagued the War Cabinet and everyone else.

But even Churchill had to submit to some modifications. The existing battalions of Home Forces frequently had officers in their forties, decidedly on the old side for Commando training, let alone raiding. As for reservists and conscripts, most of them were hidebound by Field Service Regulations, by the demands of 'the book'. And the one thing Dudley Clarke was absolutely determined about was that 'the book' should be thrown away and forgotten. The Commandos were going to be new men in a new world; a world where the humdrum would be rare and the deadly and the impossible became the normal.

But from where were the special forces to be drawn? The question rapidly became of more than academic interest.

There came a swift summons for Clarke from General Dill,

amounting to a direct order: 'I want you to get a raid across the Channel mounted at the earliest possible moment. The Prime Minister will brook no delay.' Clarke was then told to shed his present duties and take charge of a brand new section with responsibility for every conceivable form of land operation.

Fortunately, there was the nucleus of a small force already available, part of the newly formed 'Independent Companies' raised out of the Territorial Divisions left in England after the British Expeditionary Force had gone to France. Ten units had been specially trained to supplement the Royal Marines with army landing parties.

Ten units! A slim nucleus indeed, but at least it proved to Clarke that some promising material already existed. The trouble was that these ten were reckoned by some sections of the army to have outlived their usefulness. Some had fought in Norway and that had turned out to be a lost cause. Clarke realized that he had to get to the units fast before some well-meaning War Office pen-pusher disbanded them.

Clarke wheedled the promise of a free hand if he could find among the Independent Companies the sort of material he was looking for.

Meanwhile, there remained the problems of drumming up the rest of the sorely needed recruits...

One of these future recruits was blissfully ignorant of what was in store for him. A cheerful Devonian private named Ken Phillott, who had briefly been with the Gloucesters and then with the pre-war Supplementary Reserve, stared with interest at a poster on the wall of the orderly room in his depot at Bristol.

Phillott recalls: '"Soldiers wanted for special duties" is all it said. I and a few mates booked an interview with our Company Commander, followed by another with the Commanding Officer of what was later to become known as No 4 Commando.

'The Company Commander seemed interested only in whether I could swim. It seemed a bit odd at the time because I had been trained as a machine gunner originally. I remember putting it down to the lunacy of officers generally. He seemed even more delighted when he learned that, as well as being a good swimmer, I could actually cook and ride a motor cycle.

'That seemed to confirm that they were all mad, but I got a job in this new-fangled outfit that I hadn't the first idea about.'

In fact, Ken Phillott had been swept up in Dudley Clarke's other method of recruitment; one separate from the desperate search for talent among the Independent Companies.

Each of the Military Commands in the United Kingdom received a circular letter, inviting them to collect the names of those who possessed certain qualifications and were willing to volunteer for 'special service' of an undefined but 'hazardous' nature. All soldiers had to be fully trained and possess irreproachable health and strength. They had to be immune from sea and air sickness. Other qualities looked for were an intelligence and self-reliance which would enable them to carry through any unusual assignment.

The Commando leaders were to be chosen by the War Office from officers under forty, and given the rank of Lieutenant-Colonel.

Each successful candidate would return to his own Command headquarters and pick ten troop leaders from the list of officer volunteers. The troop leaders would each find two junior officers, who would help to pick a total of fifty NCOs and men from the list of 'other ranks'.

For the officers this afforded a priceless opportunity. They could actually handpick their own talent, discarding quite ruthlessly anyone they considered below the required standard.

And it could work the other way : any man would be able to leave his Commando unit on request. No explanation need be sought or given. As Dudley Clarke put it : 'It was to be at all times a force of voluntary enthusiasts, among whom there would be virtually only one penalty in the maintenance of discipline – removal from the Commandos.'

It was a judgement that found no quarrel with men like Ken Phillott. He himself comments : 'There was this old army saying, "Never volunteer for anything". The Commandos consisted of keen types prepared to volunteer for *anything.* That was the quality that attracted our officers.'

Before all this, though, Dudley Clarke had the by no means easy job of selling the idea of this new style force both to the army and the navy. He knew very well that it was one thing to assemble troops of high potential, quite another to extract from the navy the right sort of craft for raiding expeditions.

The Independent Companies were encamped on the outskirts of Glasgow; Dudley Clarke took the night train to have a look at them. He soon found that the mood of depression which seemed to be gripping the entire country was firmly entrenched in this particular corner of Scotland. Originally full of enthusiasm, officers and men had seen themselves as the saviours of Europe: knocking the hell out of the impertinent Hun. But it hadn't worked out like that. The five companies in Scotland had been formed hastily with the intention of following others into Norway. Then had come the débâcle of France and Belgium.

The stuffing went out of professional soldiers who had once been impatient to get at the throats of the enemy. Now they kicked their heels with footling guard duties in Glasgow and time-wasting watches for saboteurs and parachutists. Home Defence might be essential, but it was tame sort of soldiering. Rumours were circulating that there were not enough weapons to go round to fit out a brigade, and a lot of men openly voiced the feeling that they would have much better prospects back with their original units.

Then Dudley Clarke had a stroke of luck. Two old friends, 'Atty' Rice of the Suffolk Regiment and Ronnie Tod of the Argyll and Sutherland Highlanders, were on hand. Here at last was a chance to get things going.

At a working lunch, Clarke announced abruptly: 'I want you two each to pick a hundred volunteers and get them south. They'll be going raiding within a fortnight.'

The die was cast.

The navy, even more than the army, had good cause to be

more than slightly scornful about the whole Commando idea. It was still tied up in the perilous business of snatching the last troops from France; if the Assistant Chief of the Naval Staff of the Admiralty had proved obstructive at the prospect of playing cowboys and Indians, few could have blamed him.

The admiral listened for a few moments in silence to Dudley Clarke. Then suddenly he bounced out of his chair with a schoolboy enthusiasm that for a moment took the soldier aback.

He grinned: 'So the army wants to get back into the fight already! It's the best news in days. For that you can have anything you like in the world.'

Clarke felt guilty at having doubted the Navy; after all, sailors were pirates at heart and could not resist the mere scent of mischief.

In Whitehall, clerks were soon busily inscribing files with the prosaic title 'War Office Section MO9': the secretariat that would organize and direct the formation of the special new force.

In a series of clandestine meetings, many of them held in flats and private houses, members of the newly formed MO9 got down to the practical work of planning the first raid. The Hamble River in Hampshire, near the New Forest, was pinpointed as a convenient spot to assemble motor boats with crews of yachtsmen and fishermen who would carry the Commandos to France.

But by no means all the deliberations could be carried out in a cloak-and-dagger spirit; regular meetings had to be held at the War Office. At many of them there stalked the ghost of Colonel Blimp, his moustaches bristling with indignation and doubt. *Commandos?* What Clarke and his friends were contemplating seemed to entail the enlistment of a load of cut-throats: a sort of mixture of ruthless hit men and rat-cunning poachers.

The cut-throat label was one that Dudley Clarke did not disown. He wrote cheerfully: 'We looked for a dash of Elizabethan pirate, Chicago gangster and frontier tribesman.' But he did add that he also needed the professional efficiency and standard of discipline of the regular soldier.

An official directive from the Chief of Staff himself was issued to silence the Blimps : the new force was to be known by everyone as 'Commando'. It existed and all criticism was henceforth irrelevant. The Blimps ceased murmuring for a while.

It is not known whether any German spy was aware just how many Thompson sub-machine guns were actually available throughout the whole of England when that first Commando raid was planned. In any case, he would probably have found it hard to believe. In fact, there were precisely forty such guns – and none of them had been issued. It did not take a mathematician to calculate that, even had the Commandos been given the lot, there would only have been four to each unit. Eventually, half were issued and the rest put into store.

It soon became only too clear that not more than two groups of Commandos would be able to carry out raids at the same time; weapons would have to be handed from one group to another. And if any got damaged or lost – well, that was a problem few dared think about.

As for transport to ferry Commandos from depots or training centres, that was only too simple. There wasn't any. When a Commando was called upon to move, he had to do so under his own steam.

If a soldier was told to leave Southampton one afternoon and turn up in Dover the next morning, it was entirely up to him how he managed it. He could take trains and buses, cadge lifts and even borrow a bicycle if necessary. This had a security advantage : troop trains or convoys of army lorries would have attracted far too much attention.

A Commando was expected to find his own billet and, because he was already regarded as a special sort of soldier, arrangements were made for him to be paid a special allowance.

Just how the magic sum of 6s 8d (34p) was arrived at remains a mystery, but that was the figure reckoned appropriate for maintaining a Commando soldier for one day.

Born of innovation, corner-cutting and unabashed administrative cunning by his superiors, the Commando was in being and on his way.

The target date for the first raid was set for the night of 23-24 June 1940. The strike would be made in the neighbourhood of Le Touquet with the aim of reaching the German aerodrome at Berk.

# 2

A studied air of modesty hung over the planning of the first Commando adventure. No one expected that the war would be won by a few troops landing in France. The question being asked was: would it be possible for a raiding force actually to set foot in enemy territory and do an agreeable amount of damage in the shortest possible time?

With a bit of luck, papers and prisoners could be snatched as well and some useful information of terrain and defences made. The whole thing would be something of a dress rehearsal for more ambitious capers.

Dudley Clarke was not given overmuch to introspection, but even such a buccaneering opportunist must have realized that his whole career and the likely future of his untried band would be thrown into jeopardy if the adventure turned out an unmitigated disaster.

The first raid on Nazi-occupied Europe was in the hands of a group designated No 11 Commando. It was made up of officers and men picked by Clarke, Tod and Rice and rushed to Southampton for training. Meanwhile, the search for vessels was in the hands of the tireless Captain G. A. Garnons-Williams, DSC, RN, who had already made a name for himself on an expedition to block the port of Zeebrugge in Belgium.

Garnons-Williams had secured from the RAF some fast and reliable air-sea crash boats usually used for rescue work – admittedly only six of them, and they would have to accommodate thirty men each. But if ever there was a case of beggars not being choosers, this was it.

On one thing Clarke was absolutely determined. The Commandos had been his idea and he made up his mind that he was going to see a sizeable slice of the action. This seemed reasonable enough to everyone but the War Office. Clarke was told that as War Office staff, he had no business haring over to France at the head of a group of overgrown boy scouts; anyway, what guarantee of success was there for this crazy adventure? After more than a few tussles, Dudley Clarke got himself designated an observer for MO9, which meant that he had to stay firmly in his boat and not put as much as a toe on the land of France.

The expedition began badly. It had been intended that three boatloads were to start from Dover, and another three divided between Folkestone and Newhaven. But engine trouble caused two to be left behind; the force which set out under a cloudy sky with a calm sea and a light north-east breeze numbered only 120 men.

There was a distinctly festive mood among those involved. Faces were blackened with grease-paint, and any tension there might have been dissolved in hilarity as each man contemplated the others: there were numerous and highly raucous echoes of nigger minstrel language. The expedition might have been nothing more menacing than a concert party.

But soon the mood switched dramatically. The first hint of danger came, ironically enough, from the RAF when a clutch of fighters arrowed out of the sky and dived menacingly to have a look at this curious force on its way to France. The men waved cheerfully and made the required recognition signals. But to everyone's horror, the aircraft did not seem to notice and gave every sign of going into the attack. The boats killed their motors and heaved to in a last desperate effort to hold off the fighters.

Each man flinched in wait for the barrage that never came, but still the aircraft buzzed overhead. Clarke noticed that they always seemed to peel off in a south-westerly direction. What lay there? Were the pilots now trying to warn them of something?

The fact that they were sailing in air-sea rescue boats looked a possible answer. There was probably a crashed aircraft near at hand. Sure enough, someone soon made out an object in the water on the starboard quarter in line with the course the planes were taking. Such an interruption was plainly a nuisance, but some investigation was called for. In fact, the offending object was nothing more than a buoy; the fighters, seemingly satisfied, peeled away.

Dudley Clarke realized that an important lesson had been learnt already. The operation had been wrapped in secrecy to the point of overkill: obviously more co-ordination with the other services would in the future prevent the RAF putting its well-intentioned nose into raiding expeditions.

The delay was undeniably serious. Nearly an hour had been wasted and the darkness was already gathering. Milner-Gibson felt the most anxiety. He was in charge of the flotilla and now, in the dark, all contact had been lost with the second boat. It was far too late to keep the appointed rendezvous with the parties from Folkestone and Newhaven.

There was worse to come. Milner-Gibson had to confess that he was uncertain of his position: RAF crash boats were not equipped with means of exact navigation. As for the compass, that had decided to be capricious. Milner-Gibson had made no less than nine solo landings in recces on the beaches in the weeks before the raid proper. Navigation then had been child's play; now here was fate deciding to be bloody-minded on the one night that mattered.

However, he reasoned, the French coast could not be that far away. He dropped down to half speed to reduce the noise.

Suddenly, the blinding pencil of a searchlight beam cut through the darkness and, even as the boat swung round towards the open sea, there was another sweeping arm of light.

Land had loomed up far quicker than anyone had expected. Milner-Gibson was shouting: 'Christ! We're almost in Boulogne harbour!'

Incredibly, the beams did not seem to pick up the phosphorescence from the wake of the boat. The expected stutter of gunfire never happened. Milner-Gibson sought out another landing place. Soon it was possible to make out the dark outline of sand dunes. With a small hiss and a jolt, the crash boat grounded into the sand.

The barely whispered word of command came from Ronnie Tod. The men were over the side and into occupied France.

A total blanket of silence enveloped the coast. For Clarke and Milner-Gibson there was nothing to do but wait. The timetable was rigid. The men were only to be allowed three hours on shore – cut to two now because of delays. It was vital they were back on board by half-past three so that the boats could be well clear of the French coast by sunrise.

Clarke was idly studying the patterns of light on the dunes picked out by the moon when he was jolted by the lookout's warning: 'Aircraft ahead, sir!' And there it was, flying low over the line of breakers but evidently content to do little but watch. By a miracle the crew seemed to have missed the black shadow of the boat against the reflection of moonlight in the water.

Then the lookout was at Clarke's side and pointing to another shadow further along the beach. The man's comment that 'she doesn't look like one of ours' stung Clarke and Milner-Gibson into action. They whipped out their night-glasses, experiencing a chill of fear as they remembered the dire warnings of the effectiveness of German E-boats. The darkened boat was such an indistinct shadow it was impossible to identify her as friend or foe.

But there was no time to ponder it further because of another distraction. The rumble of fire could be heard far to the south and the sky lit up with Very lights. Machine-gun and rifle fire were clearly distinguishable along with the thump of grenades.

Now the aircraft were waking up – and with interest. They roared menacingly overhead. Milner-Gibson shouted: 'Here we go! The party's started!'

Keen to join it, Ronnie Tod was wading towards the boat with one of the precious tommy guns at the ready. A brief conference followed; plainly, this was no time to stretch the schedule any further. The aircraft overhead – to say nothing of the sinister prospect of an E-boat – heralded the presence of a by no means welcome reception committee. It seemed the best time to get out.

The lookout was soon reporting figures moving along the beach. They were a German cycle patrol making their way along the water's edge. Somehow they had managed to dodge the British pickets. Tod was no more than a few yards from the cyclists, but as he cocked a tommy gun, the magazine became detached and fell to the beach with a clatter.

The German guns spoke; bullets spattered around the boat. Clarke felt as if a giant fist had come out of the darkness and knocked him into eternity. The side of his head was splitting as if from a violent blow; he pitched headlong on to the deck. As he scrambled to his feet someone was shouting with joy that the Germans were making off. In the confusion, they had plainly not realized the extent of the opposition and thought it prudent to leave for reinforcements.

Clarke was nursing a left hip and jaw, both of which were giving excruciating pain, but nothing else seemed broken and he was far from being immobile. There was a short lull. Mercifully, the E-boat kept out of the proceedings. Evidently, none of the crew had been able to make up their minds who was friend or foe, especially as there had been no large assault on the cycle patrol.

But overhead the sky was getting rapidly lighter and the clouds were dispersing. Every moment of delay spelt a real danger; so far, reflected Clarke, his boys had enjoyed far more luck than they had really deserved.

Now there were more figures on the beach. This was clearly the crunch. Slowly, Dudley Clarke edged along the boat until he was able to clutch the reassuring metal of an anti-tank rifle. It may have been the dreadful pain, but later he recalled that the scene was strangely unreal: rather like watching a sequence of film where the sound-track has broken down. Advancing towards him were shadowy outlines of troops with fixed bayonets. They closed in without a sound. No voices, not even the crunch of feet. When it was all over, Clarke was the first to admit that he had felt sick with fear.

Then he heard a croak that seemed to be issuing a challenge from far off. It was his own voice. And it received a cheerful reply from a very English NCO.

The nightmare was over.

Back they came, the Commandos, wading up to their armpits and swimming wherever possible. As they crawled aboard, the sky became alive and enemy aircraft closed in. This was followed by the deep-throated roar of the E-boat. It was all up to Milner-Gibson now. He handled the retreat with sublime skill. He ran his boat very slowly, so as to show no wake and make the least possible noise. Then, miraculously, there was the open sea and the chance of full speed.

But still the aircraft would not give up. Milner-Gibson cut the engine. It was light enough now for the streak of the wake to give their presence away. But the planes were far enough inshore for the Commandos to escape undetected. The E-boat was still there. A glimpse was caught of her bow-wave, rocketing along the coast line at right angles to the course which the British had taken. Then the E-boat's motors began to fade; there was nothing now to stop progress to the white cliffs of Dover.

The relief of getting rid of so formidable an adversary was very real; a crash boat could never have matched an E-boat either in speed or armament. A close encounter would have spelled the sure end of the first expedition of the British Commandos.

Luckily, the dark had been slow to depart. It was still around while the British put some eight miles between themselves and the French coast. Came the dawn and there were British fighters – friendly this time – to dip their wings in proud salute.

The party spirit returned to the Commandos. Blacking was rubbed off faces and some immensely welcome rum produced. Dudley Clarke was prepared to join in but was brought up short by a row of horrified faces. The whole of the left side of his head, neck and coat was caked in dry blood. His left ear was numb and to the touch it was like a badly chopped bit of wood. Somebody opened a field dressing and bound the ear temporarily. The rest of the men may have enjoyed the run home; Dudley Clarke did not. The throbbing pain was becoming unbearable.

The first Commando raid perhaps had its elements of farce. It certainly showed up some grave deficiencies in planning and intelligence. None of this mattered a scrap to those awaiting the party in Dover. Every ship in the harbour was lined with cheering men. Grimy, dishevelled, triumphant troops, many of them decidedly pickled in rum, were cheered from the crowded jetties.

A shocked petty officer was soon examining Dudley Clarke's mutilated ear. He exclaimed: 'Gawdalmighty, sir, it's almost coming off.' Then he set to work to sew it back on, adding the balm of a dressing. The Millbank Hospital in London later completed the job. After healing, barely a scar remained.

And what of the other boats? Three had returned without incident. The fourth caused anxiety for a few hours: the one which had been involved in the firing during the night. At last a signal came from naval headquarters: the boat had been held up with engine trouble and put into Folkestone. The message was laconic: 'Raid went well with no casualties except to Germans.'

This particular boatload had been in the thick of it. It had landed at the Plage de Merlimont, south of Le Touquet, edging its way towards a hut guarded by a couple of German sentries.

Both sentries were seized and killed. But the group had not yet perfected the silent despatch which was to become the hallmark of Commando killers. The scrap had been too noisy and the scuffle attracted attention. A machine gun was poked through the windows of the hotel; klaxons screeched; there were Very lights and utter confusion. But the damage done to the hotel – probably an army billet – by lobbed grenades from the Commandos had been some consolation.

So ended this first operation. British and American newspapers, longing for some colourful exploit to splash over their front pages, went to town on it.

Headquarters of Combined Operations, the integrated Command for all three services, dealt in facts rather than sensation. The communiqué it issued stated: 'In co-operation with the Royal Air Force, naval and military units yesterday carried out successful reconnaissances of the enemy coastline. Landings were effected at a number of points and contact made with enemy troops. Casualties were inflicted and some enemy dead fell into our hands. Much useful information was obtained. Our forces suffered no casualties.'

Of the British newspapers, *The Times*, while not exactly niggardly with praise, was not prepared to heap heavy laurels on the shoulders of the Commandos.

Said the paper's leader: 'The point is that this incident shows the offensive spirit, which is exactly what the public wants ... No extravagant claims are made in the Communiqué and none should be made elsewhere.'

It was a judgement with which the men themselves probably had no quarrel. But what precisely had been achieved?

Three lessons for the future were of value: the need for means to identify friend from foe, always difficult in night actions but particularly so for a small party on a hostile shore; the problems of co-ordinating secret operations with the regular forces – the delay caused by the well-meaning Spitfires was a case in point; the difficulty of pinpoint navigation.

But what above all had been proved was that landings on the enemy coast *were* possible. No men had been lost. And a sentry's body was almost brought back to identify his unit. Unfortunately, overcrowded conditions aboard forced the raiders to tow the body, which sank.

As a morale booster, the raid came to the newspaper readers of Britain like a tonic. 'It gave Englishmen a better breakfast for a morning,' was one judgement.

The men who wore the Commando shoulder flashes – and from 1942 the green beret – would not have asked for a better epitaph.

# 3

The little foray at Boulogne may have put heart into soldiers who a few weeks before had despaired of ever seeing action, but it and a subsequent small raid on Guernsey which had been conducted with two 1918-vintage destroyers found decidedly less favour with Winston Churchill.

The war lord fumed that 'Storm Troops' and 'Leopards' were to be worthy of better things. Both Boulogne and Guernsey had Keystone Cops elements which annoyed the Prime Minister. At Guernsey, for example, the landing craft used by the Commandos were too noisy, stood too high out of the water and were too crowded. What was needed was an overall commander of sufficient energy and ruthlessness to get rid of any inefficiency and give the force a good back-up in men and materials.

Churchill was conscious of this; all at once a fresh breeze swept through Combined Operations. It took the form of a new Director, Admiral of the Fleet Sir (later Lord) Roger Keyes, GCB, KCVO, DSO, MP, who, in World War One, had leapt to fame as the hero of the Zeebrugge and Gallipoli campaigns. Keyes was sixty-eight at the time of his appointment, but his superb ability as an organizer and his total dedication to the Commando ideal attracted Churchill. Keyes found himself in overall command of a force numbering four thousand and increasing daily.

If enthusiasm had been enough, Keyes could have been the greatest Combined Operations leader alive. But he had one fatal flaw that was not in the Churchillian mould. Whereas the Prime Minister could charm, bully and wheedle service chiefs and government departments into doing things his way, Keyes had no gift for co-operation with ministries.

It was a weakness that his opponents were only too willing to exploit.

These backstage bickerings remained unknown, of course, to the eager young recruits, but they sensed the numerous frustrations of their chiefs as one seemingly promising campaign after another was set up with high hopes and then cancelled. Keyes' big operation was the proposed capture of the Azores. After a series of seemingly endless exercises, it was cancelled. The next objective selected by Sir Roger for a Commando raid was the island of Pantelleria, between Sicily and Tunisia, but this scheme too was aborted.

Those in charge of supplies for the three service ministries were openly hostile to the whole conception of the Commandos. Officers commanding conventional forces saw Keyes' plans as an impertinent attempt to steal their best men.

Across the conference table, Churchill frequently met the attitude: 'What is it they can do that my men cannot? This plan robs the whole army of its prestige and its finest men. We never had it in 1914. Why now?'

Churchill was prepared to press hard for change. Fortunately, he had an invaluable ally in Brigadier J. C. Haydon, DSO, Commander of the Special Service Brigade. Haydon was a man with scant interest in the susceptibilities of politicians and service chiefs. He was intensely interested, however, in creating good Commandos. Part of the fault, Haydon was willing to concede, lay in the organization of the forces, which badly needed streamlining.

The Commandos were reorganized into a headquarters and six troops, rather than ten. Commanding Officers, faced with fewer underlings, now had a ready-made and painless method of getting rid of some of the dead wood which had collected. Each troop was now to consist of three officers and sixty-two other ranks. Haydon had found a central weakness. He picked up the whole unwieldy structure, gave it a thorough shake and remoulded it. A few careers doubtless crashed in the turmoil, but in every good military leader there had to lurk something of the butcher.

It felt like realism at last.

One man who felt a keen disappointment at the cancellation of the Pantelleria project was Lieutenant-Colonel John Durnford-Slater, Commanding Officer of No 3 Commando, which was set up in June 1940. A professional soldier whose habitual bluntness was much to the taste of Roger Keyes, Durnford-Slater did not hesitate to communicate his sense of frustration to his sympathetic chief.

Keyes could not vent his feelings with the freedom he would have liked. But this did not stop him taking Durnford-Slater aside and confiding: 'Don't worry, I've got another one up my sleeve for you. No 3 Commando is my first choice and I will guarantee to have you in in it.'

Ken Phillott, then stationed in Weymouth, Dorset, was conscious of the restlessness then coursing through No 4 Commando, to which he belonged.

Phillott recalls: 'In such an uncertain period, it was scarcely worthwhile finding the troops regular billets. You always had this feeling that you would soon be moved on. With our 6s 8d a day we were expected to find our own places to lay our heads. As became traditional with the Commandos, you slept wherever you could – in my case, more than once it was the theatre on the pier at Weymouth – and I got my food from the various cafés. I had complete freedom, provided I was on duty during the hours required.'

The feeling of being on the wing was justified. Soon the troop trains, carrying Commandos on long journeys where speed was all-important, were running north to south-west Scotland. The destination was the old seaport of Troon in Ayrshire. This curiously shaped promontory on the Firth of Clyde had already played an important naval role in World War One. Now it was destined to become virtually a fortress as the home of No 4 Commando.

Ken Phillott and some three hundred of his mates did not so much take over Troon as blend with it. They found comfortable billets with only too willing families.

The British landlady, along with the mother-in-law, obstinately remains a music hall joke. Veteran Commandos might concede the point about mothers-in-law; many will not, even now, tolerate a word against landladies.

For the landladies of Troon became second mothers overnight to total strangers – changing sheets regularly for stinking, mud-caked men home after a day's hard training so tired that they could barely summon the strength to tumble into bed. Meals were cooked at all hours and hot baths run. Landladies even inspected equipment and carried out stern unofficial parades. Some cleaned rifles and bayonets while their owners slept upstairs.

To Troon landladies, Commandos were nothing less than heroes in the early 1940s. And to some daughters of landladies, too. There was a healthy blossoming of engagements to local girls. Everyone took to their hearts these strange roughnecks with their seemingly endless bouts of vigorous training.

Troon was not just a home, it was a strategic sweatshop, a training centre that no one who served there is ever likely to forget. Certainly not Ken Phillott. Along with the rest, he discovered soon that decidedly more was needed than an ability to cook and swim.

A man was required to march for sixteen miles at a stretch every Saturday morning with full kit and rifle straddled across the shoulders. With grim humour, this marathon was known as 'the strength through joy', a slogan borrowed from Hitler's Germany. The tag had an extra irony; there was precious little joy about it. This super-gruelling feature of Commando training was also known as 'the speed march'.

Phillott remembers : 'You started off with the CO's parade and then you went on the jog and the sight of the boots of the bloke in front was the only evidence of humanity you saw until the march was over – eight miles out, then straight back without a breather.

'You couldn't bank on dismissal after that, either. You stood to attention while your feet felt they'd been thrust into hot coals. The blood trickled around your toes. You thought of only one thing : the beer that was waiting for you.'

And, sure enough, for each troop the pints were lined up on favourite bar counters. The Troon bus driver who passed the returning marchers tipped the wink to the publicans.

Ken Phillott says : 'I kept my bicycle on the parade

ground and leapt on after dismissal – anything to take the weight off the feet. I pedalled straight to the pub and the routine was three pints and, believe me, it took two to put the fire out in your throat before you actually tasted anything.'

Then the men would return to their billets and sleep the rest of the day away. Those who felt like it – and many did – were up and fresh for the evening dances.

The Saturday marathon had other purposes than toughening up; the men served as useful guinea pigs for such refinements as rope-soled boots designed to get a grip on surfaces encrusted with snow and ice.

Despite its toughness, the jog around Troon was regarded by some cynical souls as almost a rest compared with the training activities of other groups – notably No 6 Commando, which tended to regard Nos 3 and 4 Commandos as somewhat effete.

The men of No 6 had their toughening process in the form of regular runs up the three thousand feet of Goat Fell on the Isle of Arran, west of Troon. Invariably, the exercise was carried out with needles of rain driving into the eyes; more than one shivering private doubtless reflected ruefully that the west of Scotland seemed to exist in a perpetual downpour. Goat Fell boasted a sheer drop into the sea; it was ideal for Commando training.

When the mountaineers of No 6 were rash enough to gaze down from Goat Fell they saw canoes bouncing on the treacherous choppy waters. These were not pleasure craft, but the Special Boat Section attached to No 8 Commando going through its own highly individual form of training.

Canoes may seem more relevant to the days of the Red Indians than to Hitler's war – and indeed there were some misguided men in Whitehall who so regarded them. But Lieutenant Roger Courtney had worked out a scheme which was to confound the critics of the canoe in highly dramatic fashion. A former big game hunter who was later to make a name for himself in the Middle East and the Mediterranean, Courtney personally paddled out one summer night in 1940 to a carrier ship moored in the Clyde. Its captain was more than disconcerted next morning to receive one of his own gun covers dripping wet from a grinning Courtney. The rascally Commando had coolly stolen it single-handed and unnoticed.

The point went home with the founding of the boat section. Canoes, it was conceded, would be invaluable in gathering intelligence on enemy strengths and fortifications. Photographs were not always reliable; they gave only some of the story. But a small boat getting in close was an invaluable tool.

Salutary lessons were being learnt elsewhere, too. The various troops felt a new spirit. A comradeship had been firmly established, not least because the officers shared every experience with their men. The feet of the CO bled every bit as freely as those of his men when it came to 'strength through joy'.

The exploits at Boulogne and Guernsey, whatever their true value to the war effort, had delighted the press. Reporters had become as demoralized as anyone with events in Europe, which seemed to suggest that it was only a matter of time before the swastika fluttered triumphantly over Buckingham Palace. Commandos, said the reports of the more lurid scribblers, were ex-jailbirds and nightclub bouncers who had vomited out of the underworld with knives stuck firmly between discoloured teeth. They were thugs who would be more than a match for the Hun hordes currently raping civilization. The Commandos themselves paused during their vigorous training to laugh into their beer and reassure their startled families that they were no more cut-throat than other professional soldiers.

Nonetheless the image of a cross between Genghis Khan and Jack the Ripper persisted – and it had to be admitted that there were certain Commandos who did little to demolish the legend.

Lieutenant-Colonel John Durnford-Slater was a Devon man who seemed to have been picked up by some fiendish time-machine in the age of Elizabeth I and flung unceremoniously into the more prosaic world of twentieth-century combat. Bald, stocky, red-faced and a thirsty veteran of the messes of India, this genial firebrand was just the sort of Commando other Commandos earnestly tried to kid everyone did not exist.

But Roger Keyes was not prepared to disown him; the original promise that No 3 Commando would get its share of the action was about to be kept.

And that was why, early in 1941, Durnford-Slater received a signal to make for Troon and team up with Colonel Dudley Lister, commanding No 4 Commando. The pair were met by the admiral's staff officer; there was hasty adjournment to the Marine Hotel. No time was lost in outlining the objective: 'Nos 3 and 4 Commandos are to carry out an attack on the Lofoten Islands in northern Norway. The object is primarily to destroy all the oil installations; secondly, to destroy shipping; and, thirdly, to bring back prisoners and volunteers from the Norwegian navy. The project will be known as Operation Claymore.'

The Nazi-occupied Lofoten Islands, 850 miles from Scapa Flow, were well inside the Arctic Circle. The key ports were Stamsund, Henningsvaer, Brettesnes and Svolvaer, the capital. Before Durnford-Slater and Lister could wonder what was the point of hammering some obscure islands when the real action surely lay on the mainland, the staff officer explained gleefully that it would mean the Germans lost no less than half of Norway's herring and cod oils. The oil was made into glycerine for explosives and vitamins A and B for the use of the German army. In addition, the Germans were living on an unacceptably generous quantity of fish and salt, chilled and fresh from the islands. They must be deprived of these benefits.

Durnford-Slater confessed later to a sense of exhilaration. This would be no boy scout romp: the raid would be a marvellous present for Keyes to take to Winston Churchill.

It was just as well that the Royal Navy was prepared to give the Commandos the fullest co-operation: it was going to be the navy's job to get the men to the islands, in an area often buffeted by gales and subjected to temperatures which seldom rose above freezing. Snow could be expected as well.

U-boats hunted in packs, but fortunately no aerodrome

north of Trondheim was fit for mid-winter operations; the only enemy air activity, so Intelligence suggested, was from an unarmed reconnaissance JU52 which was known to patrol three times a week.

Most of the inhabitants of the Lofoten Islands had burned with hatred ever since the Germans arrived and requisitioned the fishermen's boats and ships. The Gestapo had embarked on a programme of mass arrests; it had its headquarters with the army at Svolvaer. There were known to be an unhealthy number of collaborators: called Quislings after Vidkun Quisling, the turncoat Norwegian leader. Intelligence further believed that defences were light; there was a telephone link with the mainland.

Durnford-Slater and Lister learnt that the starting date would be in late February but there were several postponements and the final day chosen was 4 March 1941. The starting point was Gourock; the party would then sail north to Scapa Flow in the Orkneys for final preparation and training, notably with landing craft, with whose vagaries many of the troops were largely unfamiliar.

The craft were slung on the davits of converted cross-Channel steamers, the *Queen Emma* and the *Princess Beatrix*, now dignified with the function of infantry landing ships.

Ken Phillott remembers: 'The steamers weren't exactly designed for the North Sea in winter. They did everything but travel upside down. There wasn't a single man aboard who didn't feed the fishes.'

Seasickness is no respecter of rank; Durnford-Slater was soon vomiting with the best.

Black-bearded Commander Joe Brunton of the *Beatrix* took him in hand sympathetically and started him on a cure immediately after he unceremoniously jettisoned a breakfast.

'Beginning now,' he said, 'every morning at eleven you will consume with me a couple of bottles of beer with some cheese and pickled onions.'

If it had been possible, Durnford-Slater would have been sick again. He merely groaned. Brunton's tone took on an edge. 'That,' he said deliberately, 'is an order.'

The beer-cheese-onions treatment worked like a charm; Durnford-Slater's days of seasickness were over.

Relief came after four days of mercilessly heavy rolling. Once the party had passed into the Arctic Circle on the last day before landing, the weather turned warm briefly and there was a lolling respite on the sun-kissed decks. All possible preparations had now been made.

But, summoning all reserves of training and discipline, the men let only a little of their minds surrender to tempting torpor. These after all were the Lofoten waters – enemy waters. Did the Germans know they were coming? Was the peace of the skies suddenly to be shattered by enemy aircraft? Fathoms below, HM Submarine *Sunfish* edged into position. And there were the reassuring shadows of the covering force which included HMS *Nelson*, HMS *King George V*, two cruisers and five destroyers. The Commandos also had with them Norwegian volunteers who had crossed originally to Britain in fishing boats, many of them guided by their own resistance movements.

The early hours of March 4 brought a nasty shock. The Admiralty had fed the raid organizers with a succession of weather reports. These had been accurate so far, but now everyone noticed that the darkness was beginning to fade. Every time the clouds broke, the day got brighter. The leading landing craft from the *Beatrix* was in charge of a Canadian Flotilla Leader. Anxiously, he asked Durnford-Slater if he could increase speed; getting ashore now under the cover of any sort of darkness was impossible.

To make matters worse, the sinister grey mass of an armed German trawler was spotted pulling away from the harbour at Stamsund. The sound of gunfire shattered the early morning. The British escorting destroyer *Somali* knifed through the water to engage. Conflict was bitter and brief: fourteen of the trawler's crew were killed and five wounded.

The landing craft of No 3 Commando continued their unflappable progress. Utterly absorbed though he was at reaching his objective, Durnford-Slater felt a lifting of the heart as in the little harbour he spotted Norwegian fishing boats raising their national flag. Such an act had been specifically forbidden by the Germans; it was the first blatant act of defiance by the gallant islands since the occupation.

Durnford-Slater found his landing craft protected by a fish jetty. As he scrambled ashore, he slipped, spreading his length in a three-feet-high pile of frozen cods' heads. But he barely noticed the indignity. What worried him was that the main street of Stamsund, ribboning away in front of him, was suspiciously empty. It would have been much more reassuring if it had been teeming with Germans.

A hasty conversation with a disconcerted local postman revealed that the town was full, not of troops, but mostly of Gestapo and local businessmen plainly unaware of what had happened.

It was intensely cold in the little town with its wooden houses and fish factories, but the Commandos scarcely noticed. Durnford-Slater's men were gripped with something like a holiday mood; they hastened to obey an order to seize the local post office.

A certain Lieutenant R. L. Wills saw no reason why he should not make use of the available facilities. Soon he was rattling out a wire:

YOU SAID YOUR LAST SPEECH GERMAN TROOPS WOULD MEET THE ENGLISH WHEREVER THEY LANDED STOP WHERE ARE YOUR TROOPS?
WILLS 2-LIEUT.

The telegram was addressed to A. Hitler in Berlin.

The assault had been planned in three waves. Three landing craft went in as the first flight. Bringing up the rear was Lister, complete with a phalanx of adjutant, signals officer, intelligence officer, MO, runners and sapper sections with high explosives. After disembarking the assault party, boats turned back and dashed to the parent craft, bringing on the full strength of five hundred Commandos.

Ken Phillott, in the thick of it with No 4, recalls: 'The two things I remember most were the twinkling, oddly friendly lights of Svolvaer, our main objective, and the sudden appalling cold. I suppose it was according to regulations to wear steel helmets. Some Commandos did, but there were also thick oilskins and woollen comforters to protect the ears.

'The landing craft were odd looking things – like a box without a lid and with a hinge at one end and out of which we all poured.

'It wasn't a steady progress because as the craft hit the water, so the spray came straight at us. It hit our capes and it was as if we were wearing overcoats made of nothing but thick ice. Like a lot of others on landing, we had to edge our way past the treacherous slippery fish on the jetty. We must have been an odd looking invading army. By now the Norwegians were going to work and most of them took us for Germans and raised their right arms in the Hitler salute. My job with the other blokes was to block off the back exit of one of the hotels. All of which was a bit of a joke because my fingers were so frozen I wouldn't have been able to pull a trigger if a German had suddenly appeared.'

Near the hotel was a stack of cut wood. Phillott snatched a small piece and rammed it through the trigger guard of his rifle. He reckoned that he could just about manage to pull on that if he needed to fire.

As casually and politely as if they were booking rooms for the night, an officer, a batman and a knot of Norwegian officers who had accompanied the raid walked into the hotel and asked the manager if there were any German guests. Two civilians – propaganda professors on a special mission from Dr Goebbels – were conveniently in residence.

The quaking manager was ordered speedily to round up his staff and keep everyone in the kitchen.

The two professors slumbered innocently in their beds. Suddenly, they were blinded by the overhead lights, then found themselves staring straight into the eyes of highly determined individuals bristling with cocked weapons.

The officer caressed his revolver lovingly, pointed it beneath the bed and sent a couple of bullets into the chamber pot obligingly in the line of fire.

The two professors rose from their beds as if a giant spring had thrust its way through the mattress. Their arrest was a peaceful, courteous sort of affair.

Indeed, many of the activities at Svolvaer were decidedly gentlemanly. A number of Germans rounded up in the street by an utterly unexpected group of Commandos raised their hands almost with relief.

There was even comedy. An officer's batman who took the popular image of the Commandos seriously – rifle and bayonet slung over his shoulder, revolver in his belt and Very pistol cocked at the ready – advanced menacingly on one isolated German soldier and marched him proudly down the street. A Ministry of Information photographer, if he had been on hand, would have been delighted with such a gift of a picture for the recruiting posters.

Unfortunately, this fine image of Commando implacability was destined to be rudely shattered.

The snow and ice of the Svolvaer street was something to be treated with respect; the batman suddenly slipped. When he crashed to the ground, the Very pistol rolling away from him towards the German prisoner.

The German swung round, regarded the falling Commando gravely, picked up the Very pistol and advanced. Suddenly, the Commando found himself yanked to his feet by his well-built prisoner. The Very pistol was thrust into the Englishman's hands. Politely, he was asked if he was all right. Then the German continued his progress down the street towards the improvised prison compound, his hands thrust above his head.

At Brettesnes, the task was to seize and set fire to shipping, while at Svolvaer the main forces destroyed factories and oil installations. There could be no discrimination: Norwegians who had collaborated with the Germans lost their property along with those who had remained loyal. Oil factories were blasted to the skies; the main object was to leave nothing that could be of any use to the Germans.

A Mr Johannsen, owner of the largest factory in the town and the general store adjoining it, protested volubly that he had never sold oil to the Germans.

'Then where the hell has all your oil been going?' demanded Durnford-Slater, stung into anger by the man's prosperous appearance and air of injured innocence.

Johannsen stared back in sullen silence. Durnford-Slater turned away in contempt. 'Blow the place up,' he commanded.

An elderly Englishman, Mr Hawes, the manager of another factory who had never concealed his hatred of the Germans, greeted the news that his installations were to go and that he was to be evacuated to England with phlegmatic calm.

He shrugged: 'If those are your orders, you had better carry them out. But what about the rest of the factories?'

It was a fair point. Obligingly, Hawes guided the Commandos to more installations. More boilers were blown up and machinery wrecked.

Not everyone was prepared to give up without a fight. One vessel which served as a factory ship had a determined First Officer who, at the first sight of the advancing Commandos, pitched the ship's log and records over the side.

The solution was simple. The officer found himself frog-marched along the length of the deck and shoved overboard into the icy water with the injunction that he had better retrieve the papers if he ever wanted to see dry land again.

The head of the local police appeared most obliging. With a pathetic desire to please, he escorted the Commandos and his fellow Norwegians around the various oil installations. He was tireless in his denunciation of Quislings. A solid figure resplendent in fine frock-coat and astrakhan hat, he positively exuded loyalty and expended much energy on voicing his hatred of the Germans.

As the Lofoten operation drew to a close, he walked confidently towards one of the landing craft, dreaming of the comfortable billet that he felt was his right back in England.

'What are you going to do with the bastard?' shouted one of the fishermen.

A nearby Commando looked puzzled, then hurled himself at the policeman as he heard someone else shout: 'He's the biggest Quisling of the lot.'

The police chief's features contorted into fury and he began sweating with fear. By now two or three Commandos were shoving his fat bulk into the destroyer *Tartar*. The newly unveiled Quisling promptly burst into tears. And his crying never stopped until he reached England and an internment camp.

The results of the Lofoten raid were highly satisfactory. Some three hundred volunteers were taken back to England to swell the Norwegian forces.

One splendidly exuberant Norwegian soldier emerged from his home in full uniform, rifle in hand – precisely as he had been dressed when fighting had broken out in 1940. German prisoners, the bulk of them Luftwaffe personnel taken by No 4 Commando, totalled two hundred and sixteen.

Eleven ships with a total tonnage of more than twenty thousand were sent to the bottom; one trawler was manned and another taken back to England.

There was no room to take all the Quislings off. Some sixty shuddering specimens were rounded up. As for the rest, Durnford-Slater marshalled them and delivered himself of a memorable harangue. The fact that little of what he said could be understood scarcely mattered; the tone conveyed the message clearly enough.

In his breathless high-pitched voice, the colonel stormed: 'Yeah, well, I don't want to hear any more of this bloody Quisling business. It's no bloody good, I'm telling you. If I hear there's been any more of it, I'll be back and next time I'll take the whole bloody lot of you. Now clear off!'

Nos 3 and 4 Commandos left behind them an ecstatic population, who had touchingly presented small gifts such as tobacco, wool, sugar, sweets and soup.

The Englishman, Mr Hawes, later recorded for the BBC an impression of his last look at the Lofoten islands – taken from the safety of a British boat.

He said: 'I remember when the oil-dump blew up there was a great sheet of flame from the benzine and lighter oils and there came black smoke as the heavy oil started to burn. As we sailed away, we could see the black smoke hanging over the horizon behind us. I cannot believe even today that I am free . . .'

Understandably, German broadcasts played down the success of the Lofoten raid, tossing it aside as a mere pin-prick that the Reich would soon forget : 'Light naval forces destroyed several fishing boats and landed Commandos in the Norwegian skerries, where they took prisoner some Germans and Norwegians.'

It was a tribute of a sort : even the Germans had allowed the word 'Commando' common currency.

Following this, the first of two Lofoten raids, the Germans hastily consolidated their position on the islands but, apart from burning a few houses, they did not shoot any of the inhabitants who had welcomed the Commandos so warmly.

On Svolvaer, where No 4 Commando had landed, stands a memorial to eight of the volunteers who had sailed for England in the *Princess Beatrix.* They were to lose their lives in later theatres of war.

The success of Lofoten had been tangible but scarcely significant : after all, there had been no opposition.

Veterans of Nos 3 and 4 Commandos who went to Norway on that March night were later to look back on it in wonder : it was kindergarten stuff compared to what was to come.

# 4

Although the first of the two raids on the Lofoten Islands made even the most sneering critics of the Commandos sit up and take notice, the fledgling force was still far from gaining the desperately needed acceptance of the Whitehall mandarins.

In 1941, there was also a Commando raid in Spitzbergen, north-west of Norway and east of Greenland. Once again a snook was effectively cocked at the Germans; 450,000 tons of coal were set on fire, along with 275,000 gallons of fuel oil, petrol and grease. But there were no opportunities for serious raiding. The mission was unopposed and the Germans only learnt of it when the Commandos were on the way home. Matters were not to remain so easy for much longer.

In North Africa, a very different sort of war faced the new special forces. Here, the Germans were only too aware of the strength of the opposition and there were failures for the brainchild of Dudley Clarke and Roger Keyes. Often, when plain defeat stared the Allied armies in the face, it was the Commandos who were hastily sent in to mend the fences; they got precious little reward when the job was done.

In March 1941, disaster was very much in the air. Hitler's armies seemed to bear a charmed life; Rommel was even regarded by some of his enemy as a fox touched with magic.

On to the stage of Combined Operations strode the highly charismatic figure of Lieutenant-Colonel Robert Laycock of the Royal Horse Guards, to whom discipline and good order were a way of life and not simply items in a military manual.

Laycock was one of the very few senior officers of the Commandos who had enjoyed the benefit of a course at the Staff

College. But such a seeming advantage had proved a disappointment: it had brought him only the prospect of being Anti-Gas Staff Officer to General Headquarters, Middle East.

That sort of job had no appeal whatever for Bob Laycock. He was above all a doer who had set his sights on command. Clearly, someone else would have to be persuaded diplomatically to become Gas Officer. Indeed, by the time Laycock got to the Middle East a substitute had been earmarked. Laycock was seeking a formidable brigade all his own; eventually he got it.

With high confidence matching the freshness of spring, a force of Nos 7, 8 and 11 Commandos set out for Egypt. The group was known as Layforce and was joined speedily by Nos 50 and 52 (Middle East) Commandos. The force was initially used as a reserve Brigade of the British Eighth Army.

Bob Laycock was given the order to scoop it out for a special mission: a raid on Bardia, an enemy-held port lying on a forbidding coast some two hundred and fifty miles west of Alexandria.

Since the Germans were within fifty miles of the British Imperial Headquarters in Cairo, Bardia was beyond British fighter cover.

The prospect of a major raid against Germans and Italians with the prospect of opposition! It was the sort of chance of which Bob Laycock had dreamed.

On the night of 19–20 April, men of A Battalion (No 7 Commando) crouched aboard HMS *Glengyle*, escorted by an anti-aircraft cruiser and three Australian destroyers. The Royal Navy submarine *Triumph* was to be a reassuring presence two and a half miles off Bardia, showing a white light as a navigational aid.

Then came trouble – and in a form that showed Commandos still had a great deal to learn when it came to preplanning and intelligence. Out of the skies swept British aircraft whose crews had become highly suspicious of the *Triumph*. Their buzzing, as it happened, amounted to little beyond nuisance value, but the harm was done. The progress of the *Triumph* was impeded. Nor was that the whole extent of the misfortune. Roger Courtney, who had indulged in the schoolboy prank of stealing a gun cover undetected from a carrier ship moored in the Clyde, now found himself with a mission infinitely less satisfying. His job was to show a green light from an offshore inlet, but the waves were savage that night. They smashed his helpless little canoe just as he was launching it from the conning tower of the *Triumph*.

The navigational lights upon which *Glengyle* counted were simply not there at the critical moment. And she was in trouble, too. The release gear was tangled and the run in for the landing craft was fifteen minutes behind schedule. All this was wearing on the nerves: the wheels of the planning machine should have been turning smoothly but now everything seemed to go wrong.

The landing on the beach became a shambles. Men dressed in ankle puttees, battledress and gym shoes who had been designated for one beach never made it. One of the landing craft was stuck firmly in the davits. Annoyed at being cheated of action, they made for another landing position, contrary to orders. An officer moving among knots of men on the beach failed, when challenged, to give proper identification and was promptly shot. A number of Commandos made for a spot where no landing had been planned at all – and blundered straight into the enemy.

It was a humiliating experience for Layforce. Pre-reconnaissance and intelligence had evidently produced precisely nothing; at none of the beaches was there any opposition. The country up to within two miles of Bardia was in the tender care of just two motorcycle patrols.

The total bag was some forty-five Italians killed or wounded and twenty-five vehicles ignited. The barracks of solid stone were left alone in disgust. In a mood of frustration, the Commandos contented themselves with blowing some Italian naval guns' breaches. A sharply timed withdrawal was vital; the naval force had to clear the coast before daylight.

The whole affair had caused the Germans only mild anxiety; an armoured brigade at nearby Sollum to the east was yanked back in some haste.

Up to now, the sole role of the Commandos had been to follow a programme of small-scale raids on the enemy's lines of communication which ran for so many miles along the coast. But events changed all this.

First signs came a fortnight before Bardia, when the Axis powers had sprung their advance through Yugoslavia and Greece. The whole situation in the eastern Mediterranean went from bad to worse. Allied troops in North Africa were sent on a mercy dash to the hard-pressed Greeks.

Here was an enemy so formidably armed and so superior in numbers that victory was impossible. Withdrawal had to be in anything and everything that floated. Infantry landing ships had more important tasks than transporting raiders; besides, they would have been at the mercy of greatly intensified air attacks and there was no Allied fighter protection to spare. Ships were no longer available for the Commandos; in this part of the world, at least, dreams of future raids were forced to languish.

But there was other work and plenty of it.

The disaster of Greece was followed by the German invasion of Crete, curtain-raiser to further humiliation. Between 20 May and 1 June 1941, Crete was subjected to merciless bombing. Then the skies above the island were filled with the shape of parachutists and airborne troops.

This was no time for a purist interpretation of the Commando role: the special forces must fulfil whatever tasks were needed, whether or not raiding was involved. No 11 Commando was sent to Cyprus to form part of its garrison. Nos 7 and 8, with the two locally raised Commandos, were kept as general reserve.

But not for long. Crete was getting desperate. Rapidly the order came for the four reserve Commandos: get into the island and fight a rearguard action. Was this going to provide Bob Laycock with the glory that had eluded him at Bardia?

Soon after the landing on 26–27 May sheer hell came from the skies above the main road going south to Crete's evacuation port of Sphakia. German Ju 87 dive bombers had previously played havoc with British shipping; now they swept in for a ripe new kill.

The nerves of Layforce held up well under the seemingly endless onslaught. With the departure of the bombers came the chance for No 7 Commando to leap at the throats of the Nazi victors of Crete.

Captain F. J. R. Nicholls of G Troop prepared to assault some of the enemy established on a hill to the extreme left flank, where it was in a position to enfilade the Commandos. Came the order: 'Fix bayonets'; then G Troop, fearsomely belligerent with all that reassuring cold steel, stormed upwards to run the Germans through.

To Nicholls it was the most exhilarating experience of his life. Within a few days he was writing home: 'One thing I am certain about after Crete is that, man for man, there is not any question as to who is the better. Although the Germans have every advantage of air support, etc., whenever they counter-attacked or got to close quarters, which in our case was twice, they dropped their weapons and fled before us – a very heartening sight.'

The victory of the Germans in Crete could not long be delayed. But the Commandos were determined that the enemy would pay dearly for it. Laycock was in no mood to give his opponents either mercy or rest. Just before dark he would launch a few light counter-attacks, fighting patrols of no more than seven or eight men. The desperately fatigued Germans stumbled on. Laycock's forces seemed to appear from nowhere, harassing the forces at every turn.

From the morning of 27 until 31 May, the Commandos kept the German forces heavily engaged – a rearguard action which made some evacuation of Sphakia possible.

On 28 May, the Germans hurled themselves at the point where Laycock had established his headquarters. The strength of HQ was down to just three tanks. Ahead of these was the invading force. Bob Laycock did not hesitate. He and his brigade major leapt for one of the tanks, cranking it into action and hurtling it straight into the face of the Germans.

And so the Commandos slogged their way to Sphakia

itself, only to find that most of the evacuation craft had left and only a quarter of the unit had survived. A large proportion of survivors were taken prisoner; those that remained free were determined to get back to North Africa.

One party of Commandos stumbled into a landing craft, only to find it empty of fuel. Feverish scrambling aboard produced a blanket; somebody discovered bootlaces. Up was hauled a makeshift sail and the craft took to the water, sailing for the African coast throughout six nerve-racking days. Improvization had indeed been part of Commando training; the effectiveness of all that spade work back in England was vindicated.

Now the only effective Commando muscle left in the Mediterranean was represented by No 11 Commando. It was to be hurled east from Cyprus to the Litani river.

Australians advancing north from Palestine were held up near the mouth of the Litani. No 11 was given the job of unlocking this line. The objective was a strong redoubt covering the bridge at Kafr Bada, the bulk of whose garrison belonged to detachments of the French colonial army, the 22nd Algerian Tirailleurs, part of the Vichy forces.

In charge was fire-eating Lieutenant-Colonel Dick Pedder, whose sense of discipline probably exceeded that of Bob Laycock. Pedder's second-in-command was Major (later Lieutenant-Colonel) Geoffrey Keyes, son of Admiral Keyes, Director of Combined Operations.

The first landing attempt was called off because of a full moon which was inconsiderate enough to turn night into day. The force returned to Port Said. No sooner had it arrived than it was promptly ordered to sea again with instructions to carry out the operation forthwith.

Pedder decided to land his men in three detachments on the north side of the mouth of the Litani. He would then strike inland with the object of taking the French defences in their right flank. Intelligence reports had indicated that the French had blown up the bridge at Kafr Bada and withdrawn their detachment from the river's south side.

At dawn on 9 June, the landing was underway. Something of the fiendish misfortune which had bedevilled Layforce at

Bardia had struck again: Major Keyes and his men now found themselves put ashore by mistake on the south side. But Colonel Pedder, who was with the centre detachment, and Captain George More, commanding the left, were landed successfully on the river's north side.

In with the rest of No 11 Commando was twenty-six-year-old Charles Mellows in shorts, shirt, pack, steel helmet, rifle and two bandoleers of about one hundred rounds each. Mellows was a wiry little Londoner who was nevertheless fiercely proud to be a member of the only Commando group to have been raised in Scotland. Ahead of him and moving in slow, unfussed, highly-disciplined order was Peter Foulger, six foot of bone and muscle.

The moment of landing was unopposed, but the enemy did not leave the Commandos alone for long. A French truck manned with a machine gun squatted menacingly on the road ahead. The tough Commando training which Mellows had undergone in Ayrshire was never put into practice – a trick of fate he curses with colourful versatility to this day.

He recalls: 'I wasn't conscious of being hit at all, only feeling when I heard the almighty row of the gun that I must press myself hard into the earth. But I had already stopped bullets in the chest, ankle and backside. Then there was a quick burst from Foulger's anti-tank rifle. He saved my life, because the enemy gunner was killed instantly.'

Meanwhile, Keyes, on the wrong side of the river, managed to secure a boat from an Australian battalion. His men piled into it and Keyes himself ferried them successfully across the Litani while the enemy kept up a cruel barrage of fire. The Commandos were now tackling the very obstacle their landing had intended to outflank.

Pedder, who lived on a perpetual short fuse, cursed and blasphemed his men forward. He was shouting orders to his officers when the bullets slammed into them all, killing Pedder instantly and wounding all the others.

The hour belonged to Regimental Sergeant-Major Tevendale: he took command and propelled the advance ever forward. Ahead of them was the local barracks and a number of men about to reinforce the key redoubt.

For Captain More there was elation. His detachment had done well, taking a number of field guns and howitzers. He commented later: 'At one point it was really rather embarrassing. The number of French Algerian prisoners we took outnumbered the Commandos.'

But the enemy was not finished: its fire power was suddenly stepped up and Geoffrey Keyes had to reorganize the attack. It was lunchtime when the redoubt eventually fell.

For the fiercely proud 'Scottish Commando' the price of victory was high. When No 11 went back to Cyprus it left behind a quarter of its strength with one hundred and twenty-three casualties.

For Layforce the writing was already on the wall. Commandos would have stormed on with the utmost cheerfulness. But the escort ships were simply not available. And the prejudice against amphibious raids by senior commanders was still very potent. They were happier with the broad sweep of battle: a highly trained army hurling itself at a foe equally proficient. Anything else smacked to them of banditry.

Except for a successful attack on two Italian strongpoints known as the Twin Pimples outside Tobruk, major amphibious raids did not figure largely in the history of the Mediterranean war during the summer and winter of 1941–1942.

Nevertheless, the adventure of the Twin Pimples is part of Commando legend: a highly creditable action in the frustrating, untidy, thankless war in Africa of those years.

Twin Pimples was undertaken by No 8 Commando, which had been formed by Laycock himself in June 1940 with men from the Household Cavalry, the Foot Guards, the Somerset Light Infantry and (accompanied by inevitable teeth gnashings from the army) the Royal Marines. No 8 was to be disbanded just over a year later, but its short life was worthwhile.

A small detachment consisting of five officers and seventy men was given the job in Tobruk of harrying the enemy in an unabashed bid to tear its nerves to shreds. The result was a small-scale raid which put the wind up the Italians to a highly gratifying degree.

No 8 was to zero in on the Italians at the Twin Pimples. Indian troops holding the forward positions had found the Italians a thorn in the flesh. So it was No 8's task to wipe out the offending garrison's presence from the two hills. Out went the reconnaissance parties: scouting missions carried out by Commandos and Indians seeking to get an intimate knowledge of the ground.

Captain Mike Keely of the Devonshire Regiment commanded a force which was to slip through the Italian lines, along the main road and hurl itself at the Twin Pimples from behind. The 18th Indian Cavalry Regiment was to put in a frontal assault from the hills.

Forty commandos were to take part, taking with them a demolition party of Australian sappers.

It was, stated one of the party, 'like an English summer night' as the raiders set off, moving silently but quickly in their crêpe-soled boots. They carried tommy guns, rifles, bayonets and grenades. Some had ground sheets to use as stretchers. The road leading to the Twin Pimples ribboned ahead. The party skirted the two hills until it found itself in the Italians' rear.

The Indians began their diversionary attack; the Italians let loose their flares. The bullets rained into the Indian positions. No 8 struck. Right into the face of the enemy machine guns it advanced, getting within a mere thirty yards of the nests, the Commandos shouting their password 'Jock' to prevent fighting one another in the dark. The Commandos were everywhere, killing Italians assiduously. Those of the enemy who had no stomach for the fight scurried in vain to their foxholes. The grenades went in after them.

Keely was everyone's dream of a Commando that day. He leapt like a creature possessed into one machine-gun nest and brought the butt of his tommy gun crashing down on the heads of the occupants.

Control of the two hillocks was imminent. The Australian sappers blew up the ammunition bunkers. The whole area was rent by explosives; the dump went up in one angry red ball. Italian trench mortars joined the booty. The whole thing was over in fifteen minutes. The Indian cavalry serenaded the departure of the rest with an angry fusillade of shells into the Twin Pimples but most of the enemy had been dislodged triumphantly.

The toll for No 8 Commando was four casualties, one of whom died later of his wounds.

Layforce was disbanded in the late summer of 1941, most of the men returning to their regiments. Six officers with fifty-three men remained in the Middle East under Bob Laycock as a raiding force attached to the 8th Army.

It was this little group which was now to embark on one of the most bizarre and dangerous gambles of the Commando war.

# 5

Even as implacable and resolute a soldier as Bob Laycock felt a twinge of anxiety at his new assignment. It was chilling in its clarity: strike deep into the heart of Rommel's headquarters, kidnapping or if necessary killing Germany's most celebrated soldier.

Laycock was to be in overall command with Geoffrey Keyes in charge of the detachment which would strike the vital blow. In no way, Laycock reasoned, could there possibly be a single survivor from such a hazardous enterprise. It would be quite literally a suicide mission; the chances of being evacuated afterwards must surely be nil.

But for Keyes, now a Lieutenant-Colonel, it was all high adventure with the prospect of a magnificent prize. He begged Laycock: 'Please keep your doubts to yourself. Otherwise the whole thing will be called off.'

General Rommel's headquarters were thought to be sited at Beda Littoria in Cyrenaica, some 125 miles from the coast and 500 miles from Alexandria, where the adventure was to begin.

The disappointments of the desert war to date might as well have been written in the sands as far as the Commandos were concerned. Here was a mission to appeal to the schoolboy in all of them.

In high spirits and fevered impatience for action they embarked in the submarines *Torbay* and *Talisman* on 10 November. The choice of date was deliberate. The attack was meant to coincide with the opening of General Auchinleck's offensive against Rommel. The weather was splendid. It matched the soaring spirit of Geoffrey Keyes and his little band.

Those Commandos in HM Submarine *Torbay* were the first in. The stretch of coast was indeed desolate, but ahead was the friendly torch-flash signalling the start of disembarkation.

Desert Reconnaissance Group, a highly efficient intelligence outfit, had done them proud, dropping into the territory the cool and resourceful Captain John Haselden, who had arrived masquerading most effectively as an Arab.

The party landed in small rubber boats, which were treated with fierce contempt by the considerable swell. One wave slapped viciously into a little knot of boats, pushing four of them into the sea. The delay seemed endless, but eventually Keyes was on shore with a sterling partner, Sergeant Jack Terry. Behind them came Captain Campbell, Keyes' second-in-command, and those of his party who had survived injury on landing.

They presented a miserable spectacle; they were drenched to the skin and their gear was completely useless. Haselden, however, treated the new arrivals as honoured guests. With supreme courtesy, he ushered them to a roofless stone ruin nearby; soon he had a cheerful fire blazing.

It was more than welcome, for the weather had suddenly changed very decidedly for the worse. Keyes and his men had it very cushy for a while, which is more than could be said for Bob Laycock. He and his detachment were desperately trying to land from the *Talisman*. The heavy seas churned and raged; most of the boats capsized. Eventually, Laycock and seven other ranks struggled ashore.

The storm blew itself out next day and the sun shone on the men's clothes.

The forces were divided into two. Keyes was to lead the first detachment and storm Rommel's house. Lieutenant Roy Cook had an essential role : he was to lead the second detachment with sixteen men, cut the telephone and telegraph wire south of Cyrene.

Laycock would remain behind with a sergeant and two men. They would form a beach-head and stand guard over the rations and ammunition dump. There was a group from *Talisman* that had been unable to land : perhaps they would have some success on the following night. If so, they would be welcomed as friendly faces.

The rain returned and with it acute discomfort. But Commandos did not seek feather beds; it was the inactivity which nettled them.

At 8 p.m., Lieutenant-Colonel Geoffrey Keyes set out on his last journey.

The party trudged inland across the inhospitable country, the sheep-tracks rock-strewn and often barely perceptible. Keyes cursed his compass and indifferent map with equal volubility. At the top of a small hill they stopped for sleep in the rain-soaked scrub. They awoke to a shock. Towering over Keyes and his men was a posse of Arabs, brandishing short Italian rifles.

Keyes muttered: 'My God, whose side are they on?' Hesitation could easily mean death. In a flash, he had spotted the leader of this singularly unsavoury band. Captain Campbell later recalled: 'He was a very villainous looking Arab with a red headcloth wound round his head at a raffish angle.'

Keyes, a man of considerable persuasive charm, advanced with what he hoped was a winning smile. Fortunately, Corporal Drori, a Palestinian who spoke perfect Arabic, was one of the landing party. To the intense relief of the other Commandos, the parley seemed to go well. The 'seedy brigand' (Campbell's description) was disposed to be welcoming. Soon he was promising to supply food and at nightfall to act as a guide to a cave which was a few hours away from the headquarters of the Desert Fox.

When it came to friends, Keyes and his men certainly could not complain. For now an Arab boy was produced and sent ahead to reconnoitre the objective and give Keyes enough of a description to draw a usable sketch map.

But by the time that the party moved off, the weather had turned foul and vicious. A series of thunderstorms raged; the terrain seemed to consist of nothing but smelling, oozing mud. A march would be nothing but long, cold and wet. And this before the objective had been reached!

Keyes, however, remained resolutely cheerful. He pointed

out : 'Nobody is going to suspect that a group of Commandos will attack in this weather. They'll be taking shelter and that means less opposition.'

The ground up to this point had been manageable, even if the men did slip and stagger, trying desperately to keep in single file so that they did not knock each other over and tumble into the mud's sticky embrace.

But even that comparative luxury was to be denied them. Soon they found themselves faced with a 250 foot escarpment of muddy turf and rock. Up they stumbled, realizing that they were bound to be making some noise which sooner or later would be noticed.

And so it proved. Suddenly, there was the sound of a dog barking. A stream of light issued from a door of a hut straight ahead. A man shouted; then the door was slammed shut.

At the top of the slope, they followed a track towards the headquarters. Keyes and Jack Terry edged on fifty yards; Roy Cook set out for the telephone pylon he was due to demolish.

Keyes, Terry and Campbell were pushing ahead through a hedge and running up some steps. They shoved open the front door of a building, coming face-to-face with a German soldier. Campbell reached for his .38 pistol and fired. The German dropped and the party sped through the hall. An empty room led from the hall and as the raiders catapulted towards it, another German appeared on the stairs.

A tommy gun barked viciously. There was a second door; behind it a knot of Germans took the full force of Geoffrey Keyes' weapon. Campbell wrenched the pin from a grenade, aiming to complete the work of the Colt. But the Germans had come to. There was short, sharp fire. Keyes slumped to the floor.

Campbell related : 'The grenade burst with a shattering explosion. This was followed by complete silence and we could see that the light in the room had gone out. I decided Geoffrey had to be moved in case there was further fighting in the building, so between us Sergeant Terry and I carried him outside and laid him on the grass verge by the side of the steps leading to the front door.

'He must have died as we were carrying him outside, for when I felt his heart it had ceased to beat.'

Then Campbell went back through the hall and round the back entrance. A trigger-happy Commando opened fire; one of Campbell's legs felt like a mass of searing flame. Horrified Commandos gathered round, offering to carry him the twenty-five miles to the beach. But Campbell – whose leg was to be amputated after he was taken prisoner – would not allow so drastic a departure from schedule; the party must go back and leave him behind.

Now the entire responsibility for withdrawal lay with the ever-faithful Terry. He guided the dispirited raiders back to Laycock. Now they would all await Roy Cook and his demolition party.

That was to prove another disappointment: Cook had been captured. There was a further blow. *Torbay* edged her way towards the coast after dark, flashing a Morse message which told Laycock that the sea was too rough and that she would return the following night.

There was nothing for it but to hope that the weather would change and the Germans would keep away.

The weather did decide to be kind; the Germans were less accommodating. Soon sustained fire was directed at the beach; it obviously came from a force far superior in numbers. Laycock and the party crouched in caves, wondering how long it would be before they were forced to break out.

Then Laycock made his decision : the party must split up into small groups and streak across the open to the cover of the hills inland. There they would either get in touch with *Talisman* or hide out in the wadis, the rocky watercourses which were dry except in the rainy season. Reinforcements would surely come.

It was now a case of Laycock and Terry struggling for their own survival and somehow reaching the Eighth Army. The rest of the forces had scattered. The country was wide and open, and concealment impossible. Sniping was continuous and merciless but by a miracle neither man was hit. Fortunately, the Arabs they encountered were friendly.

Other members of the raiding party had not been so lucky. Their throats had been slit and their bodies handed over to the Germans.

Laycock later recorded: 'Our greatest problem was the lack of food, and though never desperate we were forced to subsist for periods, which never exceeded two and a half consecutive days, on berries only, and we became appreciably weak from want of nourishment.'

At other times, the two men fed well on goat and Arab bread, but developed a marked craving for sugar. Since it rained continuously, water was never a problem.

Colonel and sergeant linked up with the British forces at Cyrene, forty-one days after setting out. Bob Laycock was able to enjoy his Christmas dinner before setting out for Cairo to make his report.

Although the story he told was one of high courage, the overall achievement was precisely nil. Once again, a hugely spectacular Commando success had somehow dodged Bob Laycock. For the blunt truth was that the house that had been attacked was in fact the headquarters of German and Italian supply services. Rommel had been nowhere near. True, he had started off in the house at Beda Littoria but he disliked it and after ten days, he handed it over to his quartermaster's staff and moved to a position near the battlefield with his troops.

At the scene of the attack, the Germans examined the body of Roger Keyes, finding Egyptian and Italian money, a girl's photograph and a leather diary which helped to establish identity.

Rommel himself later scanned the reports of an attempt to kill him by 'an English Commando killer band'. A fellow officer told the Desert Fox: 'The Führer has ordered all those captured to be shot immediately.' Rommel snapped: 'I consider otherwise. Let them be treated as honourable prisoners of war.'

And they were. For Roger Keyes, there was to be the Victoria Cross – and a remarkable tribute from the Germans. Although of course aware of the object of their mission, Rommel admired both its cheek and its courage. The chaplain of the garrison church at Potsdam conducted Keyes' funeral with full military honours.

It had been no fault of Laycock, Keyes or their men that they had been misled. Initial intelligence had been unreliable. But if the raid had come off, the prize would have been spectacular indeed. Rommel's capture would have been a sufficient blow at German morale to have made the operation supremely worthwhile. It was a classic bit of Commando impudence that went tragically wrong.

The situation in North Africa remained black and frustrating for the special forces in 1941.

# 6

Lieutenant David Stirling was a giant of a Scotsman with a lean athletic figure which could never stay still. Inaction invariably put him out of temper, and when the somewhat ill-starred Layforce was disabled young Stirling was in a very foul humour indeed.

He had gone to the Middle East at the time Laycock had amassed his force of five Commando units to do battle with the Axis.

Stirling now felt like a stranded whale. He was damned if he was going to share the fate of many of his fellow officers who had been sent back to England. So in Alexandria he fretted and fumed for fresh orders.

Layforce, he recognized, had had many faults. It had been too big and unable to move with sufficient speed. Commando units, he felt, should work in small, mobile groups that would strike the enemy swiftly from behind its own lines. Above all, there must be the all-important element of surprise.

Normally, an officer in the middle of fighting a war does not have much time for speculation, certainly not on such seemingly airy-fairy projects as raising what amounted to a private army. But fate took a hand and gave David Stirling ample opportunity for cogitation – from a hospital bed.

It all began with a chance meeting with Jock Lewis of No 8 Commando who had come into possession of a consignment of parachutes delivered by mistake to Alexandria. Parachutes were not exactly in generous supply in the western desert, so Stirling decided to investigate.

He came straight to the point with Jock Lewis: 'We could use these parachutes if only we had the manpower at our disposal.' He added with studied casualness: 'I was thinking some sort of Commando unit.'

It was a daring idea and equally attractive to Lewis. Putting it into effect proved quite another matter. Both men discovered that there was precisely one ancient Valencia aircraft available. Worse still, there was not a single instructor in the Middle East capable of teaching anyone parachute jumping.

Stirling shrugged: 'Very well, we must do the job ourselves.'

Stirling, Lewis and six other men made their way to Mersa Matruh and ruefully inspected the Valencia. Everything they had heard about it was depressingly confirmed: it was a tired, clumsy old hulk about as suited for paratroop operations as a cart-horse in the Grand National. For one thing, it did not even boast proper static line attachments. These would have to be clipped on to the passenger seats.

In some trepidation, they all clambered aboard. When the time came for Stirling's jump, he felt an ominous tug at his back as the static line on the parachute pulled open at the back. White silk blossomed out. But it had happened too soon. The billowing silk caught on the tailplane. For a few seconds, Stirling dangled like a malefactor on the gallows. Then came the ripping sound which every parachutist dreads: the parachute canopy tearing in shreds.

Now he was hurtling to the ground with a speed that made even prayer impossible. Below him blurred the desert wastes; the air tunnelled through the canopy's widening gap.

He hit the ground with a jarring thud. The pain was unspeakable; the merciful black of unconsciousness enveloped him. The result was temporary paralysis of both legs and a violent injury to the back.

But he was alive, and in hospital his brain raced with a fresh intensity. He lay there, planning, scheming, formulating. Obviously, it was not going to be any use just commandeering the odd aircraft and going out on jumps; the whole thing had to be plotted much more scientifically.

From his bed in the Scottish Military Hospital in Alexandria he studied maps of the Western Desert. Plans of attack on German and Italian installations were worked out. He dwelt on numbers of men and types of explosives.

As he grew stronger and was able to hobble around the hospital, he became increasingly more impatient at the inactivity. How on earth was he to get his ideas even looked at, let alone accepted? He could, of course, put the whole thing in a memorandum. But that would mean going through the bureaucratic army machinery; his memo would end up in some pigeonhole and that would be death to it.

So on one July day in 1941, he decided on direct action. He hobbled out to his car and drove straight for Middle East Headquarters in Cairo.

General Neil Ritchie, Deputy Chief of Staff, Middle East Forces, stared with astonishment at the dishevelled giant who barged into his office waving pieces of paper covered with almost illegible scrawl.

Stirling had managed to penetrate the headquarters by tricking the sentries and hobbling into the building. He gasped out his apology. But Ritchie scarcely heard him. He stared at the papers for some time in silence. Then he stared coldly at Stirling.

He declared: 'This might be just the sort of thing we've been looking for. Leave this with me and I shall discuss it with the Commander-in-Chief and give you our decision within the next few days.'

Mercifully, Ritchie's hatred of red tape was every bit as profound as the young Scotsman's. Within hours, the idea had gone to General Auchinleck, the Commander-in-Chief. Stirling was told to present himself for briefing within three days.

Auchinleck was succinct: 'You will recruit six officers and sixty men to be based in the Suez Canal Zone. You will only have time for a crash training course because I want a swift raid on German airfields the night before there is a major offensive. By the way, you are now a Captain.'

Stirling had forthwith under his command the L detachment of the Special Air Service. Until then, no such organization had existed; it was literally his own baby.

Getting together the talent for SAS was the least of the problems. Jock Lewis was an obvious choice; soon he was joined by an Irishman named McGonigal, a Scot called Bill Fraser, and Thomas and Bonnington, two Englishmen. Some other likely non-commissioned officer talent was drawn into the net.

In addition, there was Paddy Mayne, a vast block of an Ulsterman who had probably been born for just such a scrap as this. There was, however, one rather serious snag to Paddy Mayne. The former international rugger player was at that precise moment under arrest for hitting a superior officer. Stirling considered the matter to be less than important; Mayne was told to behave himself and was promptly released for 'special duties'.

Training, in a hastily constructed camp at Kabrit, a desolate, forbidding territory some one hundred miles from Cairo, was tough indeed. Men were sent out night after night to put into practice Stirling's marksmanship training. Armed with a variety of Italian, German and British automatic weapons, the men of SAS made the darkness their friend and became expert in firing blind, shooting on sound rather than sight.

The desert obeys few of the laws of nature as most of us know them. By the day, the men sweated and cursed in the iron heat of the rock-strewn desert. At night, the temperatures plunged to ice; everyone muffled up in greatcoats but carried on Stirling's particular brand of weapon training.

Of course, there was parachuting; drops were made by the SAS leader along with everyone else. On one of the drops came tragedy : two of the men were killed when their parachutes failed to open.

Masking his feelings, Stirling permitted no time for sentiment, no pause in training. Too much was at stake; SAS had a number of enemies in orthodox military circles. One hint of failure would bring about the collapse of the enterprise.

Ingenuity by the individual Commandos was encouraged. Stirling was anxious to fashion a bomb which could be both an explosive and an incendiary. It would not only have to blow up an aircraft, but also to burn it completely so that it became useless.

To Jock Lewis it proved a challenge. He experimented with a variety of explosive substances. The desert shook to fearsome explosions, all to no avail. Then came an impressive alchemy of plastic, thermite and oil which were mixed together and kneaded into a small bomb. With great glee, Lewis placed his toy on top of the oil drum. The fuse was inserted and lit. The drum was torn apart; inside blazed the liquid. The 'Lewis Bomb' was born.

The SAS was now ready for its first strike. And the opportunity was at hand.

General Auchinleck was planning his first big offensive against Rommel's Afrika Corps on 18 November 1941. Tobruk was encircled by Axis forces. The push was designed as a relief; in addition, the heat was on to drive German and Italian forces out of Cyrenaica.

The SAS was to have a vital job, attacking five of Rommel's airfields on the night before the offensive opened.

Stirling's raiders, in a mood of feverish excitement, were flown to the forward base of the RAF where bombs, fuses, grenades and tommy guns were packed into special canisters to be dropped with the parachutists.

The target airfields lay in the Gaza–Timini area. It was planned that the raiders would be dropped on the night of the 16th, hide up until the evening of the following day and then go into the attack.

Afterwards, there would be a forty-five mile march into the desert. At a pre-arranged rendezvous they would link up with the Long Range Desert Group, one of the key special service units. It would take them back to the RAF's forward field.

Soon the first disappointment came for David Stirling. The weather deteriorated menacingly. Winds were gale force and parachuting in such conditions would be suicidal.

Everyone had started off with such high hopes. The blow to morale would be cruel indeed if the raid was cancelled. Besides, a Commando who waited for absolutely ideal conditions would probably wait for ever.

The men conferred. Everyone agreed that the raid was on.

Not for the first time, David Stirling found himself ill-served by aircraft. On this occasion he had to put up with Bristol Bombay transports, twin-engined heavy affairs which could only reach 192 mph. Stirling swore: 'The ruddy things were probably due for the scrap-heap before the war.' But if ever there was a case of take it or leave it, here it was.

It was a cold, uncomfortable ride. The aircraft creaked and groaned; cold air whistled through the fuselages which, more than one man reflected gloomily, probably had as many holes as a sieve.

When the anti-aircraft guns opened up, the transports banked steeply. Shells whistled alarmingly. How long would it be before they did their dreadful work on these aged hulks? On they rumbled until the targets were only minutes away. Then the doors were opened and the air whistled in. Of course, it increased the danger from enemy fire, but somehow the rush came as a welcome tonic. Static lines were hooked up. Then the green light glowed. With Stirling in the lead, each man leapt into the blackness.

Stirling floated down peacefully, but the descent was brief and soon the ground would come up to meet him. But where was he? Where were the rest of his comrades? With an almighty blow, he smashed into the earth and lost consciousness.

Being dragged along the ground hastened his recovery; there was bad bruising but nothing worse. He flashed his torch into the darkness; there was no response. His men were obviously scattered widely over the desert and he hadn't the slightest idea where. It took him more than an hour to round them up and they were a sorry sight indeed. Not one had escaped injury: there were broken limbs, gashes and bruises.

Injuries to men who should have been in top condition for fighting was bad enough, but what about the equipment? The containers holding the bombs, fuses, machine-guns, food and blankets had been scattered to the winds of the desert.

The result was total humiliating failure, a miserable

shambles for the Commando group which Stirling had founded with such high hopes. With their tails between their legs, the men trudged off across the desert for their rendezvous with the Long Range Desert Group.

Here mugs of scalding tea revived spirits somewhat. An exception was David Stirling, worn down with depression and fatigue. Of Lieutenant McGonigal's party there was then no sign; Charles Bonnington's group had all been captured. Its aircraft had landed by mistake in an enemy airfield.

It was no good blaming anyone; somewhere, the whole idea had a basic serious flaw. Stirling had to admit reluctantly that parachuting was now out. It was too hazardous a means of getting men to their target.

The LRDG group ferried everyone home and Stirling realized that a possible solution was staring him in the face. Could the LRDG function be reversed? If it could bring his raiders back, why should it not ferry them to a raid? He began to feel rather better.

But would the LRDG solemnise such a marriage? Most certainly it would, and with enthusiasm. Furthermore, Stirling had a staunch ally in General Ritchie.

Fortunes had been changing in the desert war. Rommel had retreated, certainly. But then he had turned round and hit out yet again. Ritchie was sent into the desert to get things moving. Such a link-up was just what he wanted. Stirling was given a completely free hand.

Of course, tactics were different now. Stirling had been coming round increasingly to the view that the place to set up a base was *behind* the enemy lines. The place chosen was Jalo, a malodorous spot situated near the north-west tip of the Kalansho Sand Sea. It had been snatched from the Italians just before Stirling arrived and was now in command of Brigadier Reid.

Tough and pugnacious, Reid came straight to the point: 'You can have all the help you want. All I ask is that you hit the enemy hard. We have a plan to trap Rommel in his retreat from Benghazi. I don't anticipate much trouble from him. It's the air which worries me.'

Possible opposition from enemy aircraft had to be eliminated. That meant destroying any planes on the ground; just the sort of job SAS was particularly fitted for. Stirling was delighted at the prospect of action; the slate could be wiped clean.

The enemy airfield at Agedabia looked a likely target. It seemed to pose the greatest threat. Stirling went further. There were other airfields he wanted to destroy so that neither the Germans nor the Italians would be capable of launching an effective air strike.

He, along with Paddy Mayne and two men, would go for the airfield at Sirte, some three hundred and fifty miles from Jalo. Jock Lewis with his group would shoot up the airfield at El Agheila. The other raid would be led by Bill Fraser, who would make for Agedabia.

The various groups struck out across the barren desert, a terrain positively bristling with hazards. Jagged rocks tore at tyres. Punctures caused frustrating delays because equipment had to be unloaded before the trucks could be jacked up.

Real trouble, when it came, swooped down on them from the desert skies.

An Italian Gibli reconnaissance aircraft hovered over the columns. The gunners leapt to their Lewis guns but now the Italians were diving down on the column, unleashing a couple of bombs which screeched well away from the target. The aircraft banked steeply and vanished. This was no relief; the Gibli had lived to tell the tale. Soon other aircraft would be back, unleashing destruction on the trucks and their occupants.

A patch of scrub loomed ahead. The trucks put on a burst of speed and made for the best shelter there was. Camouflage nets would be a waste of time, anyway. The Italians would know the likely position of the trucks.

Every man strained for the inevitable hum of engines.

The Italian bombers prowled the skies, scouring the desert for the sight of the trucks. Of course, they spotted them and down came the stick of bombs. Machine-gun fire raked the area. For fifteen minutes it went on. Then the aircraft regrouped and flew away.

Stirling, rising from his prone position in the sand, saw to his amazement that not one of the trucks had been hit. Casualties were nil.

It was pitch dark as they nosed their way towards the airfield at Sirte. Lights were doused. Stirling suddenly heard voices and the revving of engines. They were a few yards from the main coastal road, which was in the hands of the enemy. Obviously, the news of their approach had reached the Italians; there was every prospect of a fight.

Stirling thought fast. The best plan would be for him and one of his best sergeants, Brough, to raid Sirte airfield. Paddy Mayne would take another group and attack another Italian airfield, this time near the town of Tamit.

Stirling and Brough stole away into the night with their bombs and weapons. They bade farewell to the LRDG troops heading towards Tamit with Mayne and his raiders.

The two men moved gingerly towards the edge of the airfield where they could now see rows of parked aircraft in a long line, apparently unguarded. The temptation to plant bombs then and there was almost unbearable, but it had to be resisted. Stirling realized that it would ruin Paddy Mayne's chances of success with his surprise attack. With regret, they would have to wait.

Stirling stepped back and stumbled over an obstacle. Then all at once there was a yell : he had tripped over a slumbering Italian sentry.

The two needed no encouragement to run for it. But by now there was an excited babble of Italian. Bullets whined through the air and the airfield's heavy anti-aircraft guns joined in.

But the enemy fire was directed elsewhere. The Italians were aiming at imaginary targets out to sea, thinking that a Commando attack was coming from there.

It was a respite needed by both men. They made for a welcome ridge, waiting until the sullen roar of the guns had ceased. Then they settled down to sleep.

There was to be no attack on Sirte, no glorious SAS assault on the Italians. The two men woke to find that only a few yards away, a group of Arabs were working on a cultivated plot of land. It was an almost laughable humiliation. But worse was in store. As the day wore on, Stirling noticed that aircraft were taking off and not returning. The airfield was being evacuated.

The whole enterprise had failed. There was the prospect of a rendezvous with the LRDG after yet another fruitless adventure for the Commandos.

Stirling was convinced this was the end; he would never be allowed another chance.

Paddy Mayne fared better. Under the shroud of darkness, he and his men moved in single file across the outer perimeter of Tamit airfield. Mayne glimpsed a thin ribbon of light below a hut door and edged towards it. Inside was the sound of laughter: excellent, it would soften up the target.

The door was thrown open. Mayne levelled his tommy gun and fired. The bullets smashed into the room. The startled Italians fell in a sea of blood. Up jerked the machine-gun, spraying the lights. Then Mayne slammed the door and ran.

Inside, dazed and wounded Italians climbed over the bodies of their dead comrades. They sent revolver shots spreading after Mayne's group, who now made for the dark shapes of the aircraft on the other side. From plane to plane they darted, planting the bombs where they would do the most damage.

Mayne found himself without a bomb. It was the last aircraft of all. He did not hesitate. He leapt into the cockpit and tore out the instrument panel with his bare hands.

He and the rest of the group just made it before the aircraft blew up one after the other. It was a most satisfying inferno of fire.

Far off, near the coastal road, Stirling saw the glow from the burning aircraft; twenty-three in all were destroyed in the raid.

Stirling had not been the only one to hit bad luck : Lewis's target had turned out to be little more than an aircraft ferrying point. But there was a further sensation. Fraser's group blew up no less than thirty-seven aircraft. SAS had proved itself beyond measure.

The blood of the air services was up. In a mood of jubilation, Stirling planned and carried out scores of raids.

His next plan was to attack with jeeps, brand-new custom-built affairs with four Vickers guns mounted two in the front and two in the back. There was a crew of three, a driver and two gunners.

The target this time was the German airfield at Sidi Haneish, near Fuka.

Eighteen jeeps set off at twenty miles an hour on the forty-mile journey, eventually fanning out into two columns of eight as the moon slipped behind the clouds. Stirling strained his eyes through the dark, but could see nothing. Then suddenly the whole scene was illuminated; the airfield, its lights full on, was a bare half-mile away. A bomber roared overhead, but it was making straight for the airfield.

It was then that Stirling went in. The jeeps gathered speed into a mechanized version of an old-style cavalry charge. They opened up with their machine-guns. A green Very light was fired and the jeeps fanned out in V-formation.

Soon they were next to the banks of aircraft. The Commandos crouched, firing into the planes and igniting the petrol tanks. One by one, the planes turned red, then burst into flames.

Incendiary bullets crashed into Junkers, Heinkels and Stuka dive-bombers, while the Germans recovered and made for their defence posts. A mortar bomb smashed into two columns of jeeps, followed by the roar of a Breda cannon.

Raider Steve Hastings heard an ominous clang; then the hot oil sprayed up, covering his body. Stirling's jeep was riddled with fire. He and his companion quitted the blazing jeep and leapt into another.

All attention was on the Breda cannon. It was knocked out of action. The jeeps returned to the planes and destroyed those remaining.

Paddy Mayne found one aircraft decidedly obstinate; it

refused to blow up. He leapt from his jeep and planted a bomb in it personally. Then he and the rest roared off back into the desert.

Avenging Stukas were sent out by the Germans from other locations to deal with the jeeps. Their tally was one raider killed.

The SAS had destroyed twenty-five aircraft and damaged at least a dozen more. Two men had been killed.

This was by no means the end of the daring exploits of the man who was now a legend in the desert, almost rivalling Rommel. He became known as 'the Phantom Major'.

Raids were carried out, not only on airfields, but on every conceivable target. To the SAS fell ships at anchor, oil pipelines and enemy transports.

Luck like that could not last for ever. Eventual capture was perhaps inevitable. After four escape attempts as a prisoner of war, Stirling eventually ended up in the notorious Colditz castle. Command of the SAS went to Paddy Mayne.

But in his fourteen months of command, David Stirling destroyed no less than two hundred and fifty aircraft with minimal loss.

His Special Air Service still exists in Britain today. Its motto embodies Stirling's whole philosophy: 'Who dares, wins.'

# 7

Back in Europe, the Allies were most gratified with the effect of the first Commando raids. Not only had Hitler learnt of the existence of a new-style raiding army, but, in the case of the Lofoten Islands strike, had been robbed literally overnight of about half of the fish industry's total production in Norway.

The main factories had been put out of action; rebuilding them would take time, and the Norwegians, with new heart, would scarcely prove co-operative.

German submarine crews had their own special reason for cursing the Commandos. Fish oil is a particularly valuable source of Vitamins A and D, the 'sunshine' vitamins. U-boat crewmen, operating on the Atlantic convoy routes, had forgotten what sunshine was like. For weeks at a time, they knew no other existence than that within their tight steel cocoon – surfacing in daylight hours would invite the attention of the RAF and allied vessels.

And that, of course, was all part of the idea.

But the satisfaction to be gained from blowing up factories soon palled; still, it was better than kicking one's heels while the bureaucrats made up their minds about future objectives.

There were enthusiastic souls who believed that a permanent base on the Lofoten Islands would provide an ideal arsenal against German shipping at Narvik and the northern coast.

The Luftwaffe would have welcomed such an idea; it would have played straight into Goering's hands. The Germans could have smashed the Commandos in a series of leisurely raids, since the islands were way beyond the range of British aircraft.

It was an impracticable idea, so the chiefs of Combined Operations began looking at other possibilities.

The trouble, grumbled Sir Roger Keyes, was that it was all taking far too long. Desk-bound officials did not realize that inactivity was the death-watch beetle of the soldier's morale. Men brought to the correct psychological peak for effective battle will experience a plunging of the spirits when the action fails to materialize.

In the months which followed the Lofoten Islands raid, a number of seemingly promising plans were set in motion and then, to general anger and disappointment, unceremoniously scrapped. This had even happened when raiding parties were already embarked and in sight of their targets.

The deliberate obstructionism, as he saw it, was too much for Keyes. There came the day when, as a Member of Parliament, he fired one last salvo at those he saw as his dithering tormentors.

In the House of Commons that October he proclaimed: 'After fifteen months' experience as Director of Combined Operations, and having been frustrated in every worthwhile offensive action I have tried to undertake, I must fully enforce the Prime Minister's comments on the strength of the negative power which controls the war machine in Whitehall ... Time is passing and so long as procrastination, the thief of time, is the key-word of the war machine in Whitehall, we shall continue to lose one opportunity after another.'

With Keyes' resignation, Winston Churchill sprang a surprise. The war lord's choice of a successor was Captain the Lord Louis Mountbatten, Royal Navy, who was made acting Vice-Admiral on his appointment. He was a handsome and charismatic figure whom some people were unwise enough to dismiss as a night-club playboy, as a polo-playing cousin of King George VI who could, if he wished, spend the whole of his life licking a golden spoon.

But it was Mountbatten who in the Mediterranean had brought his ship, the destroyer *Kelly*, into harbour, riddled by German fire, torpedo-holed and riding so low in the water that most of her main deck was awash. That in itself was a remarkable achievement. But Mountbatten's devotion to the *Kelly* was such that he had her pumped dry and put straight back into action.

Then the *Kelly* was shot from straight under him. He and his crew were machine-gunned mercilessly in the water while swimming for their lifeboats.

This exploit, impressivc though it was, did not necessarily serve as an ideal qualification to lead the Commandos. Churchill was interested in his other qualities. Mountbatten had a flair for handling men – and not just fighting men, either. He could charm and flatter bureaucrats with the same infinite skill as the Prime Minister.

Dithering was now in the past. Decisions were made fast from now on. There was ruthlessness, of course, but at least there was also charm and panache.

One Commando raid was to be launched every two weeks. All right, a few such forays would be minor affairs where a handful of men in rubber boats would knock out a coastal radar station and collar a few surprised Germans. But the day would come when battalion-sized forces escorted by destroyers and even warships would hurl themselves at enemy coasts.

No more would professional men at arms have to shudder before a succession of faceless committees. There was one committee with a specific job : hunting out juicy Commando targets.

Required reading from now on were the maps of the enemy coastline, intelligence files and situation reports.

During Mountbatten's first month, the target committee drew up a list of likely objectives which stretched from the northern tip of Norway to the French–Spanish border. The Royal Air Force representatives in Combined Operation's HQ scheduled missions to get the latest photo coverage of chosen areas.

Which area, everyone wondered, would be first?

The crew of a certain twin-engined bomber with the distinctive RAF roundels may have had a shrewd idea when circling over the island of Vaagso on the Norwegian coast opposite the Faroes.

Photo reconnaissance was a tricky business at the best of times and decidedly perilous when German anti-aircraft guns suddenly started their relentless spattering. The bomber's pilot nosed around for as long as he dared. Then he made off at high speed, enemy fire whistling harmlessly in his wake.

Every generation of seamen has its love-hate affair with the cruel, ruthless boiling cauldron of the North Sea. Even fair-sized vessels can be crunched to pulp, not just by the angry waters, but by the howling winds that slap and sting and poleaxe. The elements are respected and cursed in equal measure. Where there is life, its character is bred as hard and unflinching as the climate itself.

From Norway sailed the Vikings of old, men with scarcely an appetite for the sophisticated activity of war as we know it, but possessing an insatiable thirst for primitive rape and plunder. And yet, even in these seemingly Godforsaken lands, there are whole areas of calm where men are able to put down roots, to build little towns and settlements and make the best use of tiny anchorages snuggled improbably along the deep networks of the fjords.

A clutch of islands dots the west coast of Norway; scores of them looking like mere pimples when seen on the map or from the air.

It was two of these, Vaagso and Maaloy, which were to concern the twentieth-century Commandos.

The main object of the raid was to attack and destroy the German garrison in the small port of South Vaagso. The troops had been assigned to coastal defence duties and policing of the inland waterways – numbering, so British Intelligence believed, one hundred and fifty men from the 181 Division, with a solitary tank and one hundred men of a labour corps building defences. On Maaloy, there was a four-gun battery covering Vaagsfjord. A similar battery of two guns was to be found on Rugsundo Island, but the Commandos were instructed to punch where the opposition was greatest.

On the north coast of Vaagso lay Halsor, covering the northern entrance to Ulvesund, where German convoys formed up and shipping could be expected to be heavy.

Looming like a sinister menace on the mainland was the Luftwaffe with airfields at Herdla, Stavanger and Trondheim. This was formidable opposition for the Commandos at their present stage of development.

On 6 December, the joint force commanders were appointed. The Fiji-class cruiser HMS *Kenya* was to be the headquarters ship of Rear-Admiral Harold Burrough and Brigadier Charles Haydon.

Escort and support for the force was to come from four warships from the 17th Destroyer flotilla, HMS *Onslow*, *Oribi*, *Offa* and *Chiddingfold*. Troops were to land from the infantry assault ships HMS *Prince Charles* and *Prince Leopold*. The role of navigational beacon was to go to HM Submarine *Tuna*.

The potential of the Commando clout was impressive indeed. Lieutenant-Colonel John Durnford-Slater of No 3 Commando was in charge of fifty-one officers and five hundred and twenty-five other ranks. There were also a troop and a half of No 2 Commando; detachments of Royal Engineers (No 6 Commando); Royal Army Medical Corps (No 4 Commando); Intelligence officers from the War Office and a Press Unit. Men of the Royal Norwegian Army were to be attached as guides and interpreters.

A group system was organized. There were to be five assault groups. Group 1 was to land at Hollevik on the island's south shore and clear a known defence point and villages a mile and a half from the town of South Vaagso. It would then move in to support Group 2, which was to land just south of the town and capture it. Maaloy would be grabbed by Group 3 which lay not far from the town quays.

One of the biggest innovations so far in the Commando war (carried out with tremendous success in Vaagso) was the role assigned to Group 4. This was to be a floating reserve – quite literally, since it was to lie offshore in landing craft until needed to reinforce one of the other groups.

Group 5 was to be carried by the destroyer *Oribi* to the west shore of Ulvesund, then set up a roadblock between South and North Vaagso, and send a fighting patrol into the latter town in search of stray Germans.

The Royal Air Force was to carry out bombing missions assigned to Hampdens of 50 Squadron and Blenheims of 110 and 114 Squadrons of Coastal Command.

D-Day was set initially for 26 December – the same day that three hundred of No 12 Commando were due to go ashore for a second crack at the Lofoten Islands. But that particular action was to be largely a diversion raid for the far more serious business of Vaagso.

The blueprint for Vaagso looked sound enough on paper but the almost mystical faith placed by civilian administrators in tidy-looking documents found only cautious acceptance by Admiral Mountbatten. He preferred to talk directly to the men who would do the job.

His question to Durnford-Slater at their key interview was characteristically blunt: 'Can No 3 Commando carry out this raid?'

Durnford-Slater's confident affirmative then brought forth the comment: 'This seems very ambitious. Don't you think it would be better to take on something not quite so strong? How do you intend to deal with the battery?'

Durnford-Slater knew that *Kenya* and four destroyers would be available. Training and very fine human material would do the rest. It was more than enough for Mountbatten. Questioning ceased. No longer did Durnford-Slater feel that he was a junior officer being quizzed by an ultra-conservative commander anxious to prove himself in a new job. The Commandos were trusted; they would be left to get on with it.

That human material on which Durnford-Slater was relying – and which even at the time of his discussion with Mountbatten was going through a gruelling training programme in Scotland – was apt to take some colourful forms.

Major Jack Churchill, MC, already enjoyed an honourable place in the gallery of military eccentrics. Shakespeare would have relished this Falstaffian figure who was now No 3's second in command.

'Mad Jack' Churchill had been a legend at the time of Dunkirk – puffing into the city on a bicycle across which was slung a longbow.

Such a weapon, Mad Jack bellowed to all and sundry, was ideal for killing Germans. Failing the availability of a longbow, the tried and trusted sword was the next most effective armament. This terrifying broad-hilted claymore was swung around his head as he leapt into battle.

But good-natured critics said that neither the longbow nor the sword were Mad Jack's best weapon. That honour was reserved for his bagpipes, which he frequently played with such dubious skill that the enemy fled in horror. Or such was the story. Affectionate ribbing of Jack Churchill concealed, however, the intense respect that his men had for lion-hearted courage.

His citation for the DSO later in the war read like a comic strip, but was nevertheless true. Mad Jack collared over thirty Germans in a single night, stalking them one by one and leaping out of the shadows with a cry of *Hände hoch!* (Hands up!) accompanied by menacing cartwheels from the claymore.

Jack Churchill's value as a morale booster at this particular time could not be over-emphasized. Durnford-Slater, no cardboard character himself, certainly knew how to pick talent.

His choices also included a pre-war crony, Lieutenant C. S. 'Charlie' Head, who was to be the colonel's right hand man; and Captain J. E. 'Slinger' Martin, the administrative officer who had already been hardened in battle in World War One.

Slinger was a champion horseman with a style and dash which Durnford-Slater, also a sportsman, richly appreciated. He was also a superb administrator whose corner-cutting methods frequently turned Whitehall pen-pushers grey. Originally, he had been destined for service in the Middle

East, but such a prospect had attracted him not at all. He simply went to the nearest medical officer and complained that he was too old for such exertions. However, the prospect of a Commando scrap had a remarkably rejuvenating effect; he cunningly managed a transfer to No 3 Commando.

The talent at troop commander level could scarcely be described as pallid, either. Of the six troops, No 1 Troop was led by a whirlwind of an Irishman named Captain Bill Bradley, while Lieutenant Bob Clement of No 2 was an irascible Scotsman. It was a highly combustible mixture that must have caused even Durnford-Slater a twinge or two. The unpredictability of Bill Bradley, in particular, was apt to be lurid.

Bradley still twinkles with schoolboy relish about a perfectly serious project to blow up the German Embassy in Dublin.

He recalls: 'It was during the idle period before Vaagso. What the hell was the use of all that special training if we weren't goin to get the chance to use it? We desperately wanted some Germans to take on for size. I was convinced that some of the villainous Southern Irish were aiding the U-boat campaign by tipping off Berlin about convoy movements. Much to my surprise, Durnford-Slater thought it was a jolly good idea to teach the Irish a lesson. We were just about to set it up and get the ammunition when the Colonel was whipped south smartly for the interview with Admiral Mountbatten.'

It was probably just as well.

John Durnford-Slater sat alone in his office, staring at the buff folder in front of him. On top of the pile of papers lay the RAF reconnaissance photographs. The interpreters had given them a good going over; the German positions were inked in clearly. Burrowing down further, Durnford-Slater came to the mountain of Intelligence reports – maps, transcripts of interrogations of local refugees and hydrographic tables.

The young lieutenant-colonel realized he was staring at data which amounted to an almost perfect blueprint for a classic Commando raid.

Brigadier Haydon, as the overall military commander, was called away at this stage on another assignment. So Durnford-Slater was on his own to carry out the planning of 'Operation Archery' with the navy and air force.

A key job was given to Charlie Head to make out the signals plan – a reasonably straightforward operation in normal circumstances. The only drawback was that Charlie Head had a decidedly scrappy knowledge of signals.

Durnford-Slater shuddered as he heard his friend talking airily about kilocycles. He confided to another colleague: 'Charlie wouldn't know a kilocycle if he met one in the street with a label round its neck.'

This, however, was no barrier to Charlie Head's getting himself appointed chairman of the signals planning committee. He was cute enough to let most of the others do the difficult talking; basic commonsense, organizational ability and the sort of energy which left most men wilting carried him through.

A complete scale model of Vaagso, showing every house and building, had been made up from the photographs; briefing of No 3 Commando could go ahead. But there was a significant omission from the model – there were no place names. Security was a paramount consideration in mounting Commando operations; not even Jack Churchill yet knew precisely where the target was.

Durnford-Slater then left for Scapa Flow with Admiral Burrough and Admiral Tovey, Commander-in-Chief of the Home Fleet, to complete the naval planning for Operation Archery.

At Scapa Flow there were no less than two rehearsals before Vaagso, and D-Day was put back to 26 December. These were held to decide finally whether the men of No 3 Commando could give the best possible account of themselves on an island whose shape and general configuration corresponded near enough to the Vaagso-Maaloy area.

The men sailed in on the first of these exercises; a flight of Hampdens dropped smoke floats in front of the landing points. This was an innovation not in the original plan. The floats successfully masked the landing craft at the exact moment they reached the shore.

Some fresh wrinkles showed up: a second exercise was ordered.

The name Vaagso was still a secret when the men taking part in the second exercise waded into the cold December seas. At the moment, there were no Germans to greet the invaders: only some totally uninterested black-faced sheep. Yet the dummy-run on a remote northern island was as near to the real thing as was possible without actually closing with the opposition.

The reality was to come soon enough.

Briefings had been thorough and there was really very little more to say when Lord Louis Mountbatten appeared for a final pep talk. But Mountbatten was not a man to confine himself to conventional wishes of good hunting.

'This is my first experience in telling people what to do in an action without going in myself,' he said, 'and I don't like it. You needn't be too gentle with these Germans. When my ship, the destroyer *Kelly*, went down off Crete earlier this year, the Germans machine-gunned the survivors in the water. There's absolutely no need to treat them gently on my account.

'Good luck to you all!'

At 9.15 p.m. on Christmas Eve with troop morale riding high, the seven ships of the Archery force pulled up their anchors and slipped out of Scapa Flow.

They were making for Sollum Voe in the Shetlands. From there the final run was some three hundred miles.

It was no millpond voyage. The seas rose in unrestrained fury and winds howled and lashed. The *Prince Charles* alone took on around one hundred and twenty tons of water. Everything forward of the superstructure was flooded to a depth of fourteen feet.

Certainly, the Commandos were sick in great numbers, but their training, which had included trips in small ships in rough weather, had prepared them somewhat for this particular misery. After all, these men were expected to leap from a weather-battered vessel fit and ready to fight.

There were other torments to be endured besides seasickness, not the least of them being Jack Churchill's bagpipes. Their appalling racket led someone to fling a copper on the deck and yell: 'Next street!' The coin was pocketed without turning a hair.

But it was Churchill's dress which attracted the most attention. His silver buttons had been a gift from a French officer in 1940. He wore a Sam Browne belt with a Wilkinson fighting knife in the sword frog. And he was festooned with bow and arrows. The general feeling was summed up by a sergeant who commented loudly: 'If Robin 'ood were alive today he'd be effing blushing!'

By noon on Christmas Day, the wind seemed to have spent a little of its anger. But the forecasters warned that the respite would not last; the Commandos must expect to ride out a few more hours of the North Sea cauldron.

But now there was a period of relative calm spent amid the cluster of barren and snow-covered islands of the Shetlands.

It was actually possible to enjoy Christmas dinner, although the very idea would have churned the stomachs of most of the men but a few hours before. Perhaps even more appreciated than turkey and plum pudding was the blessed relief of sleep.

But for Admiral Burrough there could only be a fretful, impatient wait for the moment when he could actually read the long-awaited signal that the storm finally looked like dying. Already the weather had meant postponement until 27 December.

The elements, though, laugh at the designs of puny men. The storm blew and crashed and rumbled outside. The raiding force played endless pontoon, smoked themselves dry and winced yet again at the dreadful squeals from those ubiquitous bagpipes.

It was late in the afternoon when the message came with the promise of fair weather tomorrow. There was no need for further delay; 'Archery' would be launched at dawn on 27 December.

And so it was that at four o'clock in the afternoon of 26 December, the force upped anchor. The crews noticed that the wind was beginning to fade. The force, with *Kenya* in the van, followed by *Chiddingfold* and the troop ships and destroyers melted into the gathering dusk.

# 8

The daily bustle begins early in the dark lands of the northern latitudes. The sun does not rise until ten o'clock and takes its time before peeping over towering white-capped mountains.

On Vaagso in 1941 the German sentries crunched through the snow and envied those they had relieved for a few hours' sleep. Ruefully, they recalled other peacetime Christmases in front of blazing fires. Now there was a schedule of decidedly unseasonable work to be done on strengthening defences.

On Maaloy, members of the coast defence battery were in a more comfortable state. They were only required to sit and listen to a lecture on military etiquette entitled 'How to behave in the presence of an officer'. Doubtless, younger soldiers reflected that the old-time Prussian standards of spit and polish died hard. Still, it was better to listen to some brass hat gassing than actually do any work in the cold outside.

Captain Butziger, lying late in bed on this particular morning, reflected lazily that there was not much to do. Still, not putting in an appearance would be harmful to discipline. With considerable reluctance, he heaved his substantial bulk off the bed, handing his boots for cleaning to an orderly. He wandered into the bathroom to shave.

He had just lathered his face when he heard the telephone ringing. The orderly scowled at the instrument and went on with his polishing. Then languidly he stretched for the receiver, only to curse when the ringing ceased. He reasoned that it couldn't be all that important and returned to the boots. The captain, he knew, was the very devil for clean footwear; it was all a question of priorities.

The call had been put through by the lookout at Husevaago Island who, a few minutes before, had snatched his binoculars to look at some shadowy shapes steaming quietly in front of him.

Why the hell wasn't the command post answering? The sentry picked up the receiver again. This time he got an answer from the harbour captain's office in South Vaagso.

He reported what he had seen, only to hear the clerk at the other end say: 'There's a small convoy expected this morning. They're probably early or you've been over-celebrating Christmas.'

The sentry protested: 'They don't look like merchant vessels to me. They're completely blacked out. They could be destroyers.'

The disbelieving laugh at the other end irritated the sentry, but before he could protest further the telephone was slammed down.

Nevertheless, he was a conscientious soul; besides, he wanted to cover himself. So he scrawled a brief message 'Unidentified warships entering fjord' and gave it to the signal orderly with instructions to pass it on to the Maaloy naval signal station.

Van Soest, the signalman on duty at the Maaloy signal tower, flashed an acknowledgement and then committed an almost incomprehensible miscalculation. Instead of alerting battery headquarters, which were a mere hundred yards away, he leapt for a rowing boat and began pulling frantically across the narrow strait for the headquarters of Leutnant zur See Sebelin, the German harbour master.

The drone of the Hampdens was now only too apparent. The batteries were waking up. They turned their full fury on the aircraft; air-raid alarms began to wail.

The British vessels nosed their way up the fjord. The two troopships pulled off the north side into the little inlet of Slaaken Bay. *Kenya* and the other warships edged into position for the introductory bombardment. Then the run in with landing craft began.

What happened next was a highly gratifying re-run of the

training exercises in Scotland. About a hundred yards from the landing place, Durnford-Slater fired ten red Very light signals. This told the ships to stop firing; the aircraft would come in now with those invaluable smoke bombs.

Durnford-Slater, leading two hundred men of Troops 1, 2, 3 and 4 (known as Group 2) from No 3 Commando, leapt from the leading landing craft.

He ducked under the roar of three Hampden bombers; they seemed so near that they would surely slice into the defenceless men below. Then they were loosing their bombs, which flashed and mushroomed in a hideous blast of noise.

To his horror, Durnford-Slater saw rolling towards him a great flaming sheet of phosphorus. He was to recall later: 'Next thing I knew, both my sleeves were on fire. Fortunately, I wore leather gloves and beat the flames out before they could eat through my four layers of clothing to the skin.'

Durnford-Slater was fortunate. What happened next to the others was sheer nightmare and horror. Anti-aircraft fire ripped into the side of one one of the Hampdens.

The aircraft was now totally out of control. Down went a bomb into an incoming landing craft. The men took the full force of the phosphorus blast and soon the air was full of screams and the smell of burning flesh. Grenades, explosives and small arms ammunition were detonated and added to that mad mixture of battle and noise.

Soon the big, friendly figure of Sam Corry, the Irish doctor, seemed to be everywhere. Somehow among that dreadful hell he managed to summon many of the wounded and to send them back to the *Prince Charles.*

Durnford-Slater had to close his mind to the obscene barbecue he had witnessed; he turned with the rest of his men into the battle.

A string of flares hung in the sky over Maaloy. The *Kenya* was firing her first salvo of shells. Little Maaloy was rapidly becoming totally invisible: one mass of smoke and flame as the high explosive ripped the battery positions. The time was 8.48 a.m.

Captain Peter Young, commander of 6 Troop, caught a glimpse of Jack Churchill, who moments before had been stowing away his bagpipes with the loving care of a mother wrapping an infant in swaddling clothes. Now, like some Highland chieftain romanticized in a Victorian battle painting, Mad Jack stood up among the swirling smoke and waved his beloved claymore above his head. Then, with a terrible yell, he leapt into the murk and was lost to view.

Young's troop, three officers and fifty-two men, advanced and fanned out. Ahead they could make out an outline of wooden huts. Then the firing began. One of the troop edged forward further than was wise; he took a bullet in the neck.

Peter Young fixed a German soldier in his sights at twenty yards and fired. The man screamed, spun round and crashed to the ground.

The advance continued to the huts. One defender snatched at Young's bayonet. The British officer pulled it back, expecting the man to surrender. But he turned and ran. Young pulled the trigger, firing from the hip. The German slumped against a wall, then took the full blast from a tommy gun. The rest of the magazine was emptied into a second German who had aimed at Young with a pistol.

The Commandos soon dealt with the rest of the opposition, then inspected the battery office and arms magazine, which were now on fire.

Peter Young clambered through the window and stumbled through the smoke. His hands tore at the bundles of files, books and assorted military papers. Then he flung them below and the soldiers stowed them into sandbags. The place was rapidly becoming too hot for further amusement. Young dived back through the window with seconds to spare. The building disintegrated behind him.

The rest of the Maaloy opposition was swept up. Peter Young felt a twinge of pity at the sight of two German sailors crouching in a cellar under the foundations of another hut. They were in navy blue jackets and white denim trousers, smart and proud of their uniforms. But they could not stop shivering in the cold of a winter morning.

As they were led away, Young glanced at his watch. He and his men had been ashore an almost unbelievably short eight minutes.

No 5 Troop, it was later revealed, had fought a short, sharp engagement and landed a fairly mixed bag consisting of one officer and twenty-four men of artillery, two naval signallers, one groom, one pay clerk and two women, one Norwegian and an Italian. The remainder of the garrison, including two ack-ack gunners who had stuck to their post, had fallen victim to the *Kenya*'s shelling.

The capture of German guns and the neutralizing of the battery had helped to make Maaloy, if not exactly a walk-over, certainly one of the easiest phases of the battle. It was all over in twenty minutes.

The war really came home to the still fledgling Commandos in the street battles of South Vaagso.

The obese Butziger, now a prisoner, and the rest of the Germans on Maaloy had really proved puny opponents compared to the combat troops who now faced the British. They were superbly trained, well armed technicians of war who could be taught little about house-to-house fighting. A certain Stabsfeldwebel Lebrenz jerked harbour master Sebelin into action. The two men scrambled together a defensive line which called on headquarters troops, sailors and just about every German who happened to be handy.

Into the buildings of South Vaagso crammed these hastily improvised snipers. They picked off British troops who burst open doors of buildings; they pursued and harried Commandos now carrying the skirmishes not just from room-to-room but into the backyards. Men groped and scratched at one another and fell into the cold, powdery embrace of the thick snow carpeting the hard ground.

Nos 3 and 4 Troops felt the initiative slipping away from them. Casualties mounted. Sebelin had thrown a ring of steel around the Ulvesand Hotel. Some of the best officers fell beneath the terrible barrage of fire; Captain Algy Forrester of 4 Troop lobbed a grenade through the open front door of the hotel. The answer was a rifle burst. Forrester catapulted on top of his own grenade, which exploded instantly.

To the surviving men of 4 Troop, Forrester's death came as a hammer blow. They seemed all at once leaderless; then one man suddenly found heart – or, more important, voice.

Sergeant 'Knocker' White of the Queen's Own Royal West Kent Regiment realized that everybody had become mesmerized. He was the first to snap out of it. He rapped out a couple of orders. To his amazement, they were obeyed and he took charge.

Bill Bradley provided the next stroke of luck. He remembers: 'I had stolen a three-inch mortar by raiding an arms store because we had no mortars on establishment. The crew certainly weren't well drilled and I'll never forget how they shrank back and covered their ears every time it fired. But at least they managed to use it.'

With a casualness he certainly did not feel, Troop Sergeant-Major Ramsay swung the unfamiliar piece of armament and blasted it a range of about one hundred yards. The first salvo evidently went home. It downed a chimney in the enemy stronghold. There were thirteen casualties.

Then with mortar, tommy gun and rifle the gallant survivors of 4 Troop and a handful of the Norwegian fighters, Kompani Linge, went in. Mortar fire and grenades rained down on the hotel and the sound of roaring flame was the sweetest music of the day.

But it was all far too protracted a business, costing too many lives. Durnford-Slater was anxious to wrap up the whole operation without delay. But how? Back at headquarters, the answer came from an immensely cheerful Brigadier Haydon.

He told the colonel: 'My chaps have mopped up Maaloy. Could you do with a reserve troop on your side of things?'

Durnford-Slater replied that he could.

Peter Young received instructions to move to South Vaagso – and fast. He was to get as many Commandos of 6 Troop as possible into the boats.

Young managed to muster eighteen men. On the other

side, Charlie Head was there to shake Young's hand with the grave politeness of a host greeting an extra special guest for a country weekend.

The grime on Durnford-Slater's face cracked; Peter Young got a warm smile and a characteristically gruff: 'Yeah, well, Peter I'm glad to see you.'

Young wasted scant time on civilities: the important thing was to get the attack moving. The row was really appalling. Small arms rattled; there were artillery exchanges between the *Kenya* and a coast defence battery down the fjord; and attacking enemy aircraft were getting badly stung by anti-aircraft fire. There was a succession of demolitions, and always the crackle and roar of flames.

Two warehouses, important targets, faced No 6 Troop. The red warehouse was held by a small party of fanatical German fighters. The other was unoccupied.

Young posted two men at a window on the third floor with orders to give covering fire to the rest of the troop while they rushed the red building.

Between the two warehouses was a small outhouse with a pile of wood beside it; it provided a useful jumping-off place from which to launch the final attack on the red warehouse some sixty yards away.

One man was wounded and a sergeant killed in the rush. A burst of fire through the door produced two Germans, ready and willing to surrender.

Peter Young, later awarded the Military Cross, advanced immediately on the red warehouse. Some ten yards from the door he spotted a German soldier, steel helmeted and in a long overcoat. Young fired from the hip, swerved to his left and crouched down behind a crate standing against the warehouse wall. The Germans erupted with three stick bombs. The Commandos replied with Mills bombs.

Thinking the opposition must all be dead, Young streaked towards the building, yelling *Hände hoch*. But the Germans were still there and slammed in a shot. Young backed away, returning the fire. Then he spotted two men dashing into the building by the front door. There were a couple of shots and the Commandos fell wounded, lying in the middle of a room covered by the invisible Germans. One of them, O'Flaherty, looked, wrote Young later, 'as if he had had a plate of strawberry jam flung in his face.'

Young dragged the wounded to the rear and yelled for firebombs. A moment later, the red warehouse was ablaze.

It was a single incident torn from the Vaagso war of which graphic accounts survive. In the confused and bloody battle it illustrated well the rock-hard mettle of the Commandos.

They had proved themselves as fighting troops at last.

John Durnford-Slater advanced down the main street of South Vaagso. Then he stopped dead and stared mesmerized at the grenade thrown from across the road.

It stopped short and then almost lazily rolled towards him. All at once, he was running for his life to the shelter of a nearby building. The grenade exploded; two orderlies collapsed with heavy wounds.

The Commandos misconstrued Durnford-Slater's sudden disappearance. They reasoned that he must have been killed. As for the sniper, he realized that with all the opposition in the street he plainly had no chance. He came out of a doorway with his hands up.

Then he caught sight of the look in the eyes of one of Durnford-Slater's men. It was pure murder.

In a voice of terror, the German implored : '*Nein! Nein!*'

The Commando shook with rage and cold hatred : '*Ja! Ja!*'

And then he shot the sniper dead.

Durnford-Slater strode over and looked down at the German's body; the blood was coursing into the road. He said softly to the killer : 'Yeah, well, you shouldn't have done that.'

In recounting the incident after the war, Durnford-Slater commented : 'Can a man throw a death-dealing grenade one second and surrender the next? I hardly think he can expect much mercy.'

There was no time then for moralizing. The houses along the main street were blazing. Durnford-Slater noted that some of his men, who could go through the most gruelling battles without turning a hair, were terrified of the flames. He walked towards the roaring inferno with his distinctive loping stride and shouted: 'Follow me! You won't get hurt.'

Charlie Head, who was with him, said nervously: 'You keep a lookout for snipers on the left, sir, and I'll take the right.'

Durnford-Slater snapped irritably: 'Lookout, nothing, I'm in a hurry.'

And on they all pressed, summoning reserves of courage they did not know they possessed.

The *Fohn* was a 250-ton fishing vessel which had been modified by the Germans to serve as a coast patrol boat and armed escort for small convoys. Her skipper, Leutnant zur See Lohr, had been told to accompany three particular vessels on this day.

He was doing just that when the British aircraft streaked overhead. One of the guns from the *Fohn* put paid to a Hampden; the crew cheered when it started streaming smoke and lurching straight for the little hill south of Maaloy.

It was exhilarating, certainly, but this was no sort of action for so small a boat. All Lohr wanted to do was get on with his escort duties while the big boys did the rough stuff.

Then came the racket of small-arms fire and grenade explosives from the island. It all sounded dangerously close and stressed the need to get the convoy out of the line of fire. He signalled to the steamers to slip anchor and run north. The *Fohn* was to be positioned between the island and the fleeing ships. Then came the instruction to open fire on the British.

The riposte was swift and effective. Two men on the island swung round a captured gun on its traverse mounting. The dull boom from the island was followed by a splash near the *Fohn*, which by this time had decided that it was possibly wise to follow the rest of the escort. She had not got far before a shell ripped her side and a second banged through the hull.

All that was bad enough, but Lohr's troubles were only just beginning. Ahead of him suddenly were two British destroyers. The killer instinct which lurked in all good destroyer skippers could not be gainsaid; here was the prospect of some marvellous sport. The destroyers now closed in for the kill.

Lohr had an overwhelming sense of duty allied with lion-hearted courage. He knew that he could not long survive an onslaught, but that did not mean that his own obligations were ended. He dashed for the tiny radio room behind the bridge and gathered up the confidential code books, which were bound in lead so that they could be thrown overboard in an emergency.

Lohr knew that to go back on the bridge meant certain death. Inevitably, he would be the main target of British fire. And so it proved. He took the full force of one of the guns, pitching across the rail, the books spilling from his hands.

There was still the crew left in the fight and they shared plenty of their dead skipper's fighting spirit. They opened up on the British with everything they had.

But nothing could stop the boarding party under Lieutenant-Commander A. N. P. de Costabadie, DSC, RN, a seasoned Dunkirk veteran now serving with Combined Operations.

He snatched a rifle lying on the deck of the *Fohn*; his men were picking up the code books littered there. More than one tribute was paid to Lohr's sense of duty and bravery in trying to get rid of the books, even though he knew that he could never survive.

Those code books turned out to be the most important intelligence find of the Vaagso raid. They identified by radio call sign every German vessel in Norway and France, and listed challenges, countersigns and emergency signals.

It was a coup that the Commandos were to be extremely grateful for a few months later when they breached the heavily defended docks at St Nazaire.

By 1.45 p.m., Durnford-Slater had been up with the leading troops on South Vaagso for more than two hours.

Now the short Arctic day was drawing to a close. To many, the adventure had seemed to consist of little beyond dodging snipers' bullets and bursting open doors. And always of course there had been the smells of battle : the sharp tang of cordite, choking smoke and the sickly smell of fresh blood.

The withdrawal began; the fjord was covered with landing craft plying to and fro ferrying wounded, prisoners and loyal Norwegians to the infantry assault ships.

Almost all the military and economic objectives had been destroyed. Among them were all the German offices, the wireless station, a German car and lorry park, four coast defence guns, one anti-aircraft gun and a tank, an ammunition store, a German barracks, a searchlight and all the huts and houses used by German soldiers.

Every other installation of value to the Germans – the lighthouse, South Vaagso's canning factory, the herring oil factory at Mortenes – had been completely destroyed. Factories had been left blazing from end to end.

The assault on Herdla airport, where the Germans rearmed and refuelled, had been carried out by thirteen Blenheims which, at one minute past noon, had unloaded their bombs on the runways. At Stavanger, more Blenheims had soundly whipped enemy shipping.

At least one hundred and fifty Germans had been killed, ninety-eight German prisoners and four Quislings had been taken. Seventy-seven loyal Norwegians were ready for shipping to England; nine ships of a total tonnage of nearly fifteen thousand tons had been destroyed.

Everyone agreed that perhaps it was time to go.

At 3.00 p.m., when the withdrawal began, Heinkels swooped down for what the pilots plainly regarded as the final assault. It was a half-hearted affair. The British machine-guns spoke; the bombs fell wide. Below decks, interrogation of the prisoners went ahead. The wounded – British, Norwegian and Germans – rested in the sick bays of the various ships.

The mood of the Commandos was jubilant – but, above

all, hungry. There had not even been a chance to eat the issued haversack rations. As for a hot meal, that was just a Boxing Day memory. But the ships' galley cooks were still at their action stations, aiding the surgeons with the wounded. Volunteers stoked the galley fires and cooked for themselves and their comrades.

Others did not concern themselves with food. Slinger Martin on the way to his cabin noticed two sailors armed with rifles standing guard next door.

Curious, Martin asked : 'Who's in there?'

The door swung open to reveal two fair-haired girls, their over-large pyjamas unable to conceal their abundant charms.

'Jerry floozies,' confided one of the soldiers with more than a suspicion of a wink. 'Yer can't keep 'em down. Me and my mate 'ere 'ave been 'aving 'eart attacks!'

Martin withdrew tactfully. A little later, he emerged again from his cabin. Two rifles with fixed bayonets stood alone against the bulkhead.

The Vaagso adventure rattled the Germans badly; more specifically, it rattled Adolf Hitler. He felt that the British would step up their raids on Norway. The German fleet, he insisted, must use all its resources for defence there. Armament was raced to Norway. Shipments of up-to-date coast defence guns and stocks of ammunition were given high priority. New networks of field fortifications sprang up along the coast.

The inflexible Führer pronounced : 'Norway is the zone of destiny in this war. I demand unconditional obedience to my commands and directives concerning the defence of this area.'

By D-Day, 6 June 1944, 372,000 German troops were tied up in Norway. They waited for an invasion that never came. For the Allies, it meant that some of the heat was taken off Normandy. The Commandos deserved some of the credit.

'Operation Anklet', the second raid on the Lofoten Islands a diversionary affair at the time of Vaagso – could scarcely have improved Hitler's temper, either.

No 12 Commando, under Lieutenant-Colonel S. S. Harrison swooped down in special Arctic kit of white overalls and hoods on two wireless stations and removed their staff.

Corporal Harry Roberts, late of the Royal Welch Fusiliers and eventually attached to B Troop of No 12, remembers: 'Just before we took to the landing craft in the eerie early light, the cook had baked everybody a hot potato in its jacket. This was wonderful fuel'.

No 12 remained ashore for two days, destroying the wireless stations. As for the staff, it was tucking into pork washed down with quantities of rough red wine. Piles of generous rations were found in a hut; they included plenty of chocolates and cigarettes, all of which were dispensed to the local population.

But Vaagso had been *the* set piece battle for the Commandos in 1941. Here had been a truly tri-service operation: a joint effort with everyone working to perfect the function of his own particular service.

The Royal Navy got a chance to practise boarding party techniques; Commandos had come to bloody grips with street fighting; the Royal Air Force had gained special experience in long-range aerial support.

The Commandos were to take their new experience to the St Nazaire docks in a matter of months; to North Africa, Sicily, Italy and Normandy.

'Archery' had been the code name of the Vaagso raid. As Peter Young commented: 'It was not inappropriate. The arrow struck the gold.'

# 9

The raids against Norway went on from 1942 to 1944 and the Commandos snatched fresh glory in a succession of actions burnt indelibly into battle history.

But one exploit – justifiably known as 'the greatest raid of all' – dwarfed the rest.

The aim this time was to strike a vital blow at the very centre of the naval strength of Hitler's Admiral Karl Doenitz, master of the U-Boat.

Doenitz was causing almighty havoc to Allied shipping. In cold statistics, the success of his U-boat war was frightening: one third of a million tons of Allied shipping went to the bottom in January 1942 alone. In addition to the U-boat, the German surface raiders spread their own particular brand of menace. Dominating these in 1942 was the recently completed forty-five thousand ton battleship *Tirpitz.*

To Hitler, she was a pride and joy. The Führer had boasted to Doenitz: 'With *Tirpitz*, we will smash the Allied navy.'

It was no idle boast and the Allies knew it. With vessels of such calibre on the loose, there was every prospect of a string of disasters. Reconnaissance aircraft kept a wary eye on this frightening Leviathan. What plans had Hitler for her?

The Führer's obsession that the Allies had further sinister designs on Norway grew and festered. On 12 January, he directed that *Tirpitz* be moved into Norwegian waters; three days later she arrived at Trondheim.

Now her threat was worse than ever. In northern waters,

she could pounce on the Arctic convoys which were carrying supplies to the Russian ports for use on the eastern front. That was bad enougn, but if *Tirpitz* was to move into the Atlantic and possibly join up with a squadron from Brest, then the future of entire supply routes would be in jeopardy.

*Tirpitz* proved mightily elusive; all attempts to engage her in battle failed. The navy then decided to adopt the tactics of the boxing ring. If a knockout was impossible, then the main hope was to keep the opponent so busy in the ring that weariness would eventually set in : victory would be on points rather than a straight knockout. There would come a time, surely, when *Tirpitz* would need a breathing space. Sooner or later, she would need to call in at a port for maintenance and repair.

And that particular luxury was precisely what the Allies, wit! the enthusiastic help of the Commandos, proposed to deny her.

But *which* port would *Tirpitz* be likely to favour? The Atlantic coast? Intelligence would have to do better than that. It was discovered that there were not many dock facilities available for a ship of that size; indeed it soon became clear that there was only one.

At St Nazaire on the jutting coastline of the Loire in western France stood the great dry dock, known to the French both as the Forme Ecluse or the Forme Louis Joubert, but which the British called the Normandie Dock because it had been built specifically for the construction of the great French liner *Normandie*.

Here could be accommodated a ship of almost twice the size of the *Tirpitz* – up to eighty-five thousand tons. It was an obvious place for such a large vessel. Indeed, it was almost certainly to St Nazaire that the sister ship of the *Tirpitz*, the ill-fated *Bismarck*, was bound when, on 27 May 1941, the British caught and sank her.

Thus the scheme being evolved in London at the Richmond Terrace Headquarters of Combined Operations was to blast the Normandie Dock out of existence.

If the *Tirpitz* was denied the use of St Nazaire, she and other vessels would be that much more vulnerable in northern seas. Certainly, the loss of the Normandie dock would seriously embarrass the Germans and weaken their effectiveness in the costly battle o- the Atlantic.

It was this reasoning which swiftly seized the imagination of Winston Churchill. On 25 January 1942, he was writing to the Chiefs of Staff about the *Tirpitz* : 'No other target is comparable. The whole strategy of the war turns at this period on this ship.'

Such a blessing was more than enough for Mountbatten's men. The Commandos had already shown a most agreeable talent for destruction; they were hungry for more.

All sorts of objections abounded from the Admiralty, and they were not unreasonable. The shoal waters were highly dangerous; the voyage in the English Channel and the Bay of Biscay would be long and the risk of detection nightmarish; the final cost would be ruinous. Worst of all, that jutting coastline was virtually a Nazi arsenal. Any force nosing around the area was holding out a clear invitation to be blown to hell. 'Combined Ops' seniors did not admit the word 'suicidal' to their vocabulary, but it was an adjective that undoubtedly passed through their minds.

When the question of St Nazaire was first raised, the objectors had their way. The papers were shoved in a file and the whole business shelved.

For Mountbatten, however, that was very far from being the end of the matter. He ordered the file to be dusted down and the whole conception reconsidered.

Other possible raiding targets were discussed by those who still hoped that the Director of Combined Operations could be deflected from St Nazaire. But, proclaimed Mountbatten, alternative targets were merely cosmetic. He gestured to the file : 'I think this is worth going into again. Let us do something a little unconventional.'

Soon there was a new order : St Nazaire, granting all the risks and the sheer certainty of appalling losses, was very much on. The scheme had been elevated from mere daring theory to 'high strategy'. It would be no mere raiding party, but a major campaign of destruction.

To Captain Bill Pritchard, Royal Engineers, explosives were something of a religion. There was no music in the world which could compare with the noise of enemy installations dancing in the air after his toys had finished with them. A happy ability to blow things up was not, however, Pritchard's sole qualification for being useful at St Nazaire. His father had been the dock master of the Barry docks of Cardiff in Wales. Not only had Bill been brought up in the docks, but he had actually spent five years working in them on apprenticeship to the engineering branch of the Great Western Railway.

It was small wonder that Combined Operations became all of a sudden extremely interested in the career of this 28-year-old captain who had already won his spurs at Dunkirk by blowing up a bridge and had received the Military Cross by way of appreciation.

To Bill Pritchard, St Nazaire looked like an interesting proposition. One of his first tasks was to seek out Wing Commander the Marquess de Casa Maury, collator of intelligence.

What did he have on St Nazaire? The answer was, plenty: air photographs, detailed engineers' drawings of the Normandie dock gates, the composition of the submarine pens. Intelligence had plainly been busy, spelling out in graphic terms precisely what the assignment entailed.

The Normandie Dock, which lay roughly north to south, measured 1,148 feet long by 164 feet wide. To control the flow of water in or out of the dock there were at each end two vast sliding steel gates, known as caissons, measuring 167 feet long, 54 feet high and no less than 35 feet thick.

'As big as a block of flats,' Pritchard murmured, appreciating that the idea would presumably be to demolish these caissons, thus making tidal the submarine basin which lay to the west of the dock area. This would prevent U-boats passing freely into their eight bomb-proof pens. In addition, it would obviously be necessary to destroy the impeller pumps used to empty the dock. These were deep in a cavern forty feet below a pump house with two winding-houses at either end of the dock basin.

The very sight of the drawings of the massive caissons brought a stab of anxiety to Bill Pritchard: how on earth were his fellow explosives experts, however skilled, to destroy utterly caissons of such incredible strength and thickness – and presumably in double quick time?

Bill Pritchard was not the only one to be worried. It soon became obvious that no conventional force had a hope of negotiating the passage to the dock area through the formidable defensive armaments which had been manned by the Germans.

St Nazaire could only be approached by crossing mud banks. A ship small enough for the task had to be found. On the other hand, such a vessel had to be accompanied by a formidable force with a big task of destruction ahead.

How could all these essential requirements be reconciled in a single plan?

Captain John Hughes-Hallett, RN, chairman of the inter-service committee set up to look into the feasibility of an all-out attack on St Nazaire, had been instructed by Mountbatten to draft a possible solution. The document which was forwarded on 6 February to Lord Louis was explosive – almost literally so.

For what Hughes-Hallett proposed was nothing less than that St Nazaire should be attacked head-on by a single destroyer. It would be packed with explosives that would cut through the anti-torpedo net and be hurled at the outer caisson of the Normandie dock. The explosives would be placed at the point of impact and the destroyer would then be blown up by delayed action fuses.

From the severely shattered destroyer, troops would land and blow up all lock-gates leading into the submarine basin. It was further proposed that Bomber Command should keep German guns, searchlight and radar fully occupied. That meant a large-scale bombing operation which would go on throughout the raid.

Bold, audacious, brutal: a stratagem that might well have been tossed aside with a laugh if it had been submitted for a comic strip. But the Allies were desperate to destroy St Nazaire.

Few quarrelled with the reaction of a Combined Operations planner who, when let into the secret gasped: 'Anyone who even thinks of such a thing deserves the DSO.'

There was naturally a great deal more thinking to be done – and that included abandoning an early plan that a second vessel would be standing alongside the battered destroyer to take the Commandos home. Instead, there would be a number of coastal forces motorboats containing assault parties, demolition squads and protection parties.

Bill Pritchard and his men were of course itching to get going with their particular brand of mischief. They were not to be kept waiting long.

Lieutenant-Colonel Charles Newman, of the 4th Battalion the Essex Regiment, radiated a geniality and warmth which instinctively attracted fellow officers and men alike. Before the war, this highly successful rugger player and building engineer relaxed amid the beer and bonhomie of the Territorial Army. But with the outbreak of war, he was given the job of raising No 2 Commando, hammered into existence via characteristically rigorous training, much of it in Devonshire and later in Ayr.

No 2 gained a reputation for regarding barracks as soft and self-indulgent: the men spent a lot of time roughing it in ditches. They chalked up recordbreaking route marches, invariably of the hill country variety at seven miles in the hour. When they swam, it was in icy water and full kit.

So dedicated a pipe-puffer was 'Colonel Charles' that he seemed to circulate in a perpetual haze of blue smoke. Certainly the whiff of John Cotton was particularly potent on the day that he, like Bill Pritchard, found himself gloating over the air photographs, the plans of the caissons, the enemy defences of St Nazaire.

A short while before, Newman's boss, Brigadier Charles Haydon, had put the situation succinctly: 'The dock demolitions are to be carried out by combined demolition squads from the Brigade that Pritchard will start training forthwith. Your Commando is to provide the fighting troops for the operation and you are to be the Military Force Commander.'

And so now here he was committing to memory every single detail of a particularly fine model of the docks which had been obligingly supplied by the RAF.

He was later to recall: 'I was filled with elation. Here was a goal as exciting as any man could wish for.'

Commander Robert 'Red' Ryder, RN, experienced rather different emotions at the first sight of this dock model.

The mildly pugnacious 34-year-old, who before the war had distinguished himself both as a submariner and by sailing from China to England in a custom-built ketch, was at this precise moment wishing that the earth would swallow him up.

He had received a surprise signal from the Admiralty which ordered him to attend a conference at the headquarters of Combined Operations at 3 o'clock on 26 February. Now here he was fifteen minutes late and being glared at by no less senior brass than Lord Louis Mountbatten.

The lateness had scarcely been Ryder's fault: the vagaries of wartime transport were notorious. But would Mountbatten see it that way? And what would be the reaction of the phalanx of other senior officers from all three services who were flanking the Combined Ops boss so imposingly?

Ryder gasped to himself: 'What the hell is this? A court martial?'

But Mountbatten seemed to be talking about some dock invasion and the need for bombers. What was it he was saying? 'The Naval Force Commander appointed for this operation is Commander R. E. D. Ryder.'

The startled commander recalled making some fatuous reply, and then he was being introduced to a genial giant who never seemed to have a pipe out of his mouth and never stopped firing questions.

Ryder queried hesitantly: 'Where the hell *is* this place

we are supposed to be attacking?'

Naval security was, of course, notorious. With a gust of laughter, Charles Newman hastened to enlighten his more than slightly bemused fellow commander.

But soon even Red Ryder found himself caught up in the general air of secrecy surrounding 'Operation Chariot'. When Charles Newman went to inspect the destroyer *Campbeltown*, which was eventually picked for the raid, he found his way barred by a determined Ryder.

The sailor reasoned that an alert German agent skulking on the quayside at Portsmouth *might* just wonder what a figure in khaki was doing on board a destroyer. Or, more precisely, *the* destroyer. For the *Campbeltown* was to be cherished and cosseted with a fervour not usually expended on obsolete four-funnel ships. In fact, the *Campbeltown* had previously been American and named the *Buchanan* ('old Buck' to sentimental crews).

Now she was to undergo a truly startling metamorphosis which, incredibly enough, included 'lending' her briefly to the German navy.

Colonel Newman had secretly been amused at Ryder's insistence that he should go nowhere near the *Campbeltown*, but in fact from now on security ceased to be a game and became as accepted as sleeping and eating.

Stores officers suddenly faced with requests for extra fuel tanks were told to mind their own business as soon as they opened their mouths.

It suddenly became vital to lay hands on explosives of strange shapes and sizes. The Director of Signals at the Admiralty was ordered to become an expert on German codes.

Charles Newman, puffing away like a furnace, darted from meeting to meeting. One particular encounter he was not to forget. On the steps of Richmond Terrace he was tackled by Mountbatten.

Bluntly, the chief said: 'This is a very hazardous operation. Frankly, I don't expect to see any of you again. If we lose you all, you will be about equivalent to the loss of one merchant ship. But your success will save many merchant ships.

'Don't take anyone on the operation with worries or home ties. No married men. If anyone wants to stand down, they've got to have the opportunity.'

Newman, who was himself married with children, smiled grimly. Of course, he would have to pass on the message to the various Commandos. It was precisely because the Commandos were a volunteer force that he had a strange feeling he already knew what their answer would be.

# 10

Burntisland, just north of Edinburgh, on the Firth of Forth, is today a highly prosperous little port given over to servicing vessels for the oil industry. But in the memory of survivors of a certain highly specialized group of Commandos in World War Two it has a somewhat different association: for here was carried out some of the key training for the planned destruction of St Nazaire.

In January 1942, Haydon's Special Service Brigade headquarters sent some fearless talent to Burntisland, where they were made familiar with the potential of just about every type of modern explosive device. Their tutor was Bill Pritchard. Some measure of his dedication can be judged from the fact that the withdrawal by the British two years before from Dunkirk had reduced him to speechless rage. At the time, he had spluttered: 'Why didn't we blow up all the Channel docks before we left them to the Hun?'

Pritchard's partner was Captain Bob Montgomery, a towering young Regular of the Royal Engineers. Happily, both had worked together in the transportation branch of the REs – one of its specialities was docks – and both had highly useful knowledge of St Nazaire. Here was a couple positively made for Operation Chariot.

These messiahs of the big bang had just about the most dependable group of disciples imaginable: first-class material picked from among Nos 1, 3, 4, 5, 6, 9 and 12 Commandos.

One of the most dashing, who was to play a decisive role in the destruction of the pump house of the caissons, was Lieutenant Stuart Chant, of the Gordon Highlanders, whose nickname of 'Stewie the Wop' referred to his swarthy complexion, hinting not at all at his proudly cherished Scots-Huguenot ancestry.

Chant and his fellows, isolated from the rest of their Commandos and in the tightest possible cocoon of security, began learning everything possible about docks: how they operated; their likely weak points; which pieces of machinery were worth destroying and which not and even how to wield an axe to do the most satisfying damage quickly.

Pritchard's lads practised on several docks of varying sizes, including another in Scotland not far away at Rosyth.

Chant explains: 'Around eighty of us were taught how to blow up caissons, swing-bridges and ships, particularly those sort of vessels to be found in a dry dock.'

Eventually, the Commandos were scooped out of Scotland and rushed in separate teams to yet more docks at Cardiff and Southampton. It was Southampton's George V Dock which turned out to be the most useful.

Anyone knowing the history of the George V Dock might have been forgiven for indulging in some interesting speculation, for it had been built after a detailed study by the owners, Southern Railway, of another interesting structure: the Normandie Dock at St Nazaire.

But St Nazaire was a name no one as much as breathed. The team at Southampton went about its series of dummy runs as unobtrusively as possible, for a mere fifty miles or so away in France lay the Luftwaffe bomber stations. German crews had reported gleefully that Southampton had been shattered enough already; no one on the British side wanted the enemy back. It was essential that Southampton be left alone.

Chant's job at St Nazaire was never less than crucial: it was to destroy all the machinery of the dry dock. To be blown up were the pumps which emptied the dock, and also the impeller pumps which filled it, situated some forty feet below ground and driven from a pumping house by electric motors.

In the case of St Nazaire, the motors could empty or fill the dock in a matter of two to three hours. The task of Chant was to get into the pumping house, descend its several flights of stairs and plant the explosives.

The men who would actually attack the caissons climbed time and again into the heart of the twin at Southampton, carrying crude little parcels and bits of string to simulate explosives and fuses. The exercises were carried out in daylight, blindfolded and then in total darkness.

Occasionally, dock officials pierced the security net and demanded to know what was going on. When that happened, the Commandos, courteous fellows all, shrugged politely and abandoned the exercise with as few words as possible. When the inquisitive outsiders had left, they stole back to the job.

While Pritchard's intensive training programme continued apace, the Commandos found their strength constantly being supplemented by a fresh intake; the general feeling was that the top brass wanted to have a pool of demolition experts at the ready should they be needed for any particular job. The actual target remained in the shadows. But, as the number of explosives experts proliferated, it at last became clear that something special was in the wind.

Red Ryder was now at naval headquarters at Falmouth in the west country surveying some very strange items indeed. In addition to charts and highly specialized explosives, he was in possession of perfect replicas of ensigns commonly carried by ships of the *German* navy. The preparations for the strange role of the *Campbeltown* were at last taking shape.

Ryder had just two weeks left to mould the expeditionary force of craft and men who would launch the glorious Commando epic of St Nazaire.

He reflected that the whole business was rapidly coming to resemble the best spy stories with a healthy emphasis on disguise and deceit. It was precisely the sort of adventure to appeal to this maverick sailor; each new problem was something to be hugely relished.

On the other hand, the normally extrovert Colonel Charles Newman, whose No 2 Commando had been selected as the main military force of the raid, was in sombre mood. He had been looking at recently taken air photographs of

St Nazaire and was startled to see four newly installed coast-defence gun positions in the middle of the dock area. This meant a hasty swelling of Commando ranks; now the total force involved would be two hundred and sixty-five all ranks.

A visit to Richmond Terrace had done nothing to lift his spirits. For his habitual optimism to reassert itself he needed to get back among his men.

Now Commandos from various parts of the country were starting to assemble at Falmouth. No 2 Commando had come from Ayr aboard HMS *Princess Josephine Charlotte*, which served as a carrying ship for Commando landing craft.

The days of training were all but over; the time for secrecy was running out.

With breezy bluntness, Newman was soon outlining to officers and other ranks what lay ahead. Mountbatten's uncomfortable instruction to him to relay the likely fate of so many men was the least agreeable part of the business.

Newman waded in: 'This is going to be a dangerous job. In fact, the CCO told me that he did not expect any of us to come back. He therefore doesn't want anyone who is married and has family responsibilities to go on it. Nobody has to go on this party if he doesn't want to. Neither the CCO nor I nor anyone else will think the worse of him if he elects to stand down.'

If even the most veiled suggestion that the Commandos would be found wanting had come from anyone other than Newman, it would have been perfectly possible for that man, officer or not, to have ended up in little pieces. As it was, something approaching a collective 'Gurtch!' greeted the pronouncement of 'Colonel Charles'.

Newman beamed happily as he left the gathering. It was clear that everyone's mood was soaring with the fine spring weather.

Security intensified during the last crucial days leading up to the start of Operation Chariot. To explain the presence of a lot of fighting men in Falmouth, an elaborate cover plan was concocted. It was put about that they were the

10th Anti-Submarine Striking Force about to depart and do what their name suggested.

As for the troops, it was plain to the good people of Falmouth that a move to a hot climate was planned. How else could those naval sun helmets and other items of tropical kit so ostentatiously displayed on quaysides be explained?

In addition, 'Exercise Vivid' was carried out against the dockyard at Devonport, to the east of Falmouth. Intended, it was said, to test the defences of the port; the fact that Devonport bore a fair resemblance to St Nazaire was significant to only a few.

The *Campbeltown* was one ship that did not take part in Vivid. As her Captain, Lieutenant-Commander S. (Sam) H. Beattie, RN, pointed out dryly: 'Ramming dock gates was not exactly a thing which could be practised very frequently.'

The Commandos had rehearsed their various exercises to the point of screaming boredom. But now the details were being filled in. The force was to consist of sixteen motor launches (MLs); two Hunt class destroyers, HMS *Atherstone* and HMS *Tynedale*; the *Campbeltown*; Motor gun boat (MGB) 314, carrying Newman, Ryder and Lieutenant Dunstan Curtis, the Captain, which was to lead the force; and motor torpedo boat (MTB) 74, which was to bring up the rear.

One further vessel was to be involved, HM Submarine *Sturgeon*, which would proceed under separate sailing orders to the mouth of the Loire. There it would surface and act as a navigational beacon by showing a light from the conning tower to lead the small fleet into the river.

The party was to storm ashore at three points: over the bows of the *Campbeltown*; on the quays to what was known as the Old Entrance and on the Old Mole, a landing slip with a concrete gun emplacement and a searchlight.

First objective was to capture quick-firing 20 mm and 40 mm guns around these positions. Then perimeter bridges leading to the south and west sides of the submarine basin and dry dock were to be held.

All that sounded daunting enough, but the position had

one particularly grim feature. Members of the squads involved were to be armed only with automatic pistols and tommy guns since each man already carried a heavy rucksack of explosives.

There could be no concealing it; for many of those involved in what had been called 'the sauciest thing since Drake', the entire adventure was nothing less than a ride direct into the jaws of death.

Stuart Chant, who was aboard the *Campbeltown* for the raid, recalls: 'At midday on 26 March, we got orders to get kitted up. We were taken from the *Princess Josephine Charlotte*, which was still lying alongside the docks in Falmouth, in small groups on to the *Campbeltown*, which was anchored midstream in the Carrick Roads.

'We had on steel helmets, wore battledress with dark blue jerseys but no other identification apart from badges of rank. The point of the jerseys was that should we be seen by German aircraft, we would be taken for sailors and not as members of any special force.'

A band of happy warriors aboard the motor launches on 26 March sailed into the English Channel under a pleasant sun and a gentle breeze. The *Campbeltown* and the two destroyers followed an hour later.

But this was not the *Campbeltown* that Newman and Ryder had first inspected: gone were the four funnels she had carried as the USS *Buchanan*. They had been replaced by two raked-back stacks which seemed to resemble to a remarkable degree those of a German Möwe class destroyer. Her bridge had been given extra armour plate. There were also steel plates amidships to protect the Commando landing parties where they would crouch on the final run.

The entire fleet with the combatants split between the *Campbeltown* and the other vessels, set a south-westerly course for the Bay of Biscay.

It sailed for thirty-six hours, well out into the Atlantic, leaving Brittany to the east, then did a U-turn and sailed straight up the mouth of the Loire to arrive off St Nazaire at 1.30 in the morning.

On the second day out a German U-boat had been spotted

on the surface. The *Tynedale* opened fire; depth charges were dropped. But, in fact, the U-boat reported only the presence of the destroyers. The MLs had evidently been too low in the water for the lookout to report.

The *Atherstone* and the *Tynedale* were moving off for their all-night patrol of the mouth of the Loire to await the return of the surviving Commandos. Newman and Ryder and the rest were soon very much on their own.

Contact was made with the submarine *Sturgeon*, which was acting as marker buoy for the party. Quiet greetings were exchanged; the *Sturgeon* then slipped away, her task completed.

Some six sea-miles on lay the port itself. Soon the Commandos could see enemy searchlights raking the sky. And the air was alive with the sullen roar of German guns.

To mask the approach of the invading force of Operation Chariot, a diversionary air raid by Britain had been launched on St Nazaire. It turned out to be a pathetic affair; light clouds obscured the vision of the pilots and they were unable to distinguish German occupied docks from civilian sections of the town.

Orders had been given by Sir Winston Churchill that the minimum of French lives were to be put at risk on all raids by the RAF. So the Whitleys and Wellingtons peeled away. Many Commandos stated later with some bitterness that if the raid had been tougher and if there had been less scruples about sacrificing French lives, then the Commando operation might have been more successful at less cost. The RAF also later claimed that it did not have sufficient bombers for a sustained raid.

But these were academic niceties to be mulled over in more peaceful times; the fact was that air activity did divert the Germans briefly. They only realized what was being catapulted at them when the Chariot force was just a mile and a half away from the dry dock.

And what the Germans saw puzzled them mightily.

They saw – or thought they saw – one of their own Möwe class destroyers, complete with German ensigns, bearing down at speed on the high tide.

The *Campbeltown*, in the clothes of the enemy, was free to move without being assaulted head on by enemy fire; the Germans were momentarily off guard. It gained essential time for the Commandos.

The fuses on the warhead of the *Campbeltown* had been set at 11 o'clock; she was getting prepared to ram. On she sailed until it was just ten minutes to zero. The whole scene was suddenly bathed in light as a searchlight beam brought the entire invading force into the German sights. There was the MGB in front, then the disguised *Campbeltown*; the motor launches and the MTB were following on.

Still it seemed that the Germans were mesmerised.

Leading Signalman Pike on the *Campbeltown*, a German speaker, had been provided by British Intelligence with the required codes. These enabled him to flash out several messages, including one to the effect that the fleet was proceeding to the harbour in accordance with orders. Pike's brazen cheek paid off; the signal was acknowledged and the searchlight killed.

But it could not last. It soon dawned on the Germans that it was a strange sort of friendly force that seemed hell bent on ramming them. They opened up; the din of battle began.

Stuart Chant remembers: 'We Commandos who were on the deck of the *Campbeltown* lay on our backs, feet forward, so that the head would not be the part of the body taking the full shock of impact. We put our steel helmets over our eyes to protect them and we lay behind the protective steel plates.'

The swastika had now vanished. In its place was the white ensign. By way of reply and with mounting fury the Germans unleashed their massive firepower. Crouched behind their steel plates, Chant and his men saw and heard a number of the Chrysler engines of the MLs flare up. Their occupants were destined never to carry out the destructive tasks for which they had been trained over so many months.

The order came: 'All quarters – stand to ram.'

The *Campbeltown* herself was soon ignited; her bow gun, a twelve-pounder, was shot into oblivion. The coxswain on the topmost of the *Campbeltown*'s two bridges was one of the first to die.

Sam Beattie and Bob Montgomery clawed their way towards the wheel. Montgomery steered the *Campbeltown* briefly, then it was Beattie in sole charge. He cursed the fact that he might just as well be blindfold for all he could see ahead among the flame and the smoke and the searchlight.

Then he caught a glimpse of the vast one hundred-foot-wide dock gates ahead. Speed inched up to twenty-two knots plus.

Shells ripped into the Commandos lying on deck. Metal tore into Stuart Chant's left leg and both arms, but he still managed to pin down the man in front who was unwisely trying to struggle up.

Chant says: 'There was no pain and it was only when the blood started to course later that I actually took in that something had happened.'

In any case, there was now a major distraction. With a crash and a jolt and a shudder the *Campbeltown* slammed into the main gate of the St Nazaire dock. The massive protecting anti-torpedo nets around the gate slowed progress slightly. But only for a moment. More than one survivor later stated that suddenly it was like being airborne.

The *Campbeltown* seemed to take off with the power of a giant bullet. In fact, it had risen out of the water and come to rest on top of the main gate.

The men's recovery was quick. Scrupulous pre-planning had determined the order in which the Commandos were to leave the *Campbeltown* and fan out to their various objectives. The MLs had orders either to pull up as near to the destroyers as possible or make the Old Mole their objective. The latter was one of the toughest aspects of the St Nazaire raid: the launches became sitting targets for the guns installed there.

Not that things were exactly quiet aboard what was left of the *Campbeltown*. The fo'c's'le was still pouring smoke; the deck was holed. There was the nightmare that the fire would reach the explosive charge and kill everyone before there was a chance to get off.

Captain Donald Roy of No 2 Commando was first and foremost a Cameron Highlander and he carried his allegiance with pride. Tall and slim and with an immaculately tended moustache, he stood out amid the controlled confusion of the sudden exit from the burning destroyer. Forward went his No 5 Troop, kilts flying. The wounded who lay in the way were thrust none too ceremoniously aside.

Normally, descent would have been by steel or bamboo ladders but most of these had been shattered and broken. So the men of 5 Troop descended by rope, crouching as they landed to give covering fire to their comrades. Then they set off with whoops of delight towards the first of their targets.

Captain Roy's prime objective was to knock out the guns on the roof of the pumping station so that Chant and his men could get on with their job.

He seized a grenade, tossed it gleefully at eight or ten Germans, who raced down a ladder and bolted in fright, a burst of tommy gun fire helping them on their way.

But German fire-power was formidable. It shattered down on the Highlanders; their numbers were soon reduced to about half their original thirteen. The cost had been high just to dislodge a few Germans from the pumping station, but the path at least had been cleared.

Chant had with him four sergeants for the attack on the station. But his wounds put him at a severe disadvantage right from the start. Soon he was faced with further drawbacks.

Clambering forward, he had fallen into a shell hole in the bows but was saved from falling below decks by his rucksack. He was hauled up by its straps. Despite his wounds, he had been able to slip on his rucksack with its load of explosives. Three of the sergeants did the same thing, but Sergeant Chamberlain, thirteen stone and six foot of bone and muscle, had more serious injuries and could scarcely move at all. Somehow, the rest managed to get Chamberlain up, and carrying his rucksack, they all struggled forward to disembark, sliding, scrambling, or falling down the practically vertical scaling ladders.

Chant remembers: 'I was limping, but I could still move around fairly freely and blood wasn't flowing disastrously. The main thing was that once the pumping station had been earmarked I was able to get my hands on the explosives.'

The Special Operations Executive, whose very skills were later in the war to help, in Churchill's phrase, 'to set Europe ablaze', had been responsible for putting some agreeably lethal toys together for the eager pupils of Bill Pritchard.

Chant says: 'There were things like limpet mines which you could slap on to a metal surface and know would stick. There were a variety of magnetic mines. We had in all about sixty pounds of explosives each.'

The party moved straight towards the pumphouse entrance – and right into the first snag.

Chant can laugh about it today. 'We'd rehearsed every bloody thing about dry docks, pumping houses and impeller pumps. But one of the most obvious and simple possibilities had been overlooked. The twenty-foot high steel door of the pumping house had been locked by the Germans! We just hadn't taken that into account because the doors at Southampton were always open in case of fire.

'At that very moment, my wounds decided to play up. Bob Montgomery darted forward and placed one of the magnetic charges and stood back. By this time, it was impossible for me to light the fuse. The blood was coursing down my hands and it was hurting like hell.'

Chant said quietly: 'Bob, for Christ's sake help me light this thing. The chaps will think I'm scared.' The two men stood away; there was a short sharp explosion and they were in. Chant and the three sergeants inched towards the enormous interior of the pumping station and began moving forward.

Sergeants Dockerill, Butler and King were in good order, and Chant felt better. But it was only too obvious that the stricken Chamberlain was going to be a decided liability.

Chant explains: 'The mere thought of taking Chamberlain, all that weight and all that size, forty feet into the darkened depths was out of the question. It would plainly be far too dangerous.

'All I could do was lay him down, thrust two Colt automatics into his hands and order him to keep at bay any Germans who might suddenly break into our rear.'

The descent into the bowels of the pumping station did not entail clattering down metal stairs, which even with pencil torches in total darkness might not have been so difficult. Instead, there were galleries, and one false step in the wrong direction and a man could hurtle instantly to his death. A miscalculation could also mean ending up against a blank wall. If that happened, then steps had to be retraced and bearings picked up again.

It reminded Chant of childhood games in specially constructed mazes of trees and bushes, but this was a maze of metal and no game. It was hardly likely that the Germans would be so obliging as to hold off for much longer. Captain Roy had to carry on with his own fighting; he and his kilted comrades certainly would not be hanging around outside the pumping station.

Somehow, Chant kept going, trying to fight the constant waves of giddiness that were threatening to overcome him.

But eventually they were on level ground below and looking at four French-built impeller pumps, the largest in the world. Chant remembers them looking rather like four giant inverted mushrooms, inside which were the fast-revolving vanes which impelled the water in and out of the dry dock. In the middle of each ring stood a shining steel shaft which was connected with the motor which drove it from far above at ground level.

Chant says: 'By the light of our torches, we took out about fifty pounds of explosives each and ten pounds for any emergencies, all specially prepared in little parcels. Out of these trailed leads of cordtex explosive charges. They were laid carefully on the pumps on top of all the casting joints.

'The exact positioning was vital. It wasn't just a question of blowing up any bit of old iron; we knew that if the *castings* went to glory it would take the Germans months to replace them. The leads were then joined up into what was known as a ring-main of cordtex in such a way that the whole formed one firing circuit.'

Each man worked quickly and confidently; now all those crucial months of training made obvious sense.

Chant could have been forgiven for finding Dockerill's insistence on singing 'The White Cliffs of Dover' more than slightly irritating. But it had an oddly soothing effect, even overcoming the lacerating pain which he steeled himself to ignore.

Then Chant was rapping out an order: King and Butler were to get themselves upstairs rapidly and move the wounded Chamberlain clear. When that was done, they were to tip off Chant and Dockerill, who were left below.

Eventually, the shout came. Chant turned to his companion and gave the simple pre-arranged signal: 'One, two, three.'

Then they pulled their igniter pins. The slow fuse began burning along its two lengths of three feet to detonator and cordtex and the men had ninety seconds to allow them to reach comparative safety outside.

Chant then allowed himself to be led by Dockerill up into the darkness and back into the galleries.

Somehow, Chant managed two steps at a time and then he was feeling the balm of the night air on his cheek and blessing the sight of Bob Montgomery.

But now Montgomery was yelling: 'For Christ's sake, get out of the way!'

All the party lay down as far away from the pumping house as they could. A few seconds later, the carefully placed charges burst with a crash and a roar. The effect on Chant was as if an almighty axe had been chopped down with maximum force on his ear drums. A great block of concrete flew through the air as if sent on its way by a giant foot, crashing down on the very spot where he and his companions had been standing seconds before.

Chant remembers happily: 'It really was a marvellous explosion, made even more concentrated because it took place underground. Such an explosion had what is known as a tamping effect – the resultant force was enormous in such a confined space.'

The plan was then to return to the carnage and destroy everything on the ground floor, including the electric motors. But the force of the bang had been such that the motors had been thrust off balance and irreparably buckled; there was very little left.

The party then withdrew and, according to plan, linked up with a delighted Charles Newman, who had been keeping one ear cocked for the expected explosion. Indeed, it had been of such force as to be heard by those aboard the motor launches in mid river.

The time was not quite two o'clock; incredibly, it was less than half an hour since the *Campbeltown* had rammed the dry dock at St Nazaire.

# 11

Fourth man off the *Campbeltown* was Ulsterman Joe Molloy of the Irish-raised No 12 Commando, which had been blooded on the second Lofoten raid. By common consent that had been a paltry affair : now they were anxious to get at the enemy on something like equal terms.

Molloy had served in the Corps of Engineers of the Irish Free State Army, knew a tolerable amount about street fighting and, even more important, explosives.

His team of demolition men was led by Lieutenant Gerard Brett who was no one's stereotyped idea of a Commando. Lean, bespectacled, studious and quiet-spoken, he looked exactly what he had been in civilian life : an assistant museum curator with an addiction to Byzantine excavations.

It might have been expected that such a seeming anachronism would either have been derided or ignored by his fellow Commanders. On the contrary, his companions respected and admired him with a genuine affection.

Brett now headed the team with the job of destroying the far caisson on the northern side of the dry dock.

Molloy recalls : 'I clambered down a steel ladder from the *Campbeltown* but it was only hanging on by one hook and I slipped and landed on my knees straight on the top of that particular caisson. A few inches and I'd have gone between the ship and the dock gate and either been crushed to death or drowned. Soon I was picking myself up and heading for the other caisson, which was our main target.

'Then there was a serious snag. We'd intended to put the explosive charges on the top of the caisson itself, but that wasn't possible because the whole of the surface had been coated by the Germans with tar and grit-coated timber. So we dangled eight twelve-pound charges over the side in the water and the ring-main was set.'

Then the team waited for news that their comrades were ready to carry out their task of destroying the caisson's winding house. But at that moment, the Germans opened up with a machine-gun concealed near an adjacent crane.

Molloy says: 'The bullets smashed straight into my guts and right wrist, while the powder sprayed straight into my eyes. I kept my head down and heard the order from Lieutenant Brett, himself twice wounded, to set off the charges.'

Brett was then out of action and other officers had been killed. Sergeant Frank Carr became the man of the hour: he snatched the initiative and masterminded the demolition teams. He activated the igniters on the caisson and withdrew. After the burning period of one minute, there was a noise, said witnesses, like the beating of a vast drum. The caisson split apart; water poured into the dry dock.

Then it was the turn of the two winding houses to be destroyed. They suddenly seemed to be snatched from the ground by an invisible grabber. After a second or two their shattered remains crashed back to earth and smoke and debris shattered and spread.

Brett, who had to be carried away, gave rapid instructions for the withdrawal. There had been seven deaths on the assault of caisson and winding-house. Most survivors, like Brett and Molloy, had been wounded. But all agreed it had been a grand bit of work.

The plan had been that, once the *Campbeltown* teams had completed all their blowing-up operations, they would withdraw to the Old Mole with the hope of being picked up by the other demolition Commandos in the motor launches.

The port group of the launches had been intended to make for the Old Mole and land their Commandos, and the starboard group to slip under the stern of the *Campbeltown* into the Old Entrance.

But it all soon became an empty dream, blasted out of

existence by the deadly accuracy of German short-range fire from automatic guns. The pitifully vulnerable Coastal Forces craft were often shot out of the water, either in mid-river or during fruitless attempts to edge into possible landing places.

There were Commandos who met their deaths when shells pierced limbs or when both boats and crews were annihilated. If a man was lucky, that was the way he died at the Old Mole on St Nazaire.

But there was another and far more horrible way. As the motor-launches blew up, inevitably pools of petrol spread wide. Their flames licked greedily at the surface of the water on which lay the crews, often badly wounded. The sea had become a host to flame and shellfire. And, above all, to burning, drowning men.

There was no way in which the pathetically flimsy wooden craft could have escaped the German guns. Shell splinters cut the steering lines while tracer set fire to fuel tanks. On the Old Mole, 20mm and 40mm quick-firing guns were on high concrete emplacements. The battery kept up more or less continuous fire; the searchlight on the tip of the mole sliced through the darkness throughout.

But some launches did get ashore. Among them was ML 11, containing Pritchard and two of his demolition team. Hard on his heels from ML 12 was London-born former boxer Dick Bradley of No 2 Commando and the Royal Berkshires. Bradley had undergone concentrated training aboard motor launches and had the supreme Commando virtue of never getting seasick. His mission was to destroy a bridge leading into the submarine base which lay above the Normandie dock.

Bradley remembers the landing vividly: 'ML 12 landed at the Old Mole perfectly. We had an Aussie matelot, Lieutenant N. B. Wallis RANVR, in charge. He got out of the motor launch, tied it up and got us out. If it hadn't been for the guns, we might have been out punting on a Sunday.

'It seemed as if we bore a charmed life, because some of the other MLs were in a terrible state. But there was no time for self-congratulation. The next minute I'd stopped a bullet right in the lungs and felt the blood spurting out and trickling down warmly front and back. Then I lost consciousness.'

That vital bridge was never blown. Elsewhere the MLs encountered disaster upon disaster.

The bullet-ridden body of Sergeant Thomas Durrant of the Royal Engineers and No 1 Commando, who received a posthumous VC, slumped dead over his twin Lewis gun aboard ML 14. Durrant had kept up a vain barrage of fire against the *Jaguar*, a Wolfe-Möwe destroyer which had swept down and harassed the launch in a series of sweeps.

Of the starboard column, only the sixth, ML 177, managed to land its party more or less intact.

The various Commandos – including, by circuitous routes, the badly injured Stuart Chant and Joe Molloy – fought their way through the hail of German fire to the planned getaway point on the Old Mole.

The MLs had been intended to carry home over four hundred and fifty miles the tired, battle-worn heroes of Operation Chariot. It was a role few of them were able to fulfil. In many cases, glowing frames were all that were left; blackened shells indicated the remains of those which had perished earlier in the action.

The appalled Commandos looked at the tragic scene of carnage. The silence was broken by an incredulous question by somebody: 'Christ! Are they ours?'

Various schemes for breaking out were discussed; Newman's idea was that survivors should split into small groups and make eventually for the Spanish frontier.

Led by Captain Roy and an assault party, they moved off, reaching the south bank of the Bassin de St Nazaire opposite which were pens bristling with U-boats.

Here Stuart Chant, later taken prisoner, was hit in the right knee by a ricochet bullet. His men carried him a little way; then he ordered them to leave him.

He relates: 'I watched the rest of the party go south, towards the old part of the town. They then dashed west across a swing bridge and I was able to see them clearly in the brilliant moonlight. Pillboxes and windows of nearby houses erupted with ferocious fire; on the roofs were German marksmen.'

Newman's force was a dwindling band by now; but they pushed on with determination. German sniper bullets sliced into them as they jumped over walls and trampled across back gardens. A German armoured car catapulted out of nowhere, its turret spitting fire on anything, British or German, which got in its way.

The Commandos staggered towards some railway lines and warehouses. But it was the moment of truth. Newman told them bluntly: 'There is no way in which we can be taken back. If we want to get home, we'll have to walk it. The alternative is to surrender.'

Newman, with twenty or so men still with him, next found an air raid shelter which, after their wanderings, seemed to them sheer luxury. It even had mattresses.

Joe Molloy, badly wounded with a five-inch gash in one shoulder, slumped against the door on the inside. 'Then someone pushed it and I was knocked forward. There was then the sound of footsteps running away, but no one dared move because we weren't sure whether we'd been spotted or not. But they came back in droves in a few minutes, shouting at us to come out.'

There was no alternative to surrender: Newman and his men left the cellars as prisoners.

The thoughts of Colonel Charles were sad as he was driven away, not because St Nazaire had ended in this way for him, but because of one particular death among that day's carnage.

Bill Pritchard had led a raiding party through the Old Town of St Nazaire in a bid to blow up a bridge. But Pritchard had seen a target he regarded as better sport: two ships berthed in the submarine basin. Pritchard selected 'Mac' McLaghlan, one of his best sergeants. With two five-pound charges they had raced along the quayside, leaping down on to the first of the two ships.

The charges were laid under the very noses of the Germans and the igniters pulled. It was a source of immense satisfaction to both men to observe that the basin was soon lacking two ships which had indubitably been there but a short time before.

Then came the Germans. Mac opened up on the riflemen with a short, brutal tommy gun blast. But it was too late to save Pritchard, who slumped fatally wounded, gasping : 'Report to HQ . . .'

And that is what was done. A few hours later, Colonel Charles was gazing at the body of one of the most skilful and courageous fighter-planners of the entire St Nazaire operation.

Depression at a single death was something Newman would of necessity have made himself overcome had he still been free. Captivity, however, encouraged introspection. Luckily, an event happened which jerked him and his fellow prisoners out of any misery they might be feeling. All the time, everyone's thoughts had remained with the *Campbeltown.* The men steeled themselves for the sublime sound of five tons of ammanol blasting powder erupting.

All at once, there was swaying and shifting as the ground danced under the feet of the triumphant prisoners. It was 10.30 on Saturday morning when the warhead blew up. With one accord, the captured Commandos burst into wild cheering.

The blowing up of the *Campbeltown* threw the Germans into something approaching panic. They opened fire in the area around the dry dock. Several French men and women were killed in mistake for Commandos.

By Sunday night, order was restored, although several Germans had been killed by their own side. The enemy had no real idea even then just what had caused the explosions, believing for a while that the Free French were responsible.

The tally of casualties contained civilian tragedies : sixteen French had died, including a child of five and a man of seventy-six.

On the dry dock itself, the scene was one of unrelieved horror. Torsos, limbs and portions of flesh splattered all around, while walls and even rooftops were bathed in blood. Dockyard workers spent days hosing away the gore; layer upon layer of sand was necessary to conceal stains of crimson.

Success at St Nazaire came through individual acts of supreme heroism: badly wounded 'Burty' Burtenshaw of No 5 Commando humming 'There'll Always Be an England' as he emptied his pistol into a knot of Germans on the quayside and falling in a cruelly unequal contest; Mickey Wynn, Commander of MTB 74, ran the gauntlet of the German guns, until he was knocked insensible across the bridge, one eye hanging loose from its socket.

And one of the five VCs awarded went posthumously to Able Seaman William Savage, who manned the forward two-pounder Pom-Pom on the MGB, until succumbing to his wounds.

The other VCs went to Commander Ryder, Lieutenant-Commander S. H. Beattie and Lieutenant Colonel Charles Newman. The other posthumous VC went to the gallant Sergeant Durrant, the only soldier in World War Two to win a VC fighting on a Royal Naval ship.

And gallantry there was; gallantry which to romantics recalled the days of Zeebrugge in World War One and, even further back, when Sir Francis Drake impudently singed the beard of the Spanish king in the harbour at Cadiz.

But it was success spelt out in copious letting of blood: the Allies lost one hundred and sixty-nine raiders killed and about two hundred taken prisoner. Three motor launches and MGB 314, with Ryder and Curtis still on board, reached the rendezvous with the *Atherstone* some miles off the mouth of the estuary. The destroyers, the *Tynedale* and the *Atherstone*, reached Falmouth, escorted by Coastal Command. Other launches made their own way home without escort, almost dry of fuel.

In the harsh, unemotional realities of total war the price was cheap and the reward eminently worthwhile. The *Tirpitz* had been denied the Atlantic, where she would have plagued the shipping routes. In fact, the dock at St Nazaire was not to be repaired until 1952. As for the *Tirpitz* herself, she was ultimately destroyed in a bombing raid by the RAF in 1944.

The lesson to the Commandos – one they were to apply to continuing large and small raids – was the absolute necessity for pre-planning that was ultra-scrupulous.

As Lieutenant-Colonel Charles Newman wrote on the twenty-eighth anniversary of the raid : 'All I could do as the military commander was to put the nickel in the slot, pull the handle and wait for the result. The jackpot came up !'

For the people of occupied France, their faith in ultimate liberation had been buttressed still further. The mayor of St Nazaire told revisiting survivors five years later : 'You were the first to give us hope.'

# 12

Achnacarry Castle, ancient seat or the Camerons of Lochiel, is a dour mediaeval hangover squatting amid the luxuriant wild of the Scottish Highlands.

Moors and lochs have their own particular beauty – or would, if you could only see them. But for most of the year the mists swirl ceaselessly. The rain driving full in the face is like painful stabs from a million metal rods.

Numerous clans down the centuries have clawed, fought, killed and raped over this land. The Camerons, fiercely intolerant of barbarian and foreigner alike, were able up to World War Two to claim that not since the Duke of Cumberland nearly two centuries before had an English soldier set foot in Achnacarry.

But now bodies were doubtless spinning in graves and indignant ghosts walking abroad; in the third year of the war foreigners were launching a continuous invasion. What is more, they now seemed to be welcomed by the Chief of Clan Cameron himself, Sir Donald Walter Cameron of Lochiel.

For not only were English soldiers allowed to crawl around castle and grounds with impunity, but other infidels seemed to have the same rights. The Cameron hills echoed to Welsh, Irish, French, American and Dutch. Cries, commands and curses were, goodness knows, familiar enough to Camerons, but never in such a babel of tongues.

Achnacarry was by no means the only training centre in Scotland for Commandos, but by 1943 it had become the Commando depot, the main training centre under the authority of the Special Service Brigade. At least, on paper. But, as every apprehensive volunteer discovered only too soon, there was only one real authority at Achnacarry. Presiding over everything as supreme master was Lieutenant-Colonel Charles Vaughan, OBE, of the Buffs (Royal East Kent Regiment).

No one was better qualified: Vaughan had come up through the ranks. He knew the smell and feel of human sweat and expressed his philosophy of war with disarming simplicity: 'We're going to 'ammer the 'uns from be'ind.'

A new intake discovered what it was in for a good couple of hours before it even arrived at the castle.

Lieutenant Bill Nash, late of the Essex Regiment and the Parachute Regiment, who was a rock-climbing instructor at Achnacarry, recalls: 'New arrivals were feted by the Commando pipe band at the station but that was the nearest thing to a warm welcome anyone got. There was no transport. Each man picked up his bulging kit bag and marched the eight miles to the castle. For NCOs it was worse. They staggered under the weight of rifles and machine guns as well.

'The first sight of the castle was unforgettable. It loomed out of the mist and ceaseless rain. You got glimpses of blokes running around in faded denims and black faces. It was like a nightmare.'

Arrivals invariably received a straight-from-the-shoulder lecture from the man with the expansive jowled face and jutting jaw who was invariably known as 'the Rommel of the North' and 'the Laird of Achnacarry'.

Bluntly, he told the Commandos they were there to work at a course which would last for twelve weeks with a break of one day a week. Instructors were of exceptional calibre; an overall total of twenty thousand men was turned into super-efficient raiding automatons.

Charlie Vaughan's instructors had all sorts of favourite tricks for the fledgling Commandos, both officers and other ranks.

Bill Nash, assisted by two uncannily nerveless sergeants, was in charge of such specialities as abseiling and scree-running.

Abseiling meant scaling down a sheer surface by rope with the feet seeking their balance by pressing against the rock. Scree-running was scorching down a rope with the added hazard of small stones.

Rivers and streams were crossed by bridges made of toggle rope – a short length carried by each man with a loop at one end and a small wooden peg at the other. Just to add spice to the proceedings, explosive charges were placed in the water and the men were fired on with the live ammunition insisted upon by Charlie Vaughan.

On opposed landings – one group of Commandos posing as Germans and using German weapons – stocks of gelignite were placed at different positions on the beach and exploded electrically.

As one troop arrived, the gelignite was exploded uncomfortably near them. It threw up mud and dirt and gave the men some idea of what it would be like in battle.

A course in unarmed combat inevitably included full instruction on how to kill a man. An effective flying rugger tackle to bring down a sentry was tame stuff. Soon a Commando was learning how with maximum effectiveness to stamp on a man or to slash his jugular.

Bill Nash, who did a course in unarmed combat along with everybody else, fully realized the limitation of even the most villainous knife. He explains unemotionally: 'It offered little defence against a bullet. But, provided you got the chap near enough, a knife thrust or a kick in the crotch was most effective.'

Everyone – officers, men and instructors – went through all the courses. Everyone learnt how to kill silently, to attack at night, to ambush and to construct bivouacs.

One of the least fair sports at Achnacarry was to manoeuvre the Americans into some of the tightest situations; by common consent, many of the British regarded the Yanks as more than a little soft.

But softness, as it turned out, was hardly a just description of the American Rangers who had come into existence that very year through the blessing of President Roosevelt. He had felt that there should be a swift formation of an American force along Commando lines. A battalion of Rangers had been recruited from American troops stationed in Northern Ireland. The appeal, put with rather strange delicacy, was for 'volunteers not averse to dangerous action'.

It had been answered by two thousand men, who, after vigorous selection had been whittled down to five hundred on the initiation course at Carrickfergus on the coast north of Belfast. They turned out to be tough, very tough indeed: their rates of pay and comparative affluence were probably what irked the Commandos.

Not that it mattered. They were a fact of life at Achnacarry. Soon they were swopping the GI's normal chow for the Commando's soup, which was invariably handed to a new arrival by a cook whose elaborate courtesy should have aroused instant suspicion.

'Do you like it?' the cook asked, indicating the dubious mass.

The delighted rookie replied: 'Very much. What's it made of?'

The cook's smile vanished as he snapped out: 'Rats.'

And it was. Rats were not just for soup. They frequently had to be killed by the men and their legs eaten. For the trainee had to live off the land for much of the time. Rations were handed out raw; the proficient had good meals while the lazy simply suffered indigestion.

And if stomach cramps did not keep a would-be Commando awake at night, then the spectre of death probably did. It was very real. Fatalities under the vigorous training conditions were only too possible, although out of the twenty-five thousand who passed through Achnacarry, deaths never rose above forty.

Live ammunition was not just there to enhance reality any more than deliberately to despatch a tiresome Ranger to another world. But real ammo did have its uses. When one Ranger persisted in sitting on the side of a cockle boat rather than in the bottom as had been ordered, he got a swift bullet in the buttock. This sort of salutary discipline did more than anything to sink differences and blur the rivalries which had greeted the arrival of the American-style Commandos.

As the training wore on, wariness of Charlie Vaughan turned to something like hero worship. For many, the first stirrings of fierce Commando pride were born at Achnacarry. If a man looked like disgracing his own particular group, discipline was a family affair and was dealt with before the point where Vaughan would have had to take action.

Judgement from the Laird of Achnacarry carried no appeal. Most fearsome of all was the order to Return to Unit, known by all as RTU. The disgrace was felt by everyone.

If an Achnacarry recruit felt like grumbling, there was plenty to take his mind off things. Landing exercises were given a new edge of terror by the grim closeness of the instructors' fire.

Men learnt that if they landed craft on the wrong beach, they just had to run and make up the time. They could spend all night clambering up a hill, only to discover that they had mistaken their objective; they simply stayed out until they got it right.

Jake Ure, first of No 12 Commando and later of No 3, found that training and sport – there were plenty of both at Achnacarry – tended to get mixed up together.

He says: 'There was something Charlie Vaughan dignified with the name of "boxing", but it was more like a series of prizefights. Two teams of ten would be lined up facing one another. Two men from each team would advance and knock hell out of each other until the loser was all but unconscious.

'Charlie Vaughan, who did the refereeing with a red flag, instructed that every man was to hit as hard as he could as fast as he could. The medicos stood by to deal with the casualties which by the end of the contest were littering the ground.

'It was nothing to be inoculated against exotic diseases in the morning, then half-an-hour later take part in the fisticuffs, followed by a football match after lunch. We all loved it.'

Most trainees found that to their considerable astonishment hard, gruelling physical exercise could become as addictive as any drug. They actually continued practising on highly dangerous cliffs in their spare time.

Like all close-knit communities, Achnacarry developed its own rules and quirks. Bill Nash recalls : 'The one thing no one ever did as a point of honour was to enter the castle after an exercise other than dripping wet. It didn't matter if the sun was shining outside and you'd done nothing more innocuous than field craft. You came home round the back of the castle and swam across the river with your kit.

'It was a constant and very necessary reminder that being a Commando had little to do with comfort.'

Yet comforts there were; rats' tails were not a constant diet. Vaughan insisted that his men off duty should eat like princes; it was the job of the mess president and his staff to wheedle the best from the Highland farms, woods and rivers.

The man who passed successfully out of Achnacarry at the end of his training eventually carried on his head what amounted to an insignia of office in the world's most exclusive private army : the green beret. The colour was chosen because of the heraldic association with hunting. Regimental badges could still be clipped to the beret, signifying the fierce sense of independence of the special services.

The beret had one rather mundane but nevertheless important advantage over the steel helmet : it could be whipped off fast and, if necessary, crushed into the pocket. But most of the time the beret was a talisman to emblazon; to wear with unbridled bravado in battle.

The green beret did not make its appearance until late 1942. Before that, the Commandos, including those who had trained at such centres as Achnacarry, had more important preoccupations. A new scheme was being shaped in Richmond Terrace and its planning advanced with ever increasing speed.

It was to throw both Commandos and Rangers well and truly into the boiling cauldron of war.

# 13

Now that the mighty *Tirpitz* had slunk off to a Norwegian hideaway and the Germans were totally unable to maintain a capital ship in the Atlantic, something suspiciously like exuberance gripped even the most arid Whitehall bureaucrat.

Fantastic Commando schemes were hatched with more enthusiasm than sense. Everyone had a vision of a mighty mailed fist rising from the sea and crashing into the hitherto impenetrable Fortress Europe.

It was not only Hitler who was mesmerised by Norway; Churchill saw a mighty offensive there as a prelude to driving the Nazis back beyond the borders of the Reich.

The victory at St Nazaire, impressive though it was, hardly provided proof that the British had either sufficient experience or muscle to cut right through to Berlin. Churchill now had to contend with Roosevelt, who was desperately keen on an all-out offensive on France during 1942 to relieve the pressure on the Russians and prevent them from being knocked out of the war.

Thankfully, the British Inter-Service Joint Planning Staff, which consisted of two officers from each of the three services and a Foreign Office political adviser, were far more concerned with realities than the fantasies of chairbound politicians and amateur strategists.

These gentlemen looked for something that would amount to a decent dummy-run for the large-scale invasion that was still far off. They favoured a hammer blow at one of the key French ports. A list of seven ports was drawn up. It was put into a buff folder marked 'Most Secret' and sent to Combined Operations.

The file arrived on the desk of a man who had been one of the key brains behind the St Nazaire raid. John Hughes-Hallett, as naval adviser, scanned the list.

He shrugged: 'Why not take a leaf out of the peacetime channel route? Newhaven to Dieppe and back. It's only seventy miles, after all.'

There was a murmur of assent from the others around the table, with someone remarking that the troops wouldn't even have time to get seasick. On 4 April 1942, the Chief of Combined Operations gave approval for draft plans to be prepared for an all-out offensive on Dieppe.

Of course, choice of the 'poor man's Monte Carlo' had not been quite so casual as that. Dieppe had a harbour used by the enemy as a port of call for convoys, on which the Germans were coming to rely increasingly for supplying their far-flung garrisons. It would prove most agreeable if the movements of such convoys could be hampered.

Besides, Dieppe provided far too many advantages for the Nazi interlopers: marshalling yards, gas works, a power station, petrol dumps and a pharmaceutical factory. It was the positive duty of the Allies to reduce as many of these as possible to pulp.

It all sounded disarmingly easy. The difficulties, though, conspired to give the Combined Operations planners a collective headache. Nature had done its very worst to bedevil the operation right from the start; man in the shape of the jackbooted conqueror had all but completed the task.

Generations of Frenchmen have given an apt name to that stretch of France's seaboard which runs roughly from Cape Gris Nez in the north and the mouth of the river Saane, a few miles south-west of Dieppe itself. They call it the 'Iron Coast'.

High cliffs rise up as sheer as castles, but far more unscalable, fractured by narrow clefts or mouths of rivers. The chief of these is the Arques, on which the town and harbour of Dieppe are built.

The beaches are stony and inhospitable, although that does not stop family picnics in quiet days of peace. Landing at low water for an invading force was a daunting prospect because of the rocks in the sea bed and the angle of the shore itself. They made the task of beaching a landing craft and taking it away an exercise in skill and judgement which indeed called for all the resources of which the Commandos were capable.

In its flat, unemotional language, the wartime official history, Combined Operations, stated: 'The clefts behind the beaches are not numerous, and those which exist are, for the most part, narrow and very easily defended. Men moving up them to the attack are at the mercy of defenders in position at their top, who can destroy the attackers with the greatest of ease as they clamber laboriously upwards.'

Difficulties enough! The Germans, with characteristic thoroughness, had added to them. Their defences could cover just about every conceivable landing place; they could summon a formidable fire of all arms from medium coastal guns to small arms. Ships would have a devil of a difficulty on any run in. Staying there for any length of time would be plainly out of the question.

The planning of the Dieppe raid developed into something of a reunion of old friends. Here once again was John Durnford-Slater saying to Peter Young in that gruff, halting way of his: 'Yeah, well, Peter, it's good to see you.' The hero of Vaagso had netted Young for the planning staff at Richmond Terrace.

Their job was specific: prepare for the launching on Tuesday, 18 August 1942 of 'Operation Jubilee'.

Robert Laycock, now a Brigadier masterminding the planners, had earlier sent for Durnford-Slater.

He told him: 'We're going to use No 3 Commando on the east flank and No 4 on the west. Your task with No 3 will be to destroy or put out of action a large coast defence battery which commands Dieppe's entire anchorage. The 2nd Canadian Division will attack the town frontally. No 4 Commando will take the battery west of the town.'

The destination of No 3 Commando was the two beaches near the village of Berneval, codenamed Yellow One. Yellow Two was at Belleville-sur-Mer. The Commando was split into two groups. The assault on Yellow One beach would be led by Durnford-Slater. Peter Young would go in at Yellow Two beach. The battery itself was sited about one hundred and fifty yards inland between Berneval and the cliff top.

Before the battery were sheer cliffs of two hundred feet. RAF reconnaissance had reported that the German defences were intensified daily; intelligence resources revealed some three hundred and fifty troops concentrated in the Berneval area alone.

For close support in the attack and to supply reassuring air cover, there were to be sixty squadrons of fighter aircraft on standby – mostly Spitfires, but including four squadrons of bombers and fighter bombers.

Lieutenant-Colonel the Lord Lovat, the twenty-fourth Chief of Clan Fraser of Lovat, had probably been a Commando before he was born. His ancestors must have been smiling favourably just now : particularly, perhaps, General Simon Fraser of Lovat, who had raised the 78th Fraser Highlanders and in 1759 commanded them at the capture of Quebec when they scaled the Heights of Abraham.

Simon Fraser's mantle now fell on the man known as 'Shimi' after 'MacSoimidh' (Gaelic for 'son of Simon').

Shimi Lovat's second-in-command at Dieppe was Major Derek Mills-Roberts of the Irish Guards. He produced a brisk pen portrait of his chief : 'A tall, strikingly handsome fellow who bore himself well and could take life seriously when necessary.'

Indeed, Lovat was to take Dieppe with super-seriousness : the business completed by No 4 turned out to be a classic piece of Commando pre-planning. So successful was it that Adolf Hitler, no less, paid him a supreme compliment. The Führer put Lovat high on a death list : 'Dangerous terrorist to be exterminated'.

Lovat received his instructions : 'At daybreak on 19 August, No 4 Commando, consisting of two hundred and fifty-two all ranks, including Allied personnel, will assault the six gun battery covering the western approaches to the coast of Dieppe.'

No 4's adventure – codenamed 'Operation Cauldron' –

was to have two arms as well. The first would be under the command of Lord Lovat. Derek Mills-Roberts would lead the other. The combined task was to knock out the Hess battery at Varengeville, some three and a half miles west of Dieppe itself. The battery lay some one thousand yards inland from the cliff top. Mills-Roberts' group would go in at Vasterival-sur-Mer (Orange One) then fan out in three prongs and hurl itself at the coastal defence guns. Lovat, to the west, would land at the mouth of the river Saane near Quiberville (Orange Two). Both groups were to be taken to their target in the infantry landing ship *Prince Albert.*

Elaborate rehearsals were mounted for Operation Cauldron. The battery area was reconstructed in outline near Lulworth Cove in Dorset. No 4 went through its paces eight times – and did it at top speed. Each man carried his full load of arms, ammunition, stretcher and demolition charge. He scanned air photographs and pored over the inevitable model.

The demolition party could blow gun breeches in its sleep. The manning of the assault craft in the *Prince Albert* had been carried out time and again.

Lovat covered every conceivable eventuality: late or wrong landings, lack of surprise, heavier opposition than had been anticipated. Somewhat to their dismay, officers were forbidden to take any papers with them relating to their jobs. Lovat's order was specific: 'No marked maps, operation orders, or any documents whatever will be taken ashore.' The whole operation had to be locked in the memory, rehearsed again and again with good solid bone and muscle.

Southern England luxuriated briefly in the smiling peace of a fine summer's evening that 18 August.

John Durnford-Slater's No 3 Commando left Newhaven in its Personnel Landing Craft (LCP) as the most easterly of the assault convoys. Some of the landing craft had four-inch guns for beach bombardment and anti-aircraft fire. There were two escort destroyers under the command of the Polish captain of the destroyer *Slazak.*

Permanently cheerful Captain Roy Murray of the US Rangers, standing next to Durnford-Slater, had trained at Achnacarry. There he had been used to the yell of the instructors and the blast of what had been jokingly called practice firing. Now everything seemed remarkably quiet and unfussed. The whip of the wind and the whine of the engines ought to have been reassuring, but they only served to make Murray uneasy.

He turned his blackened face to the Commando colonel and commented nervously: 'I never realized how quiet a combined operation would be.'

Murray would have been decidedly more nervous if he had known what was going on behind him at the radar station at Beachy Head and Newhaven. They were picking up warnings of enemy ships moving eastwards between Boulogne and Dieppe. But the warning failed to get through to the Allied vessels; No 3 just kept going on what virtually amounted to a collision course.

At 3.47 a.m., it seemed to every man on the way to Berneval that the night had been torn apart. Darkness was ripped from the sky as the whole area was lit up with starshell brilliance.

Commander D. B. Wyburd, the senior officer of Group 5, which consisted of twenty-three LCPs and a flak ship, through which four hundred and sixty troops of No 3 Commando were dispersed, yelled: 'My God, we're in for it. Better get below – quick.'

Every ship in the German convoy was emptying its guns into the Commandos; Wyburd had spotted at least five ships spread in an arc across his bows. The escort vessels had dropped badly behind. Without them, Wyburd and the rest were horribly outnumbered and outgunned.

Instructions were to keep going. Enemy fire escalated; the dead and dying lay around the turrets. Tracer bullets stabbed into their shrieking victims whose bodies were soon piling up like a scrum on a rugger field.

Somebody screamed: 'This is the end! This is the end!'

Durnford-Slater felt inclined to agree with him. He blew up his Mae West and undid his boots. But all at once the boat seemed to slow down; dawn was breaking and the enemy fire slacking off. The vessel was holed like a sieve, particularly in the engine room, and steam snaked out of the pipes.

Then all at once Durnford-Slater spotted a small boat pushing towards him in the haze ahead.

Soon he was shouting furiously to Charlie Head, his special friend ever since the days of Vaagso. Head and a companion sprang aboard. It was a stroke of luck, because Head had been a vet in civvy street.

Typically, he began his treatment of the wounded by rummaging in the gunboat's stores and producing with a grin a large jar of rum. Each man got a shot while Durnford-Slater roared mendaciously: 'It's all right, he's a doctor.'

The mood changed perceptibly. As Durnford-Slater recorded: 'By the time the last man had been attended to they were the happiest bunch of casualties I had ever seen.'

The boat did not seem likely to sink so Durnford-Slater decided to leave the wounded for the escorting vessels to pick up. The rest piled into Charlie Head's landing craft and in the surrounding chaos made for the only possible objective: the main anchorage at Dieppe.

Captain John Smale, formerly of the Lancashire Fusiliers and now of No 3 Commando, reached Dieppe as well – but not in quite the same way. He and his companions made the journey out in a wooden Eureka or 'crash boat'.

Smale explains: 'Everything with a Eureka was sacrificed to speed, getting to the objective. There was no armament, for instance, and you hoped to God you didn't meet much on the way. And that, in the nature of things, wasn't likely.

'As it turned out, our particular Eureka couldn't even guarantee speed. It developed engine trouble soon after leaving England and we found ourselves chugging through the water on our own. Mercifully, we avoided the sort of reception Durnford-Slater and the rest got.'

There were other troubles, though – such as a British destroyer looming up and warning frantically of a minefield ahead. This turned out to be an obstacle that the Eureka with its narrow draught was able to take more or less in its stride.

But the luck was not to hold.

Smale continues: 'This armed German trawler suddenly hove up out of the mist. We were near two other Eurekas at this time and we decided to make smoke by way of cover. But it was too late. Machine guns were letting loose from the trawler, which was all set to ram.

'The two naval officers and the coxswain at the wheel of the Eureka were dead and the rest of us hit the deck. Corporal Tom Gerrard, of No 3 Commando, leapt straight through the thick of the fire, grabbed the wheel of the Eureka and jammed the gear into reverse. That single action saved our lives because there was the trawler practically shaving off our edge, but nevertheless belting past and away.

'Now we were leaping for the water, while the machine-gunning continued all the time. In the water, I got off my boots and battledress denims, but Gerrard, who was with me, didn't. He cried out that the laces in his boots had swelled and he was getting waterlogged. I held him up for as long as I could but he was like an anchor and eventually slipped away and drowned.'

Smale carries to this day scars under his arms made by the close chafing of his Mae West life jacket, which had almost become a second skin. He was a first-class swimmer and could strike through the water with reasonable confidence, even though he was conscious of being swept gradually west towards the Dieppe estuary.

He was also conscious that someone else was in the water with him and recalls: 'It was one of those strange, surrealist things that happen in war because suddenly there was this American airman swimming along and we were chatting away like two acquaintances at a bus stop. He was a member of the Eagle squadron who had joined the RAF. But the waves were quite choppy and there was a mist coming down and we were separated. I never saw him again.'

Smale became hallucinatory, imagining he was still involved in pre-Dieppe training in the Isle of Wight. After thirteen hours in the water, he was hauled to safety by a German armed trawler. He never did reach the Berneval battery. But that was the fate of so many of his fellow Commandos who had been crammed in the frail boats scattered in the punishing blaze of the enemy fire.

Peter Young, as strong as a bull and with energy to match, relished unashamedly each new Commando raid. The game of spreading terror along the German-held coasts was eminently satisfying. And, it had to be admitted, the gods had grinned benevolently. He had survived Dunkirk and the forays of Guernsey, Lofoten and Vaagso. Up to now, it had been a fair run for the money; if a shell ended it all at Dieppe, the record would still be highly respectable.

Such reflections were not idle : all at once death was but an instant away. Streams of tracer homed in on the landing craft. When that happened, Young's boat, LCP 15, anxious to dodge the firing line, snaked to starboard. Now they were all on their own. Contact had been lost with the other landing craft.

Young snarled : 'What the hell can I do with just eighteen men?'

Lieutenant-Commander Buckee, in charge of the landing craft, thought it more tactful to ignore the question. Instead, he contented himself by pointing stolidly and saying : 'There you are, there's your beach. My orders are to land even if there's only one boat.'

Young warmed to the man : here was somebody equally bloody-minded. He snapped : 'It just so happens those are my orders, too. We'll go in even if we have to swim.'

Buckee arrowed the little boat towards Yellow Two. Young was apprehensive; there could be machine-guns in the gully. He asked the officer to run in about fifty yards on the right. They touched down at 4.45 a.m., five minutes ahead of zero.

The Commandos, led by Captain Richard Wills, poured on to Yellow One, whose defences bristled with wire and machine-gun posts. Guns opened up; bullets twanged and whistled towards the landing craft. Men were caught as they streaked along, bent low. Three of the landing craft braved the intense fire; they were impaled on rows of five-foot iron stakes protruding above the surface of the breaking waves.

A demolition party of No 3 Troop stepped ashore : some were machine-gunned as they crossed the beach and made for the shelter of a cliff.

Wills crouched in a ditch about two hundred yards from the cliff edge. He reflected that the hot reception which had greeted them meant that opposition was altogether too great for a direct assault on the battery. It might, though, be possible to immobilize it.

A machine gun stood in the way; it would have to be located and eliminated. Captain Wills and two men moved to higher ground. It was a useful vantage point : there was the gun, manned by a couple of Germans.

Wills snatched up a rifle and took aim. One man was hit and the other seemed to be winged. There was no time to make sure. Wills dashed back to round up the rest of his men for the advance.

It was then that a bullet crashed into his neck. At the same time, Lieutenant Edwin Loustalot was to carve himself a niche in American history as the first Ranger and US infantry officer to be killed in that theatre of war.

For the rest, there could be no question of evacuation. Three companies of a German mechanised anti-tank regiment stormed down the gully. The Commandos' riposte was courageous but ultimately futile. They fought on from cliff top, lane and ditch, not surrendering until ten o'clock. Even then, there was a group near the enemy battery which held on for another couple of hours, shelled mercilessly by a nearby flak gun.

Of the one hundred and twenty landed at Berneval, eighty, many of them wounded, were captured. The rest died. There was no escape.

Over on Yellow Two, Peter Young was fully in the fray, back with the sort of action he loved best. He catapulted ahead of his men, tearing across the shale to the base of the cliff with its rocky ledge towards the narrow entrance.

It was choked with seven-foot-high barbed wire behind a wall of thick lattice. On the other side was a pleasant-looking footpath. Altogether too pleasant. Young had a sneaking feeling that anyone suffering from self-congratulation after clipping the wire would soon be denied further interest in the proceedings. The path would undoubtedly be mined.

The Commandos turned their attention instead to the left of the gully. The German wire around it served as a rope and the iron stakes securing it made useful steps.

The barbs tore through gloves and clothing. The delay was infuriating. Bleeding and battered, the Commandos began their climb. When they got to the top, there was something worth looking at.

It was the back of a sign whose front, facing the original path, read ACHTUNG MINEN. They were away from the minefield now; Peter Young had been right. His men advanced now towards Berneval.

After expressing initial astonishment at a clutch of begrimed troops whose torn clothes made them look like everyone's idea of mounted bandits, the locals fêted the Commandos. Peter Young insisted ungraciously that this was no time to be hanging about. Still, one brief and useful diversion was allowed; the telephone wires linking Dieppe were cut.

Not everyone in Berneval was friendly, of course. Close to the church was a machine-gun emplacement on the outer defence perimeter of the battery.

The Commandos dived into the churchyard out of range. But this was not at all their way of doing things: there was not a single man in No 3 Commando who did not ache for action.

Peter Young stared speculatively at the church belfry. If only he could get some men up there it would give him a marvellous view of the entire countryside. The battery could then be picked off in comfort.

But getting to the church proved impossible and soon the whole lot were on a detour through an orchard which gave a convenient siting of the target. Young was now determined that his men would do the job: plainly, things had gone wrong on the eastern beach.

A group of some twenty Commandos against an entire battery! To any textbook tactician, the very idea smacked of irresponsible lunacy. But Peter Young was an innovator and his blood was up.

The men were spread out into three groups. Young ordered: 'Keep firing as you move and they'll think there are a lot of us.' From the sanctuary of a field of corn, they let loose at the Germans.

Later he explained: 'We had to fire from the kneeling position because of the height of the corn, taking snap shots and moving about, so as to offer the most difficult possible target to the enemy, but we were almost exactly at right angles to the enemy gun-line and any bullet that whistled over No 4 gun would give a good fright to the crew of No 1 as well – or so we hoped.'

Crews and defenders of the battery were soon thoroughly confused: just how many of those damned English were there?

The Germans reasoned that to storm the cornfield and find out would be altogether too risky. So the battery's heavy guns, designed to shoot out to sea rather than inland, were slowly, laboriously turned round. But it was a sledgehammer to crack a nut. The noise of their fire was indeed appalling but their range was such that the shells tended to land more than a mile away.

Choking amid the smoke and the cordite fumes, Young and his men retaliated with tommy guns. Not for the first time did a Commando exploit come to resemble a comic strip: a small group of tired, grimy, inadequately armed raiders grappling with machine guns, flak and, most incredible of all, gigantic coastal armament.

Nor was this the end of the atmosphere of sheer farce which seemed to dog the whole affair. Off the eastern beach, a motor launch caught the sound of fire from the heavy guns. Plainly the fleet was at risk! The gallant launch decided to make a contribution of its own and unloosed its two-pounder. The result was to send shells straight into the cornfield.

The big battery guns continued remorselessly to pound

an impossible target and were unrelenting in their fury for precisely an hour and a half.

But ammunition was running short among the Commandos; the game, which had its amusing side, plainly had to come to an end. The party, still harassed by the dedicated battery defenders, withdrew, having sent an advance guard to make sure an LCP would be available for evacuation.

And it was. By 8.20 a.m., the LCP had put out a handsome smokescreen and was heading back to England with a wonderfully cock-a-hoop group of Commandos singing all the way.

None of the rest of the forces engaged in the Dieppe operation had the remotest idea about the situation in Berneval. The general feeling was that the battery would have opened fire and blasted the fleet into oblivion – a fleet which, after all, spelled the only possible chance of evacuation for everyone in the Dieppe raid.

During two critical hours, a handful of Commandos had protected the main fleet from the big guns of Berneval.

Dieppe was not adventure of unblemished glory, but what there was had been snatched in style by Peter Young and the men of No 3 Commando during a crisp August morning.

# 14

Zero hour for landing by No 4 Commando, consisting of two hundred and fifty-two of all ranks, had been fixed for 4.50 a.m. and re-embarkation timed for 7.30. That left just two hours and forty minutes for an operation that was to turn into a nightmarish miniature war all of its own.

At 1.15 a.m. Mills-Roberts went down to the wardroom of the *Prince Albert*. Breakfast was being taken in a particularly English manner – in other words, total silence. It might have been any suburban hotel; Mills-Roberts allowed himself a wry smile as a completely unflappable steward politely accosted him with an unpaid mess bill.

Shimi Lovat's final pep talk was brief. He said : 'This is an operation of prime importance. If we fail to destroy our objective, the battery will wreak havoc among the ships in the main convoy. The German soldier isn't at his best at night and that could be our biggest advantage.'

When the Commandos had dispersed, Lovat asked Mills-Roberts : 'Do you think you'll find your crack in the cliffs, Derek?'

Mills-Roberts summoned rather more confidence than in fact he felt. 'Yes,' he replied. 'There's no need to worry.'

There was no time now for anxiety. The Commandos were sorting out ammunition and adjusting woollen caps. There was a prominence of pale green : it would merge nicely with foliage. To save weight, the men did not wear tin hats and carried neither water bottles nor rations.

Now the landing craft were lining up in two columns astern of MGB 312 and the run-in to the assault had begun. There was a good ten miles ahead of them.

One thing a Commando soon learnt was to turn every

activity to advantage, even sleeping. Mills-Roberts found a convenient corner, curled up and shut his eyes.

By 4.30 his group was approaching the beach. A lighthouse flashed its beam slicing through the landing craft. Then came a starshell far away to port, followed by the tracer bullets. Red and green navigation lights winked steadily at Dieppe's harbour entrance.

The searchlight was soon paying for its impertinence. With a mighty roar, two British aircraft came in low, strafed the offending position and put new heart into the Commandos, who were gratified to see the beam effectively killed.

Lieutenant David Style had refused to allow his concentration to be deflected. He never took his eyes off land; the point of entrance was earmarked.

The columns had broken up. Three landing craft had taken Mills-Roberts and his group straight to their beach. The rest veered off to starboard for the beach at Quiberville which was to be Lovat's landing place.

The first group ashore encountered a grim calm: far worse on the nerves than any racket of shellfire. Indeed, the only noise seemed to come from shifting pebbles under the feet of the Commandos who had run quickly under the lee of the cliffs where the enemy would have difficulty firing on them.

What did it mean? Mills-Roberts wrote when it was all over: 'It was rather like stealing round to the back door of a house where a noisy party is in progress and finding nothing but silence.'

Then up on the cliffs someone spotted the shadow of a man. For some reason best known to himself, the interloper took not a blind bit of notice, his attention presumably deflected by the noise of flash guns further inland.

There was the inevitable snag. One of the gullies was impassable; clearing the chaik and rubble and likely mines would take far too long. Mills-Roberts ordered a second gully to be blown.

David Style lit the fuse of a Bangalore torpedo, a long metal tube filled with explosive, and stood back. The silence ached painfully. What was the matter with the fuse? How long would it be before the Germans woke up? The sound from the loud report was echoed back from the cliffs. The damage should have been enough but the gap turned out to be too small.

The men cursed and scratched at it, but there had to be a second Bangalore. It blew a big enough hole to scramble through singly. A small party was told to widen the breach.

Luck was with Mills-Roberts: the noise of the action of No 3 Commando seven miles away drowned the torpedo explosion. Then, as if on cue, four Allied light bombers passed overhead just as the Commandos entered the gully.

Up they scrambled and soon Mills-Roberts and his men were in the little seaside resort of Vasterival-sur-Mer. Style looked with suspicion at the wild, unkempt gardens of the villas.

A man emerged suddenly: elderly and indignant in a long nightshirt reaching down to his toes. Some uniforms look much the same no matter which nationality wears them. Mills-Roberts tried to explain soothingly that these were British troops and not German. The old man seemed indifferent: troops were flat-footed cretins in any language and these had wrecked his hedge.

A pretty girl leaning over a verandah asked conversationally: 'Are you going to shoot Papa?' Then she shrugged at the puzzling ways of soldiers and led the mumbling old man to safety.

Explosion after explosion was shattering the village calm; eardrums were pierced as the battery opened up at the fleet lying off Dieppe. Something had to be done to stop it. It was likely to be a good hour before Lovat himself would work round inland to come up from the rear.

Mills-Roberts and his men set off at full tilt, not caring about their lack of cover. Progress was swift: soon they were within one hundred yards of the battery perimeter wire. The Commandos tensed as they heard guttural commands to the gunners.

Mills-Roberts spotted what looked like a barn; it would be a useful haven for getting a better view. But it was a yawning ninety yards away; trying to make it would amount to a life-and-death gamble at not very attractive odds. He did not hesitate, and soon with David Style and two snipers was forcing open a door and catapulting up the wooden steps to the first floor.

It was like the front row of the dress circle: almost too easy. The German crews serving the right hand guns were there to be picked off for the asking. A large German was in full view, shouting a stream of orders. Mills-Roberts made a quick gesture.

One of the three snipers from C Troop caressed his rifle with a surprising tenderness. He rested it on a table and took careful aim. But craftsmen are not to be hurried. With what seemed appalling slowness, the sniper adjusted the sights and squinted down the barrel.

Mills-Roberts cursed under his breath, willing the man to get on with it. Then he realized that once the German was shot, their cover would be blown completely. But at the same time they couldn't stand there admiring the scenery.

So the major contented himself by staring at the battery through his binoculars. Then at a range of one hundred and seventy yards, the Commando fired. The German flopped down; then the men whom Mills-Roberts had left below unleashed a cascade of fire. It looked as if the British were going to have it all their own way. The enemy was stunned, crouching down behind sandbags.

A heavy machine gun opened up from a flak tower behind the battery. The tracer bullets came in a steady stream, raking the edge of the wood near the barn.

Mills-Roberts raced below to summon reserves consisting of an anti-tank gun and mortar detachment.

Several machine-gun posts were put out of action. But the tenacity of the Germans was absolute. They replaced the machine-gun crews three times on the flak tower.

American Ranger Alex Szima, former bartender of Dayton, Ohio, recalls: 'The targets were white shirts with shiny black coalscuttle helmets on top of them. The range was about one hundred and fifty yards and you heard the commands in German given to the gunners.

'But had it not been for the sudden appearance of snipers, the entire crews of the guns would have been wiped out. The snipers started scoring and the ground was strewn with Commando casualties.

'I changed position three times and ended up in a manure heap. I lost my stocking cap twice and later found two holes through the crown.'

Corporal Franklin H. Koons, another Ranger, had found a stable from which to get a clear field of fire. He was spared the sniper exchange, and kept up a continual barrage. Then orders were given for half of the men firing on the guns to about face and fire in the direction of the enemy snipers.

Adversity, as was so often the case, worked wonders with the Germans. They recovered quickly from the barrage of fire.

Mortar and machine-guns erupted at scrub and barn with redoubled fury. The Allied snipers began a dodging exercise by shifting their positions as often as they dared which was just as well because a shell from the battery later gashed the barn apart.

A Corporal Smith was ordered to break out at 6.00 a.m., make for the beach and flash to Combined Operations Headquarters in London an up-to-date situation report.

These reports were to make progressively grimmer reading as time wore on. All right, Mills-Roberts and his men had killed a good many Germans but the enemy mortaring was becoming heavier and the forward position more precarious.

The wild ancestors of Simon Christopher Joseph Fraser Lovat, originally natives of Plantagenet Anjou, had stormed often into battle, their shields arrogantly emblazoning the 'fraises' or strawberry leaves which were a heraldic pun on a noble name. Highland Frasers had figured proudly in the war of independence, indomitable allies of folk heroes like Wallace and Bruce.

Fierce fighters, true soldiers, hard-dying men – and now the latest of their long line was touching down on the soil of France in hot pursuit of another alien conqueror.

The troops of Group 2 hit the beach dead on schedule. Mills-Roberts promptly deluged the battery with smoke and ceased fire. A green Very light signal burst overhead.

Small support craft's machine-guns now tore into the German pillboxes; troops armed with hand grenades streaked to the same targets. Others bypassed the gullies and made one headlong dash for the cliffs. Up went tubular steel scaling ladders with their four-foot sections.

Lieutenant Donald Gilchrist, a very young section leader and newcomer to No 4 Commando, was determined to be a credit to Lord Lovat and to his country. But at this precise moment of patriotic elation, he was struggling through barbed wire and his trouser buttons started protesting. Soon the trousers were sliding down.

Gilchrist wrote later: 'It was a moment of mental anguish. Clutching my trousers in one hand, tommy gun in the other, I raced inland. Those buttons had reduced morale to rock bottom. If any of my comrades had noticed my predicament and had said one wrong word, I'd have shot him dead and burst into tears.'

But no one had time for that. Gilchrist and his colleagues ran crouching like men buffeted by stormy rain. More than one Commando had memories of Achnacarry, which seemed another world away.

But somehow the experience restored Gilchrist's spirits. 'With a wrench and a twist, I made my trousers fast around my waist. I was dressed, if not properly dressed. To hell with my trousers – I was in the war again.'

Ahead of them was Lord Lovat, whose general appearance and air of insouciance conjured up visions of the laird back on his estates. He was dressed in corduroy slacks, a rifle dangling rakishly from the crook of his arm, a hunting horn slung on his shoulders.

On they all dashed, running for half a mile along the banks of the river Saane. Then they wheeled eastwards, making for a copse close to the battery which was giving Mills-Roberts such a hard time.

Thirty-five German soldiers suddenly woke up to the knowledge that here were some decidedly trigger-happy new arrivals. Then they were looking down the muzzles of the Commandos' guns. Within seconds, German bodies were tumbling to the earth in a hail of fire.

Sergeants Stemson and Szima and Corporals Koons and Haggerty of the Rangers prepared to storm a house nearby. The German who emerged from it to relieve himself never did finish transacting his business. Koons raised his rifle and fired. All four men then rushed up the stairs and made for the roof.

It was then that the Allied air strike intervened, but the cannon of the Hurricane fighters overshot the battery. The ammunition rained instead on the house occupied by the Rangers, who felt that they had been slapped off the roof by a giant fist. Miraculously, none was injured. They returned as if the tiresome interlude had never been.

Around 6.30 a.m., the air strike was over but the sudden calm was shattered by a startlingly incongruous new sound : Lovat's hunting horn voicing a highly spirited charge.

Thus with a blood-curdling yell, the men of No 4 Commandos streaked into battle and the bloody kill.

What followed was indeed a massacre that must have struck some answering chord in Lord Lovat; it was in the full tradition of the gory tribal skirmishes of his Highland forebears.

On a glorious hot summer's day, murder should have been the last thing in the hearts of either British or German. But all the sun served to do was give a fearsome glint to cold steel.

Seven German machine-guns started the carnage; the Commandos finished it. They trod over the bodies of their dead comrades and clawed their way to the first gunpit.

Major Pat Porteous, liaison officer between the two groups, reeled under the excruciating pain of three terrible wounds, but now he was like a fiend bayoneting each and every German that got in his way. Soon the severed and mutilated bodies of the gun crew lay strewn on the ground, their blood coursing into the summer earth.

For Pat Porteous, the exploit was to bring the Victoria Cross.

Courage walked tall that day. When Company Sergeant-Major W. R. Stockdale lost a foot, he simply sat down and carried on tackling a machine-gun with a rifle.

During the charge of B Troop, the air was full of smoke, the reek of cordite and the screams of the dying. This was war at its most basic and savage : wounded Commandos received morphine, wounded Germans a bayonet thrust.

Brutality, in such circumstances, can never be one-sided. A German officer's boot crashed down on the face of a hopelessly wounded Commando. Now there was no time for compassion. Eyes were dull and merciless in blackened, sweat-stained faces. Someone shot the German full in the stomach. Bayonets and knives rose in the air and slashed down on throats and limbs.

There might have been mercy for the battery commandant, alone in his office and desperately trying to destroy vital papers. The Commando who burst in stalked his enemy around a large table. The man backed eventually into a corner and made the final, fatal mistake. He moved his hand towards the pistol in his holster. The next moment he stared in dazed horror at the sharp bayonet protruding from his stomach. In his agony, he brought his hands forward to pull it out but succeeded only in cutting his hands to ribbons. Only then did he start to die.

There was to be no let up in German tenacity yet awhile. Germans were chased through the tunnels surrounding the battery, electing to fall to steel rather than surrender.

The battery cook, a strange figure with his white hat stuck firmly on his head, decided in considerable wisdom that he was no hero and came out with his hands up. Only three other prisoners were taken.

After all the preliminary training at Lulworth, it was laughably easy to lay the demolition charges.

A Union Flag was hoisted above the British dead who had been brought to lie at the foot of the flagstaff. The Germans were scattered behind the sandbag breastworks around the guns, many of the bodies badly burned. The rest slumped where they had fallen to the snipers' bullets.

The big guns were spiked and blown up. Lovat took one

last look at the knot of buildings. Instantly, he adopted the posture of the old-time Highland chief looking at castles burning in a border raid.

Then came his order: 'Burn 'em. Set fire to the lot.'

There was no attempt at German counter-attack during the withdrawal. Earlier, the enemy had missed one golden opportunity of despatching the Commandos even after victory. A squadron of German fighters had come in low. There was no time to take cover. The Commandos, in their anonymous garb, brazened it out by waving at the pilots who did not as much as suspect what had happened. Mercifully, the aircraft flew on.

Withdrawal was covered with smoke generators along the track to the beach. Bren-gun teams in pairs covered each other as they withdrew alternately behind the smoke, while their rifle squads and others moved down to the beach.

Two miles off the coast, casualties – German prisoners were made to do their share of stretcher bearing – were transferred to a destroyer as the landing craft made for home.

The assault was over. Commando casualties had totalled forty-five dead and wounded.

In pursuit of the main assault in the centre, the Royal Hamilton Light Infantry knifed across the beach in front of Dieppe and grabbed the jutting-out casino which had been the main target.

But, judged land force commander Major-General J. H. Roberts, it badly needed reinforcements if it was to get on with the job of pushing forward. The western headland was crying out for capture: flank fire from this point was stunningly ferocious.

The vital back-up job was given to No 40 (Royal Marine) Commandos under Lieutenant-Colonel J. P. Phillips. Originally a salty piece of Elizabethan panache had been envisaged: to go in after the victorious Canadian troops, help with demolition and then in high triumph snatch a few barges by way of trophies and depart for England.

But there was to be no Armada-style glamour that day.

The extent of the Canadians' plight never reached Roberts; reports were faulty. The Commandos were being tumbled into assault craft which arrowed through the water towards the Royal Hamiltons.

Most of the few who got ashore were cut down. Their mangled bodies mingled with the legions of Canadian dead. But the rest kept on, while the shells kept up their terrible cascade. Ahead of the Commandos was a blazing LCT on the beach, another abandoned alongside. One crew after another fell beneath the concentrated barrage.

Here was not war as men had conceived it up till now: sheer slaughter had come to the Marine Commandos.

It was, in the words of the official report, 'courage terrible to see'. A little earlier, Colonel Phillips had been elated at the prospect of such a magnificent assault. But now things were beyond reason.

It was true that Drake's spirit did not walk with them. Rather, there was a Nelsonian touch in the gesture witnessed by the Commandos behind the craft of their colonel.

Phillips climbed to the bows of his landing craft, which was already filled with the dead of his platoon. As casually as if he had been preparing for a dress parade, he donned a pair of immaculate white gloves so that his hands would be clearly visible.

Then he turned his back on the enemy fire, raised his hands and waved. Incredibly, his voice carried to some of the craft: 'For God's sake, go back.'

There could be only one outcome. The tracers homed in, clawing at the selfless Commando who had given his life to save as many as two hundred from certain slaughter.

Even so, some did streak ahead. A pitiful number of Commandos got ashore, sheltering from the fire near a burnt-out tank. Resistance was futile; within an hour all were dead.

The assault forces were withdrawn. The raid was over and history had gone on to judge its planners harshly.

A service force of six thousand had attacked the heavily defended port. The assault cost three thousand six hundred and seventy killed, wounded and missing. The Royal Navy had five hundred and fifty casualties and the Royal Air

Force one hundred and fifty-three. A destroyer, twenty-nine tanks, many landing craft and one hundred and six aircraft were lost.

The lessons as usual had been spelled in blood; the price of taking a defended port was altogether too high.

The sacrifice of Colonel Phillips had saved many of No 40 (RM) Commandos for further battles. Shimi Lovat and Peter Young had drawn the sharp teeth of enemy fire where they had threatened to bite the hardest.

On the night before the Dieppe raid, Lord Louis Mountbatten on board the *Prince Albert* had been brutally frank.

'Tomorrow we deal the Hun a bloody blow. We expect over sixty per cent casualties. For those of you who will die tomorrow, may God have mercy on your souls.'

But the Commandos did not go into Dieppe in a mood of fatalism. Ranger Alex Szima, nearly forty years after the raid, declares: 'Every life has one high point. Dieppe was mine.'

Two years later, the Allies would be back in Europe for D-Day. The glorious saga of the Commandos in France had yet to run its course.

# 15

The attackers in their buckskin jackets edged in uncanny silence through the dark of the forest, not so much as a twig snapping before their moccasins. Then they were at the timbered walls of the enemy fort.

Up they scaled, still without a sound; the knives were out and flashing before the lookouts had suspected the presence of fearsome black-faced patrols.

It might have been a scene straight from the pages of Fenimore Cooper. This, though, was not infant America, but a typical example of Commando-style combat in war-time North Africa, reeling in 1942 from the triumphant offensive of the British Eighth Army at El Alamein and Rommel's rout in Egypt.

Hassling the enemy forces that remained were the men of the United States Rangers who were to carve such a name for themselves in North Africa that additional units were eventually formed for fighting in Sicily, Italy, France, Germany and the South Pacific.

Their inspiration was William Darby, a fire-eating West Pointer from Fort Smith, Arkansas, whose standards of training impressed even some British veterans of Achnacarry.

Houston-born former Ranger Lieutenant Gene Philpot now recalls: 'The most pleasant thing about working for Bill Darby was when you went into combat after training. It was a rest cure.'

Those clean-limbed American boys who survived Dieppe had returned from that holocaust older, wiser and harder.

They were all superb professionals now: seasoned veterans who were entrusted with spearheading on 8 November 1942 the invasion of North Africa, codenamed 'Torch'. The operation involved fourteen thousand Americans in thirty-five transports. There were to be a series of landings to envelop Oran in the Vichy French colony of Algeria.

Bill Darby's briefing was swift and concise: 'Our job is to land at Arzew, some thirty miles west of Oran. We will clean out two forts dominating the approach to the harbour.'

Visibility was bad on the night of 7–8 November. On to the *Royal Ulsterman* piled the Rangers, appreciating the presence of twenty British warships to protect the transport.

Bill Darby led his four companies up the two and a half-mile steep cliff path from the beach destination. D-Company pushed its rubber-wheeled trolleys carrying mortars.

Scouts ahead were soon reporting four machine-gun positions and two double aprons of barbed wire. Clearly, Darby reflected, the French knew how to dig themselves in. Then tracer was flicking the ground. The Rangers opened fire with mortars and machine-guns.

The plan had been to get the action over quickly. At a given time, the fleet was to open up and blast this particular fort whether or not the Rangers had taken it.

But the timetable had gone awry. Darby did not have the luxury of radio communication to explain how things had changed; the only transmitter that would have netted the Rangers into the fleet frequencies had been lost at the outset.

The sweat was pouring down Darby's face, but all at once the skirmish line was moving forward to where the wire had been cut by the scouts. With an exultant yell, the Rangers went through and leapt in the half-light on the machine-gun crews who had left their guns and joined the battery team in the dugouts.

At 4.00 a.m., Bill Darby's Very light was streaking through the sky as a signal of success. The two companies had shot the sentries on the jetty and caught some of the garrison asleep.

But there was trouble elsewhere: American combat teams

were up against it at St Cloud, south-west of Arzew, where the French had fortified a village and were holding its stone and concrete houses with the muscle of a 75 and 155mm gun. A French battery not far away at La Macta was holding an American assault force.

Ranger C and E Companies fanned out. A few half-tracks attacked the battery from the flank with HMS *Farndale* giving supporting fire. The guns were seized in triumph. Darby's Rangers had added St Cloud and La Macta to the campaign roll of glory.

Heaping laurels on the heads of Bill Darby and his men had but one outcome: more training for everyone.

Early in 1943, there was special emphasis on ship-to-shore landing craft exercises. By February, Darby reckoned that the one hundred and eighty men of three companies of 1st Rangers were ready for a fresh overland trail.

Their mission now was to destroy German and Italian held positions guarding the Sened Pass, where the road to Sfax on the Tunisian eastern coast ribbonned between the Majoura and Biada mountains.

It was a silent night march at seven miles an hour; the Rangers went on it with equipment that had been pared right down. Besides weapons, there was a groundsheet, a small ration pack and a single water canteen. The need for silence on Commando exercises did not apply just to men but to equipment also. So boots were made squeak-proof with saddle soap; clips on webbing were taped down; cap comforters took the place of tin hats.

In a pre-reconnaissance, Bill Darby had selected a bowl-shaped saddle between two peaks as a bivouac area where his men could sit out the day. The period of waiting for the dark now had to be endured virtually without movement. This was no disciplinary formality: a German aircraft which flew over failed to spot the Rangers who sweated and cat-napped through the heat of the day.

But for Bill Darby there had been no rest. When the time came for briefing, he showed section leaders the Sened Pass, a cleft in the mountains behind three hills six miles to the east across a plateau. It was here that he had seen four enemy armoured patrols crossing during the three hours of daylight. There was borne in on the Rangers the menacing rumble of tanks or heavy vehicles.

The Americans moved forward in the darkness forming line by companies, as Bill Darby monitored progress by radio.

Single Germans encountered on the way died silently to Rangers' cold steel, but the Americans got to within fifty yards of the enemy wire without concerted opposition. It was a situation that any Commando-type soldier regarded with deep suspicion.

Then came the long raking burst of machine-gun fire to the left towards A Company. As if on cue, a dozen more machine guns opened fire, spewing green and red tracers in the plains.

Ahead the Rangers could hear the jabber of Italian as the enemy scurried to its positions. But still there was no direct frontal fire. The Americans moved on; incredibly, they seemed to be undetected.

The hillside screamed into life. Hot, searing tracers zipped over the heads of the Rangers, ricocheting into the rocks of the plain beyond them.

Ranger James Altieri of F. Company, who was trying desperately to forget his own Italian extraction, had dived for the ground. Sharp rocks tore into his legs from an ear-splitting blast less than two yards to his right. Earth and pebbles covered his head.

Then there were two shells ahead of him. But these, mercifully, passed over his head. The Ranger lines were now being raked with direct fire from the enemy's 47mm cannon.

If they stayed where they were, they would all be cut to pieces. Altieri yelled: 'Let's go! On your bellies!' The instruction was passed back to the rest of the squad. Now Altieri was cradling his rifle in his arms and slithering forward into that hell of fire.

Above the cacophony, he heard two sets of voices: the

Italian words of command and the screams of death agony from his Ranger comrades.

Rifles and machine-guns kept up their rain of slaughter. On pushed Darby's Rangers – edging forward for what seemed an eternity.

Altieri felt the ground rise slightly. They had reached the bottom of the enemy's position on the forward slope. The guns maintained their fire, but the bullets were not finding their mark with anything like the same devastating effect.

Altieri yelled : 'Get into skirmish lines !' Into their assault positions went the US Rangers. Another Ranger spat out damp mud and pebbles and bawled above the dreadful din : 'Give 'em hell.'

Then Altieri pulled out the pin of his grenade and hurled it towards a machine-gun and its stabbing killer fire. He relates : 'The explosion threw dirt down on us, and the earth ahead shook convulsively as a dozen other grenades hit home.

'Swiftly we were on our feet, screaming at the top of our lungs, charging up the slopes, firing our rifles and tommy guns from our hips.'

When James Altieri had applied to join the Rangers he had been asked pointedly : 'Would you be prepared to kill Italians?' He knew that the merest hesitation would have put paid to his Commando career. He had replied that it was not his place to make distinctions within a common enemy. It had been the best reply in the circumstances, but for a long time the question haunted him.

No longer; these were would-be killers of himself and his comrades. What helped him to make up his mind was the sight of one fellow Ranger, named Garrison, who was firing on his knees towards a blasting 47mm cannon.

There was a sudden extra blast. After it, Garrison was still on his knees, his torn and jagged neck, minus the head, was cascading blood on to the ground already awash with mutilated bodies, whose entrails were inevitably crushed beneath the feet of the defensive Rangers.

In a blind fury, Altieri pitched himself forward, only to

find that he was falling. There was a moment of fear when he was convinced that he had been hit. But he had only tumbled into a deep slit trench; as a companion he had an Italian soldier.

Both were equally surprised. Altieri was probably the first to recover. He had his rifle, but it was useless: the trench was too narrow for him to bring it from his hip and fire.

Thankfully, there was the Commando knife. It took a matter of seconds to grab the handle and bring it up with maximum strength into the man's stomach.

The Italian screamed: '*Mamma mia! Mamma mia!*' Altieri rammed the knife in again and again. The hot blood spattered his arm. The Italian gave one final groan and slumped. Altieri found nausea almost robbing him of consciousness. Then he was jerked awake at the feel of his own warm vomit down the front of his clothes.

And the battle went on. The Rangers were killer machines by now. They grenaded, bayoneted, shot. Gradually, it was borne in on everyone that the guns had stopped firing. There were still the moans of the dead and dying; the Rangers were calling for the medical men.

If the Rangers' assault had undoubtedly become sheer brutality, they were only replying in the enemy's kind.

Eighteen Rangers were badly wounded; they left the battle area in supreme discomfort on improvised stretchers slung between rifles.

In their sharp vicious attack, the Rangers had expended all energy but the former French post to which they were due to return was twenty desert miles away.

The supply of water had been given without thought or question to the wounded. Everyone's tiredness was so great that few could have put up any resistance if enemy tanks had arrived suddenly and surrounded them.

Altieri's F Company had seven wounded; those, along with others who could, limped to the medical post. There they were greeted by a delighted Bill Darby.

He enthused: 'A helluva shoot ... every company came through. A beautiful job. Now we got to get our tails out of here.'

The wounded men had to be moved – and fast. Survivors were divided into two columns; off they set along the criss-cross spines of the mountain ranges. It was a journey to the end of a nightmare. Up steep mountainsides they inched, carrying the stretchers and supporting the walking wounded. Skin had been scratched from hands that felt like balls of fire. And there was fire elsewhere : the fire of parched throats that could not be slaked.

No man would have dreamt of flagging : they only had to look at Bill Darby. This was no text-book soldier, only at his best with a campaign map. This was a born leader, a man who carried stretchers with the best, who never stopped a flow of reassuring chat to the wounded.

Darby knew the Ranger rules better than anyone else and was quite prepared to break them. When a man first joined the Rangers, it was made clear to him that if he was wounded on a hit-and-run Commando raid, he could not expect able-bodied troops to be delayed in helping him. That would put every survivor at risk. It would be a war for the sure-footed and the unencumbered; the maimed would often be on a par with the dead and written off quite ruthlessly.

But, no matter the rule book, that was never Bill Darby's way. Any wounded Ranger left behind that day would have been slaughtered where he lay. So as many of Darby's Rangers as possible made the long trek home.

Then came the moment when tired eyes and intelligences teetering on the edge of delirium thought they espied buildings far ahead. Many dismissed the sight as a mirage, as a product of their own half-crazed imaginings.

But it was true; there was the French outpost. Bill Darby snapped : 'Now is the time for discipline, Rangers. Get in line. There will be no ragged columns. We're marching in.'

And they did, those men who were still not carrying their wounded comrades or prodding the protesting captives. Or they stood to attention until instructed otherwise.

Then they knew it was no hallucination. The taste of hot broth and bread from friendly French was real enough.

The direct military gains from the raid were one hundred

Italians killed, six quick-firing cannon and twelve machine guns put out of action.

The secret army of Intelligence had perhaps gained most: a great deal was learnt about German and Italian dispositions in Tunisia. Furthermore, it was shown that the Rangers, an élite force which went in with stealth and had the useful knack of staying alive, could carry out this sort of operation with maximum effect.

Even German radio was reluctantly impressed. Darby's Rangers were dubbed 'the Black Death'.

It was an appellation Bill Darby did nothing to disown. Two days later, on 14 February, the Rangers were back in the thick of it.

The iron fist of Axis armour proved suddenly that it still had plenty of clout. Enemy tanks knifed through the American lines. Death-and-glory raiding was out for the moment: the Rangers fought as infantry, plugging thinning ranks.

The enemy was now at the Djebel El Ank gorge in the mountains of El Guettar in northern Algeria. It could boast two Panzer and four Infantry divisions. The gorge was on Patton's line of advance. The nest of strongpoints there would make frontal attack a formidable undertaking.

The pulse of every Ranger quickened on learning that the job was going to be given him; Darby's men were up there again in the front line.

The enemy was known to be stuck firmly on a pass commanding two key roads leading east. Out of a solid rock positions had been blasted which covered all approaches with heavy machine- and anti-tank guns. With barbed wire, road blocks and mines, it looked impregnable. There was, of course, a temptation to charge this impressive fortress head on. But then the enemy would open up with everything it had. And that was plenty.

A major stumbling block was the seemingly impassable cliff-top mountains which formed a useful protective barrier for the enemy. If they could be scaled and a surprise assault made, the day could yet be won.

What was needed, in the words of James Altieri, was 'Indianlike craftiness, guile and great daring'. In other words, the sort of low cunning not unfamiliar to Darby's Rangers . . .

The man put in charge was Lieutenant Walter Wojic, who led Ranger scouts on two nights to reconnoitre the mountains with their small cliffs, saddles, cuts and fissures.

Lieutenant Wojic and his team found an incredibly complicated link between them all. It led them to a rocky plateau directly behind the enemy positions. What was more, it was totally unprotected. The Rangers reckoned, not without justification, that they were one up. And without a single shot having been fired.

The Americans began their long march on the night of 21 March. It was a hazardous journey in total darkness, roughly comparable to going blindfold through at least a score of mazes in an amusement arcade. Dawn had not yet broken when they reached the rocky plateau which overlooked the enemy.

Seldom could a morning have been hailed so dramatically. Barely had the first streaks of dawn illuminated the rough outlines of the mountain rocks before the bugle call shattered the silence.

The mood of exhilaration was total. It was as if the Rangers had forgotten they were Rangers : instead they had become Sioux and Comanche, Cheyenne and Cree. The American Indian had come to North Africa and the effect was bizarre and bloody indeed.

In long lines of skirmish, the black-faced hordes swooped down on Italians full of sleep. Leaping from rock to rock, knives flashing, the Rangers let fly with grenades, small arms and bayonets.

In the mêlée, Bill Darby stood out. Time and again he shouted : 'Give them steel ! Give them steel !'

Italians of the Cantaura Division littered the rocks; their hands had reached too late for their weapons. Machine-guns were knocked out by the score; a battery of 88s was annihilated.

Darby's triumphant message went out to the Patton warriors : 'Send in your troops. The pass is cleared.'

At this point a new figure enters the Ranger story. Father Basil, the men's Roman Catholic chaplain, a man of lion courage who could say Mass perilously near a battlefield with elaborate unconcern, talked an Italian officer into surrendering his unit peacefully.

It saved many lives; no one quarrelled with that, for the Rangers had been up to their elbows and beyond in blood. Suddenly, they were sickened by it.

The battle of El Guettar stands high in the Rangers' roll of honour. The Allies had secured a pass which many thought lost; one thousand four hundred prisoners had been taken.

The cost to the Rangers had been one man wounded. Daring, impudent raiding, the very essence of the Commando ideal right from the days of Dudley Clarke, had paid off yet again.

The Torch landings ignited a powder keg which eventually blew the Axis powers out of this bitter land of harsh sun, driving rain, rocks and yapping Arab dogs.

Nos 1 and 6 Commandos, after Torch, served throughout the Tunisian campaign as part of the field army. It had been proved again that Commandos, although raised for amphibious operations, could turn their hands to anything.

This was indicated graphically by No 1 Commando, which on 30 November sailed to hold sections of the Bizerte to Mateur Road in northern Tunisia. The object for the Commandos was to block a vital supply road to the enemy's forward positions.

Signal Sergeant Tim Regan, of No 1 Commando and the Royal Welch Fusiliers, recalls: 'We were at the base of a nine hundred-foot enemy stronghold called Green Hill. We had taken over from the Durham Light Infantry to hold the front – some one hundred and fifty of us in dug-outs and trenches.

'Nevertheless, we felt very vulnerable and there wasn't much comfort in the single heavy, old-fashioned water-cooled Vickers machine-guns left behind by the DLI. Not many of our blokes knew how to handle them.

'Then the worst happened. A German patrol sneaked around the flank of Green Hill behind us and came in firing on a machine-gun post.'

Regan was hunched some distance away in a dug-out with his radio, but he heard the initial enemy fire. Then he heard something else : the stutter of the Vickers.

Guardsman Albert Baker and Lance-Corporal Jack Scantlebury found themselves in the front line, almost literally looking down the enemy's throat.

Scantlebury, of the Middlesex Regiment, recalls : 'They kept coming and they had plenty – rifles, grenades, potato mashers. Baker in the gun pit reached for the Vickers. I guided him to the correct arc of fire.'

Scantlebury was above the gun pit and there was no protection whatever. Miraculously, both men survived; the action was so swift that there was no time for a major reinforcement. Time and again, the Vickers raked across the close ranks of the firing Germans; still the Commandos held on.

Gradually, the ground was littered with enemy dead from the sixty-strong patrol who, it was later learnt, were an advance guard for some sappers who were going to mine the road.

For this action, Jack Scantlebury received the Military Medal and Albert Baker, who was later killed in Burma, was awarded the Distinguished Conduct Medal.

No 1 Commando stayed in Africa until the following April, then returned to the United Kingdom to flex its muscles for the Japanese in Burma. For the rest of the Commandos, the war was returning slowly but inexorably to Europe.

# 16

General Miles Dempsey, whose 13th Corps was to launch the invasion of Sicily, sat in his Cairo office and stared searchingly at Lieutenant-Colonel John Durnford-Slater of No 3 Commando.

The object of the meeting was to discuss the assault. Sicily had to be snatched from two crack German divisions with armour attached and a sizeable number of Italian troops. The Commando role was a classic one : get in and capture one of the batteries covering the beaches.

Dempsey shot out : 'Have you ever done any of these Commando operations, Slater?'

Durnford-Slater concealed feelings that were a mixture of indignation and amusement. After all, you couldn't expect a general of Dempsey's calibre to dwell all that much on your past achievements, however noteworthy. So the colonel stood politely to attention and said : 'Yes, sir. Guernsey, Norway twice and Dieppe.'

It was an impressive catalogue and Dempsey knew it. But this was no time for the past. He had established a small planning headquarters run by his corps which was to launch the attack on the south-east corner of the island, according to plans drawn up by General Montgomery. The legendary Monty was finishing off the North African offensive. The entire responsibility for Sicily had fallen on the confident, broad shoulders of Miles Dempsey.

The general outlined No 3 Commando's role, which was to be put ashore on the flank below the main landings so that the beach defences could be softened up and the battery captured. This would aid the main assault force to get ashore with as little trouble as possible and capture Syracuse, on which the entire army plan depended.

Commandos were to land a few miles south of Syracuse and go some three miles inland towards the battery, which was in an olive grove behind the village of Cassibile covering a key beach.

Durnford-Slater would lead the attack on the battery himself. Peter Young and the remaining three troops would be left to deal with pillboxes and beach defences. These were of a kind that No 3 Commando had seen duplicated time and again in those early periods of training: they were all professional enough to carry out the entire operation speedily and with consummate ruthlessness.

Durnford-Slater deliberately took his time pouring over the plans, conscious of the bright, impatient eyes of his superior officer.

Then Dempsey spoke: 'How long is it going to take you, Colonel?'

Durnford-Slater snapped crisply: 'We could put that battery out of action ninety minutes from the time we touched the beach. The pillboxes could be dealt with in forty-five minutes.'

For the first time, Dempsey relaxed. He held out his hand and said: 'Right, carry out your final training and I'll come and see you in a week's time.'

Durnford-Slater's men moved to Suez, where the ships that were to take them to Sicily lay in the bay.

The colonel wrote: 'At Suez, we built a dummy battery at exactly the right distance from the sea and reproduced as many of the features of Sicily as we could. We held twelve full-scale rehearsals, trying out every single detail. Each man knew the number of paces from the beach to the forming-up place, the compass bearing for each leg of the advance, and every detail of the plan.'

A visit from a now totally trusting Miles Dempsey came as a marvellous tonic to Durnford-Slater.

The general said tersely: 'I shan't have to worry about you.'

It was the only praise No 3 Commando needed.

In the late afternoon of 10 January 1943, the Commandos were approaching the coast of Sicily. Morale had never been higher, despite the rough sea. There were prolonged cheers at the first sight of Mount Etna. Then came the transfer to small landing craft and, on beaching, there were the familiar obstacles of wire and pillboxes.

Fire from the Vickers K guns mounted in the bows of the landing craft silenced puny Italian opposition. No 3 Commando was soon through and forming up inland.

Durnford-Slater forged ahead, flashing a shaded torch into the advancing column; it acted as a handy marker. They sped along at a fair crack, the only sound was the shuffle of feet and the occasional shifting stone. Each man was heavily laden, carrying extra ammunition.

When the battery opened up, parachute flares were shot over it. Then the assaulting troops poured in heavy additional fire. Durnford-Slater's batman, Charlesworth, sounded the advance on the bugle and in they went for the final assault, firing from the hip. The Italians opened up with automatic weapons; soon bayonets were flashing.

In a spirit of bravado, some over-enthusiastic soul decided to blow up the ammunition supply to the battery for good measure, but no one was hurt from the debris of a thousand shells.

The battery was blown up eighty-five minutes after landing; Durnford-Slater's promise to Dempsey had been redeemed with a comfortable five minutes in hand.

The Commandos moved on in triumph into Cassibile itself. The high spirits which had given the whole affair something of the air of a boy-scout outing were far from evaporating.

Charlesworth and another ex-bandsman named Lofty King decided that some form of raucous celebration was definitely called for. From somewhere in the village, musical instruments had been found. Soon the racket of a trumpet and a brass band shattered the air, which vastly pleased Durnford-Slater's triumphant marauders.

With decidedly different feelings, a Scottish regiment suddenly turned up in the town from the beach. The Jocks had been hell bent on getting to Cassibile first and now found that some Sassenachs had beaten them to it.

The Commandos, bloody-minded as always, decided to add salt to the wounds. The trumpet and the drum, with various attempts at musical expertise, were soon producing a tune called 'The Same To You'.

Peter Young, meanwhile, was in a foul temper. He remembered Dieppe and considered that success should prove infectious. This time, though, he considered there had only been ignominy. His landing craft had been badly handled; it had landed in the wrong place.

He begged Durnford-Slater: 'Please give me something to do.'

Sympathetically, the colonel sent him off to deal with some Italians skulking in a fort nearby.

Peter Young returned in a vastly more sunny mood.

Elsewhere in Sicily, other Commandos snatched their share of the glory.

Commandos who had trained at Achnacarry even rehearsed street fighting in bombed-out sites of London's severely mauled East End.

The role of No 41 was to effect a surprise night landing at Cap Passero on the southernmost tip of the island and overcome the beach defences. The way would then be open for the dawn landings of the 1st Canadian Division.

It remains to this day a source of pride to 41 (RM) Commando that it was the very first in at Sicily in the transports *Derbyshire* and *Durban Castle.*

Even so, at three o'clock on the morning of their mission, the Commandos were half an hour behind schedule. They were drenched with spray, and water slopped into the craft from the strong swell. The radios were severely damaged. As pillboxes loomed up in the semi-darkness, machine-guns were trained on wire defences at the rear of the beaches.

Fire turned on Captain J. A. Taplin, who was leading A Troop. He was wounded severely. Major J. McCann, second-in-command, just made it across the wire defences before he fell to the deadly barrage.

In a sharp dawn action, pillboxes were wrestled from the enemy. An observer from 41 (RM) Commandos recalled: 'We could look seaward and see a vast armada of ships sending troops and craft of all descriptions to the beaches, where they landed unopposed.'

Sicily was regarded as so strategic that the very top brass of Combined Operations turned up for the kill: among them Brigadier Bob Laycock, who, the following October, succeeded Mountbatten as Chief of Combined Operations with the acting rank of major-general.

Laycock and his cohorts came in with No 40 (RM) Commando, whose CO, Colonel Phillips, had made the great sacrifice at Dieppe and saved the day for so many landing craft.

Confidence soared throughout the entire special forces. As for No 3 Commando, it was not to be permitted to play drum and trumpet for very long.

Durnford-Slater was ordered to Syracuse: a summons which came, not from Dempsey, but from Montgomery himself.

Monty, several people had noticed with satisfaction, went out of his way to sport the green beret. He and Durnford-Slater talked in the summer sunshine on the bomb-shattered quay at Syracuse.

The British aim was to push on to Catania in one swift thrust. There was a single road running from Syracuse to Catania. Monty's plan was to cut this at two points, thus disorganizing the only main line of communications between the Germans and Italians and their bases. An airborne drop would seize and hold the Primasole Bridge, a few miles from Catania.

No 3 Commando's job would be to seize another bridge, the Ponte dei Malati, which was over the Leonardo river, two miles north of Lentini. The advance would then be open for the 8th Army.

'When do we go in, sir?' queried Durnford-Slater.

Monty riposted briskly: 'What's wrong with tonight?'

Intelligence staff stated confidently that the opposition

was likely to be half-hearted : just a few Italians and not a hint of a German anywhere.

Such breezy optimism made Durnford-Slater uneasy. But the colonel kept quiet; he could hardly contradict Monty's experts to their faces. Still, he decided to take nothing on trust. An inbuilt instinct for danger had never let him down yet.

Monty must have been aware of the extent of the gamble, though. Success depended entirely on the capture of that bridge, and the operation could turn into a monumental disaster. Supposing the Intelligence people were all wrong and there was plenty of opposition after all? Too few Commandos with too light arms would be cut to pieces. On the other hand, a main army could not be expected to lavish limitless armour on an advance guard. Of a line of retreat should the whole thing go wrong, there was not a sign.

If anyone else but Monty and Dempsey had been in charge, Durnford-Slater would have been a lot more worried. But these were a pair of gamblers he trusted. Still, the truth was written in letters a mile high : No 3 Commando would be out on its own with no one to help.

As if conscious of this, Dempsey later took Durnford-Slater aside. 'You won't be left in the lurch,' he promised. 'Our leading troops are the 50 Division. If they don't get through to you by first light tomorrow morning, clear off and hide up for the day.'

Durnford-Slater reflected that a few hours before, he had been resting after Cassibile, enjoying a few gins on the *Prince Albert*, the ship which had taken No 3 Commando in. It had only been a couple of modest glasses before Dempsey's signal had come and he was off again.

Monty was clearly a general in a hurry. Indeed, his parting shot had been : 'The enemy is nicely on the move and we want to keep him that way. You can help us do it. Good luck, Slater.'

That sort of optimism was infectious, as the men of the 8th Army knew only too well. Monty had told his men at El Alamein the previous October that hitting the enemy a crack would be 'quite easy'. Durnford-Slater was not sure if he would go as far as that over Ponte dei Malati, but he hurried back to the *Prince Albert*, gin forgotten.

Now there were briefings for the landing at Agnone, a small village seven miles due east of the bridge. Then No 3 Commando would push inland some five miles to the Ponte dei Malati and keep the enemy from destroying it.

The bridge was about two to three hundred yards long, including the causeway leading to it from the north east. It lay in a shallow valley with a low range of hills to the south-east. The south-western end was protected by orange groves and cypress trees which offered useful cover.

Plans had to be made fast. Two stages were decided upon for the landing. The first would involve Headquarters and Nos 1, 2, 3 and 4 Troops. The second would be of Nos 5 and 6. Headquarters and No 2 Troop would concern themselves with holding the beach. The vital bridge would be seized after one swift advance by Nos 1 and 3 under Peter Young. That would leave No 4 with the job of sending out two patrols. One would go north to make contact with the airborne troops attacking the bridge at Primasole. The other would be off to the south to link up with 50 Division, the advance guard of the 8th Army. Nos 5 and 6 Troops would follow Nos 1 and 3, all helping to hold the bridge.

Commander Peate, RN, captain of the *Prince Albert* found himself being rather more than a chauffeur to No 3 Commando. For all at once there hove up a threatening E-boat, torpedos blasting. A swift touch on the helm and the *Prince Albert* snaked out of the firing line. But the noise everywhere was hell : there was thunder from the low-flying Dakotas overhead taking the Paras to Primasole bridge. To the south, it was possible to see heavy anti-aircraft fire driving Axis planes from Syracuse.

The transfer to a flotilla of landing craft under the command of Lieutenant Holt, RN, was smooth; the vessels moved forward steadily line abreast, the Commandos crouching in readiness.

Then came the enemy fire : pillboxes erupting violently with machine-guns in an enfilade which was vicious and unending. Light opposition, be damned! Now everyone was blasting away furiously. Durnford-Slater noticed a sailor whose weapon muzzle was literally a few inches away.

Lieutenant Holt yelled: 'Don't shoot the colonel's bloody head off!' The noise was so appalling that words of command were quite useless.

Then all at once, Durnford-Slater was conscious of a familiar sensation: the momentary prickling of fear he had sensed when death stalked at South Vaagso and a grenade rolled at his feet.

It was fear borne of being defenceless. Lieutenant Holt had been instructed to beach the colonel's boat first, and he put Durnford-Slater at least two lengths clear of all the others. An officer carrying a Bangalore torpedo jammed it across a ramp leading from the boat. For a while, no one could move.

The colonel was alone on the beach and only too aware of it. He related: 'The sand boiled up around me as the bullets struck. Somebody also started throwing grenades down the cliff at me. I thought the bullets were enough without those extras.'

But at last the boats were beached. The craft pulled away to pick up more Commandos. Inexplicably, Durnford-Slater was to be spared massacre from the flying bullets.

Lieutenant Holt was less lucky: the fire got him in the neck and he died swiftly, not quite out of range of the shore.

On the extreme right, Peter Young landed moments later. Italian fire seemed to be tiring. Its accuracy was sporadic, probably because of the moonlight which made distances deceptive. But soon Young was taking on a German machine-gun position, and the opposition harried the Commandos all the way to Agnone. There were other irritants: a small party of British parachutists ballooned out of the sky, confidently expecting to be at Primasole Bridge.

Young cursed roundly at a spatter of Italian grenades, the noise they made mingling incongruously with the hunting horn carried by the men of No 1 Troop.

An Italian machine-gun was spewing at Durnford-Slater's ubiquitous adjutant, Charlie Head. There was no time to draw a revolver: Head's boot crashed into the side of the machine-gun and sent it toppling.

Durnford-Slater shouted to his men to stop straggling. There was a good three miles of rough country to be covered before the bridge could be struck. Off went the Commandos, conscious that the lack of cover at least precluded ambush parties.

But soon the terrain changed and they were struggling through bramble thickets, over stone walls and, after that, olive groves. Then, two hundred and fifty yards ahead, Durnford-Slater spotted the white bridge, prominent in the moonlight. There appeared to be four pillboxes at the end of the bridge nearest to the Commandos but not an enemy in sight.

Evidently, they felt reasonably confident; a lorry with dimmed lights crossed in front of the British. Were Germans or Italians or both in control?

There was only one way to find out: clear the pillboxes. Bill Lloyd, a badly wounded veteran of Vaagso, and Lieutenant Brian Butler, commanding the leading section, rushed each pillbox with their men. The din of the grenades was replaced by shouts and loud groans.

Lieutenant Butler stalked the first of the pillboxes. Then there was a frightening moment as the split pin in the grenade jammed. But eventually he pulled it out, flinging it through a slit.

Then Butler recoiled in horror as a walking sheet of flame appeared at the door. The Italian, a human incendiary, screamed loud and long, eventually crumbling as a heap of charred and burning flesh. Durnford-Slater shrugged: 'Well, there's no doubt they're Ities.'

Within ten minutes the pillboxes were cleared. Durnford-Slater was prepared for a little self-congratulation on behalf of No 3 Commando: 'I thought we had done well to get there. We were out on our own, ten miles ahead of the 8th Army, right across the enemy's only line of communication.'

Chatty and excitable Italian prisoners were lined up in front of the colonel. Their loquaciousness could be dangerous for all of them: the position could be betrayed. A Commando fist crashed into a jaw to silence one particularly hysterical captive.

There was time for rest after this spirited little exercise. Durnford-Slater snatched a catnap – rudely shattered by a mortar bomb attack, starting with a single explosion.

Now the Commandos were facing Germans as well as Italians. The mortar assault lasted some hours. Casualties were high : the men of No 3 Commando could not all take cover in pillboxes only designed to hold about a dozen.

As if the mortars were not enough, a clump of evergreens beyond the far end of the bridge suddenly parted. Out of the gap lumbered a German Tiger tank, its 88mm gun scorching all before it.

My God, what had happened to Montgomery's intelligence? How many more of these monstrous leviathans were there?

Durnford-Slater, conferring with Charlie Head, ducked as a branch from the olive grove scattered to the ground, sliced by an 88mm shell. He felt his hair parted by another missile from the Tiger.

And then it seemed as if every German in Sicily had taken it into his head to lumber through the area. The lorries rumbled along in endless procession, making south from Messina. It was an arrogant procession; Durnford-Slater decided to knock some of the cockiness out of it.

Troops dashed quickly a hundred yards ahead up the road; the lorries were picked off as they passed. The air was full of bursting ammunition and the stench of rubber.

It was a luxurious revenge but it took its toll. One young lieutenant fired his PIAT (anti-tank weapon) into a German half-track ammunition carrier and the resulting explosion killed him as well.

There was considerable consolidation, though, when No 5 Troop succeeded in setting up a PIAT on the bridge. A round fired from it put paid most effectively to a German ammunition truck and trailer, which went on exploding for quite a time.

Durnford-Slater looked around at the dead and dying

among the olive groves: whatever happened it would be a bitter victory.

But at all costs the bridge must be saved; it was crucial to Monty's plans. No 3 Troop was detailed to move under it and remove the demolition charges the Germans had placed there. A line of German paratroops fired into the sixty-strong troop; there were eight casualties. But their action saved the bridge.

The enemy assault continued with escalating casualties from mortar fire. Of Dempsey's 50 Division there was not so much as a hint.

Durnford-Slater was not to know it at the time, but there had been a major battle at Lentini which had held back the relief. At Primasole Bridge, too, there had been fierce fighting.

No 3 Commando, already badly mauled, could not hold out indefinitely: indeed, there was a total of one hundred and fifty-three casualties during the operation.

The decision was taken to move into the low hills of the east, lying up possibly until the arrival of either the 8th Army or the advance guards.

Durnford-Slater and Peter Young were among the last to leave, remaining in some cactus bushes with a party of No 4 Troop. But gradually everyone peeled off, harried by enemy fire and, above all, by the Tiger, which had rumbled over the bridge in hot pursuit.

Peter Young was deeply pessimistic: 'I had hoped that when we were reorganized we would advance and attack the bridge from both sides but, with tanks about, this would have been to invite destruction in such open country. In the hills we would be comparatively safe from the Panzer troops.'

Indeed, Durnford-Slater was soon suggesting that the best course was to break up into small bands and make their way across country to Augusta, which was directly on the east coast, roughly half way between Syracuse and Catania.

The colonel's party of four found an olive grove to snuggle in during the day, but it was not long before the bullets from the Germans were kicking up clouds of dust and the party was forced to move on at the double.

Durnford-Slater had been a sportsman all his life, but now he confessed : 'I began to change my previous views on fox-hunting disastrously. We were the quarry with a vengeance.'

The hunters were the 4th German Parachute Brigade, whose lofty standards of training and discipline won the reluctant admiration of many of the Commandos it took prisoner.

Durnford-Slater had to get back intact to report to Dempsey. Lesser mortals decided to have a little fun during their retreat. Sergeant Taylor and Corporal Pantall in gleeful mood swooped down on a party of Italians in a farmhouse.

They edged their way along the wall and came face-to-face with sheer luck : standing unattended among some shrubs were two medium mortars trained on the beach. To make things even more interesting, there was a shed nearby stuffed with ammunition.

The two men fixed their bayonets and stormed in. Two sentries were disarmed. Then they removed the sights and put the mortars out of commission.

Around the corner, the Italians were tucking into a meal in an outhouse with more devotion than they ever expended on Mussolini. Taylor and Pantall crept up and turned the key in the lock. Next, they dashed to the shed, seized forty-four grenades and the bolts of all the rifles and flung them down a well.

Then they legged it to the hills, looking for the British lines. A couple of nights later, they heard vehicles and the tramp of infantry. Gingerly, they crept forward from a hiding place only to hear a North Country voice say : 'I'm effing browned off with this.'

There could be no doubt they were among friends.

By the time 50 Division reached the bridge, No 3 Commando had all but pulled out. Opinion was divided as to whether the Commandos, severely depleted by casualties, could have held on and taken it. But the important thing was that the enemy had been prevented from destroying the bridge. In addition, much confusion had been caused in the German rear.

Durnford-Slater and his party stumbled on, suddenly on the Agnone–Lentini road to be challenged by an enemy post. In the bright moonlight, the very last grenade was lobbed at the post. It failed to explode.

In his book *Commando*, Durnford-Slater wrote : 'We ran across the road in groups of two or three. Each time there was a brief burst of enemy fire. Again we were lucky and none of us was hit. The rest of the way was plain walking, but plenty of it. Finally we reached an 8th Army anti-aircraft position.' The last thing Durnford-Slater remembered was one of his men draping a borrowed greatcoat over him with the tenderness of a mother at her baby's cot.

Peter Young already knew that No 3 Commando had nothing to fear from Dempsey as a result of the Ponte dei Malati action.

The general had driven up in a jeep during a fiendish argument between some Bren-gun carriers and German parachutists. Dempsey ignored all this, merely saying taciturnly to Young : 'I'm pleased the bridge hasn't gone up.' Anyone who knew Dempsey was able to translate this into high praise.

Later, Dempsey was much more explicit : 'The men of No 3 Commando are the finest body of soldiers I have seen anywhere.'

Such praise was seen to be even more merited when the 50 Division reported that it had identified in the area between the bridge and the beach, among other enemy forces, three battalions of Panzer Grenadier Regiment Koerner, together with guns of the Hermann Goering Division; tanks of the 101st Italian Tank Battalion and an unspecified number of Italian infantry.

The road to Catania remained unbroken. Monty, as was his wont, had the last word. He barked : 'I have an order for you, Slater. I want you to get the best stonemason. I want you to have him engrave "No 3 Commando Bridge" on a good piece of stone. Have this stone built into the masonry of the bridge.'

The instruction was carried out. According to *The Green Beret* by Hilary St George Saunders, 'In the summer of 1948, an unexploded mortar bomb was still lying on the top of one of the pillboxes guarding the bridge, the last evidence of a most gallant battle.'

Monty showed appreciation in other ways: Durnford-Slater received a bar to his DSO; Peter Young a bar to his Military Cross. There were three other awards of the Military Cross and two of the Military Medal.

They had been gained with copious lettings of blood. No 3 Commando had gone in three hundred and fifty strong. Of these, five officers and twenty-three other ranks were killed, four officers and sixty-two other ranks were wounded and fifty-one other ranks missing, mostly prisoners of war.

Truly, it had been a brutal bridge to preserve.

# 17

Sicily in summer is no place to be thinking about war. Bougainvillaea blazes proudly from little balconies in countless windows. Tomatoes grow to healthy ripeness beneath a sun which shows up with seductive sharpness the rich cobalt blue of the sea.

The summer of 1943 was particularly glorious; there were moments when the war could be forgotten briefly and the eye of British Commandos, invariably peeled for the merest suspicion of an enemy, could roam indulgently over gorgeous olive-skinned Sicilian maidens.

This slumbrous idyll was shattered, not by the conventional crudities of war, but by the outlandish squeals of the Scots bagpipes. For on 22 July 1943, Lieutenant-Colonel J. M. T. F. Churchill, MC – 'Mad Jack' of Vaagso – swept back into the Commando story with his own special panache.

Jack Churchill was now in command of No 2 Commando, which had undergone restructuring since its glorious action at St Nazaire. He was now to summon all his formidable resources for the Italian assault and he had the blessing of General Dempsey ringing in his ears: 'Let us know everything. Keep piping. Good luck!'

There followed a number of small-scale raids on selected points on the Italian mainland but these were mere curtain-raisers for the big one – securing a main foothold in Europe at Salerno. Sicily was to be the jumping-off point for 'Operation Avalanche'.

Pigoletti, La Molina and Dragone are villages nestling beguilingly near the gulf of Salerno. The honey-coloured temple of Paestum and the sands which ribbon away from it beckon the visitor seeking a quiet interlude from the noise of Naples.

But to Commando veterans there will never be anything quiet about these points north of the gulf of Salerno. They think instead, the surviving Rangers and men of Nos 2 and 41 (RM) Commandos, of map locations like White Cross Hill, Hospital Hill, Castle Hill and, most unromantic of all, Pimple.

The gulf of Salerno provided landing beaches of sufficient width and length to put ashore a whole army – it was chosen for the main assault on Italy in the dying days of Mussolini's Fascist regime. Salerno, of course, was to be one stop on the triumphant road to Rome, but, before that, the 5th Army, consisting of the 6th American Corps on the right and the 10th British Corps on the left, would make the assault landing, then hurtle towards the first of the great prizes – Naples itself.

The shortest route to Naples passed through the towns of Salerno and Vietri and then switched north-westwards through a belt of mountains before debouching on to the Naples plain. Roads arrowed through the mountains, but there were also narrow passes at the south-eastern and north-western ends which could act as sinister sentinels against the unwary. Before the liberating Allies could march in pride to Naples, the area had to be free of the enemy.

Plans went ahead for two subsidiary landings on the left or western flank. Three battalions of Rangers, under Bill Darby, would capture and hold the northern beach-head boundary, known as the Nocera defile. Two Commando units would capture and hold La Molina defile to the south. These Commandos would have another job: wiping out a coast defence battery commanding the western portion of the bay of Salerno.

The Commandos were part of the muscle of what was now No 2 Special Service Brigade, consisting of four Commando units sent out from England in June 1943 for the Sicily assault.

Now it was divided into equal parts. Two units were put under the command of 5th Army for Avalanche. Two were allotted to the 8th Army for an assault on the toe of Italy.

At Salerno were No 2 Commando and No 41 (RM) Commando, both under the man now known as 'Lucky' Laycock – for him, it was already a long, long way from the awkward days of Layforce.

The Commandos embarked at Palermo in Sicily on the afternoon of 7 September 1943. The assault craft were already being swung with a metallic clang on their davits and lowered into the calm waters for the run-in when a rumour surged through the ranks that the Italians had surrendered. Now the whole operation would be no more difficult than a Sunday afternoon spent in front of the fire with make-believe battles fought by toy soldiers.

As it became apparent that the news was true, there was cheering and whistling – and a general relaxing of tension, which made the officers gnash their teeth.

More than one senior Commando roundly cursed Eisenhower, who had made the announcement in a broadcast. It could seriously undermine discipline. Would the men who landed at Salerno from such widely scattered points as Tripoli, Palermo, Bizerta, Termini, Oran and Algiers fall victim to complacency? Had they forgotten about the Germans, fanatically determined to hold Italy to the very last drop of blood?

As it turned out, no one need have worried: the realities of battle destroyed illusion quickly enough.

About two hours after midnight, the landing craft with most of the men and brigade headquarters of No 2 Commando were lowered. The flotilla arrowed for Marina cove in the still inky black. Minesweeper, destroyer and gunboat were ahead.

Twenty minutes later, came No 41 (RM) Commandos, heading for La Molina defile, detaching two troops to clear the village of Vietri.

A shore battery opened up. The guns of HMS *Blackmore* spoke, the orange fire ripping into the beach. Rock and sand erupted to the heavens. Then there was silence; there at least the Germans would give no more trouble.

Out there in front and in paradise was Jack Churchill. A string of blasphemies and obscenities poured from his lips as, inevitable sword in hand, he forced No 2 Commando forward.

A couple of Germans from a battery stared in astonishment at the figure before them who looked like a cross between a Highland bandit and mad mullah. They recovered too late: their flares and Very lights proved every bit as ineffective as their spasmodic and inaccurate fire.

On the way to La Molina defile, No 41 (RM) Commandos had paused only to knock out a German Mark IV tank which had lumbered forward inquisitively.

Vietri was an attractively untidy jumble of gaily painted houses, the yellows, pinks and whites fractured by the green copper dome of the church which soared over the uneven tiled roofs. Brigade headquarters dug in at the German barracks which had once been the school.

Now there were all the signs of a hasty evacuation by the enemy: abandoned uniforms and equipment were everywhere. A cascade of paper littered the stairs. In the main square stood a destroyed German medium gun, its dead crew around it.

It was Lieutenant-Colonel Bruce Lumsden, Commanding Officer of the 41st (RM) Commando, with two troops under Major J. M. Edwards, who completed the capture of Vietri.

A little further away, Lucky Laycock came within an ace of losing decidedly more than his nickname. His staff and batmen and a number of signallers bumped straight into an enemy patrol. Laycock flattened against the nearest building, edging round it. He found himself looking down the business end of a German soldier's pistol. In a flash, Laycock's own weapon had fired. To his chagrin, he missed. Then the German fired and missed too. Later, someone asked: 'What did you do then?'

Laycock snapped: 'We both turned and bloody well ran, of course.'

With Vietri taken, the Royal Marine Commando pushed on for La Molina, that all-important route for Naples. Soon they had seized positions dominating the road and the railway. Here they would hang on, awaiting the main force.

On the beach at Marina, things were getting nasty. The German mortars and guns kept up their deadly assault. Landing craft trying to get in with stores and kit met a succession of barrages. Many had to beat a hasty and undignified retreat to their parent ships without unloading.

The psychological mood of an invading force can change as quickly as the wind. Somehow, the idea got about that Vietri had been lost, that the Commandos had been driven out. The headquarters ship received the false news and reacted with consternation.

A message was flashed to Laycock : 'At all costs you must retake Marina beach.'

The nerveless brigadier riposted with a terse : 'Impossible. I have never lost it.'

In the valley between La Molina and Vietri, things were scarcely happier. The Germans fought with a tenacity not encountered before, flinging every man and every stick of ammunition into the ranks of the Allied forces wherever they appeared.

In the village of Cava near Liberatore Hill, north of Vietri, German reinforcements bolstered the line. Out went the urgent call to brigade for ammunition. The Americans sent 4.2 inch mortars.

The valley reverberated to the crash of the enemy's mortar; the hills echoed to machine-gun fire. This was dense, thick country; picking out the German observation posts and fire positions was difficult and took up valuable time.

The Germans showed their mettle in startling fashion. A British forward troop saw a man advancing in British battledress, hauling a reluctant German prisoner.

There were vintage Cockney curses : 'Keep quiet, you little bastard, or I'll cut yer throat ! Shut up or I'll have yer liver for supper !'

The Commandos were delighted at this pungent whiff of East End London. But the next moment they were flat on the ground. Bogus captor and captive had got within yards, firing their sub-machine-guns and reaching for grenades to be tossed in the British trenches.

It nearly came off, but the Commandos' reflexes were good. Soon the bullet-ridden bodies of the impostors stained the ground.

Italian civilians were inevitably caught up in the no-quarters-given slaughter. Into No 2 Commando's dressing station were carried three young girls, their dresses dripping with blood. Strong men who had thrust Commando knives into enemy bellies now wept. The relatives carried away the small bodies for burial.

Marine Commando headquarters fell to mortars, wounding the commanding officer and the signal officer and his staff. Then it was the turn of Laycock's headquarters, and the death of a sergeant.

On Dragone Hill, to the north-west of Vietri, the enemy was moving forward on a wide front and passing above the posts manned by the Commandos. There was a very real danger of their slicing through to the town. Hastily, two Commando troops were snatched from the top of Liberatore Hill and put straight into the attack.

Fighting spilled over into the following day and then No 2 Commando on Dragone Hill was in trouble, with the enemy attacking under a creeping barrage of mortar.

All at once, the Germans were through both flanks of the Commando position, established on a small hill to the south-east of Dragone village and shooting into the British rear.

This was serious enough. Then, just to add to the Commando burden, the artillery observation officer found himself suddenly staring helplessly at the vehicle containing his precious wireless set. It had suddenly careered out of control down a hill and overturned. Retrieval was out of the question. Now there was no way of requesting urgently needed fire power.

A time-wasting chain was inevitable: fire orders were passed by the CO on his wireless to brigade headquarters, who in turn relayed them through an artillery link to the guns.

Eventually, up came 71st Field Regiment with the required defensive fire. The Commandos had new heart: they stood and took everything the Germans threw at them – and chucked it back again. Still the enemy steamrollered, passing inexorably between each troop position, even overrunning the dressing station at unit headquarters.

A troop of the Royal Marine Commando and the reserve troop of No 2 Commando were now together: the counter-attack was on and the prize was the steep hill of Dragone.

German battering was so intense that it seemed certain the enemy would break through. There was little prospect of reinforcements for the Commandos.

Every man devoutly thanked God for the presence of 71st Field Regiment of the Royal Artillery: its guns at least postponed the agony of what looked like inevitable withdrawal.

Jack Churchill snarled with delight. Summoning the reserves, he launched a counter-attack. In the gallant charge, the leader, Major Richard Lawrie, fell at the head of his men. In his place came Captain the Duke of Wellington.

The Commandos hurtled into that seemingly impenetrable wall. Inch by inch, the Germans fell back, giving no quarter on the way. By noon, they had abandoned the position. On sped the Commandos in a glorious counter-attack on Dragone Hill, but the Germans were too badly mauled for further fight.

It had proved a costly scrap for the Commandos: nearly one hundred men had been killed, including five officers killed and one wounded. But the enemy had received a highly satisfactory whipping: it had scurried off down the slopes, leaving a large number of dead.

The action at Dragone Hill brought one eagerly welcomed reward for the Commandos beside victory: there was the luxury of twenty-four hours' rest before they were back in the still blazing inferno of southern Italy.

Brigadier Tom Churchill, MC, of the Manchester Regiment, Laycock's chief of staff, wrote: 'On 14 September, the men could be seen stark naked at the wells washing and scrubbing their shirts and shorts, but as the town was still being shelled and mortared this necessitated undignified rushes to shelter from time to time.'

The next afternoon, they were back in action, but the day undoubtedly belonged to Jack Churchill.

As far as was known, ebullient 'Mad Jack of Vaagso' had not a single drop of Scottish blood, but this did not stop him going into action as if he could claim generations of bloodthirsty Highland ancestors.

Laycock had once seen Mad Jack on his way to battle with bow and arrow and had demanded what the hell he thought he was doing sporting a mediaeval weapon in a twentieth-century war.

Highly indignant, Churchill had demanded : 'Show me a target.'

Laycock found out a tree a hundred yards or so away. The arrow zipped through the air with unerring accuracy. As it shuddered in the tree, Churchill commented with a grin : 'Think how frightened you'd be if a shower of those descended on you !'

As for the sword, someone else had been unwise enough to enquire as to its actual benefit, only to receive the indignant reply : 'Any gentleman without a sword is improperly dressed.'

Now Mad Jack was to give the enemy a taste of his highly individual medicine. The Germans had occupied the village of Pigoletti and dug in on three hills : White Cross, Pimple, and another, later dubbed 41 Commando Hill. The brief was to get in and capture Pigoletti.

It looked like turning into just another bloody fight for high ground. The tired Commandos grumbled among themselves that here was another case of doing the conventional army's dirty work. The role of fall guy was not appreciated by the special forces; besides, in this case, nobody seemed to have the slightest idea of the strength of the enemy forces.

The point was made forcibly to Mad Jack. He grinned slyly. Well, a virtue could be made out of uncertainty. He would try a fine bit of Commando bluff. Going would be hard and slow, an advance up a thickly wooded valley through dense vines, in pitch darkness.

Jack Churchill divided the force into six columns of troop strength. The men were ordered to fan out across the whole valley.

Boyhood memories of P. C. Wren's *Beau Geste* were stirring. The idea was to make the enemy think that there were a lot more Commandos on the way than there actually were. The men were instructed to yell : 'Commando ! Commando !' at the top of their lungs. If enough of them kept up sufficient noise, no one in the darkness would know just how many there were. The scheme had another benefit : it was a highly effective way for each man to keep in touch with his fellows.

Jack Churchill grabbed the front position as of right. He advanced with sword flashing, cursing roundly at his escort, Corporal Fussell, who was quite incapable of keeping up. Churchill's eyes scanned every inch of ground, every rock. Now he was in the village, moving along with the soft-footed assurance of a cat.

All at once, he froze at the sight of a doorway ahead. Two red dots glowed. Above the cigarette butts, he discerned the outline of German steel helmets. An excellent first target! Too easy, perhaps, but one must not be fussy. He prepared to pounce.

Then the two Germans suddenly turned to chat to a villager. Courtesies were extended; there was an invitation to a drink. Churchill swore long and loud but eventually the two men came back – to just about the most menacing sight they had seen in any theatre of war.

The fearsome figure of Mad Jack Churchill stood before them, waving his sword like a crazy Dervish.

A stream of execrable German issued, of which only two words were comprehensible : '*Hände hoch!*' They obeyed without a word. The next flood of blue language was reserved for the wretched Fussell, who had only just managed to catch up.

Churchill was impatient for the next bit of fun. He snapped : 'Guard these men !'

Ahead of Mad Jack now was a mortar pit, its crew asleep around the weapon. The colonel crept towards the pit. His boot crashed into the backsides of several dozy Germans, their slumbers shattered rudely by the bellow : '*Hände hoch!*'

And now the bag was a highly satisfactory six.

Churchill inspected it with the air of a bishop confronting leprous mendicants. They were a poor lot of miserable sinners, except for one who looked as if he had a glimmer of intelligence. While the rest were marched off, the exception shuddered with fear as Churchill, in hideous German, threatened to decapitate him at the slightest excuse.

In fact, the man was much more useful alive : he knew the relevant passwords. With Churchill's sword poking at his back, he was trotted from one sentry post to another. Out tumbled the Germans, to be greeted by the sword-waving demon. In this way, thirty to forty men were taken into captivity without a shot being fired. This and similar actions were eventually to win Colonel Jack Churchill the DSO.

It all had been good schoolboy fun; but the serious stuff of war went on.

Off sheered the Commandos for Pimple Hill, which had been a decided nuisance to the infantry. The Germans dug in there listened in horror to the constantly repeated : 'Commando ! Commando !'

By now the reputation of the special forces had travelled widely. All sorts of imagined terrors gripped the enemy. They stayed quietly in their positions hoping the threat would go away, but soon the Commandos were upon them. One hundred and thirty-six prisoners were grabbed at a cost of one man killed and two wounded.

Pigoletti and the Pimple had to be held. The enemy had recovered its nerve; the moon was up and visibility good.

Resistance around Pigoletti was furious. As if embarrassed by their poor showing at the Pimple, the Germans had hastened reinforcements there. Up the hill the Commandos stormed for the second time in twelve hours, the Duke of Wellington leading. Casualties were appalling; the Duke fell at the head of his troop, adding further lustre to a noble name.

Weariness descended on each and every one of the survivors and daylight caused their eyes to smart. They had fought to a standstill; not even Commandos could proceed without rest. The blanket of tiredness enveloped them more heavily with each minute. And, unknown to them, the spectre of disaster awaited them with the new dawn.

Fresh orders came that No 41 (RM) Commando was to throw all it had at the Pimple. Zero hour was fixed for two o'clock on the morning of 17 September.

This time it was resolved that not a single man would be risked unnecessarily: a vicious artillery concentration would presage the attack for a full eleven minutes.

But there had been a serious miscalculation. The barrage stopped four hundred yards short. Most of the shells straddled the front line of the Commandos. Men who should have been advancing now leapt for cover. The acting CO was killed and many others wounded.

It was one incident in a bloody engagement – and the saga of slaughter was not yet over.

Indeed, it went on for two more days. The Commandos fired without rest by day and patrolled by night. But there was a slow falling off on the night of 18 September; the stuttering of German fire dwindled away.

A healthy sprinkling of Bill Darby's forces had learnt low cunning at Achnacarry. They put to good use what they had learnt under Charles Vaughan. Working in small groups and dodging everywhere, they fooled the Germans into believing that their strength was great.

On 9 September, they had landed at Maori, well to the west of Salerno and east of Amalfi.

Ranger Alex Szima, who was an ammunition sergeant, recalls: 'The Maori landing was sprung as a complete surprise. We were able to drive five miles inland and set up gun positions in the mountains overlooking a narrow pass. In that position we were able to cut off the German retreat from Salerno.'

Szima's job was to get the ammunition from the beaches up to the gun positions. It had to be counted, sorted and moved rapidly. The Germans soon began a severe counterattack and never let up for eleven days.

In this area at least, there were Italian civilians willing to help the Allies. Szima explains: 'Some nine hundred of them filtered through the German lines to give assistance. We would never have held that pass without them. Each of them carried one round of ammunition on his shoulders and hauled it across mountain tops to our guns.

'Some men even carried 105mm shells and took a day and a half to reach the position.'

The British finally relieved the Rangers at Maori and prepared the way for the Allied push on Naples.

A loosely organized Panzer reconnaissance company had been annihilated, even though an observation post of 16th Panzer had reported 'six ships offshore' at 1.58 a.m. There were six steep miles of slog but eventually the Rangers were above the Nocera defile in triumph. Bill Darby laconically radioed a successful landing.

When fresh troops moved in on the Pimple they found it evacuated and strewn with German dead. The battle was over.

The flowers for the valiant belonged to the entire 5th Army, but the ultimate glory shines most surely on the units of No 2 Commando and No 41 (RM) Commando.

It had been ten days of dire carnage: thirteen officers and fifty-four men killed, and fifteen officers and two hundred and twenty-five men wounded, while one officer and fifty-nine men were missing. Since the landing at Marina on 9 September 1943, the brigade had lost nearly half its strength.

It was the finish of an engagement which at one time had seemed so critical for the Allies that Royal Navy ships were on fifteen minutes' notice to re-embark the forces.

No one counted the cost. At least, not then. What mattered in the cold, passionless climate of total war was that the road to Naples lay open.

# 18

Field Marshal Albrecht Kesselring, German Commander in southern Italy, was in the position of the hunted fox on a day when the scent was excellent; snapping at his heels was the 8th Army, which would settle for nothing less than an out-and-out kill.

But Kesselring was able to leave plenty of annoyance in his wake in the shape of demolitions and mined roads. He also had a bolt-hole from which he was prepared not simply to skulk, but to turn and fight.

As the Germans withdrew along the eastern slope of the Apennines, they reached the river Bifurno, running into the sea two miles south-east of the little town of Termoli.

The place had once been a fishing port, but it was scarcely a peaceful spot. Over the centuries, when there had been no wars, earthquakes had taken their toll. The inhabitants asked only to be left alone, but fate constantly decreed otherwise. And Termoli experienced its greatest upheaval in the hours before dawn on 3 October 1943.

Kesselring adopted the technique of maintaining a few posts along the snaking coastal roads, harrying the enemy while he pushed ahead with his main forces.

Montgomery reasoned that the Commandos must go in first and sweep up whatever nuisance was in the way, thus securing a clear path for the big advance.

This reasoning worked well with the melodramatically designated Special Raiding Squadron at Bagnara, on the toe of Italy.

The German post had retired after losing Bagnara in a heavy battle; the 8th Army had been able to move straight in and for several miles beyond.

Now was the time to look at Kesselring's new bolt-hole. His forces were showing all the signs of making a stand on the river Bifurno, which offered a good defensive position.

Monty's decision was to outflank it. He would make a landing with the Commando Brigade – now consisting of No 3 Commando, No 40 (RM) Commando and the Special Raiding Squadron – and land two miles north of the river at Termoli. With Termoli and its useful harbour in Allied hands, Kesselring would be forced to withdraw even further north.

It was a challenge welcomed particularly by John Durnford-Slater. The seasoned warrior of Vaagso and No 3 Commando Bridge was now in overall charge as brigade commander.

The plans for the assault were simple and the manner in which the Commandos' role was drawn up and discussed would have been regarded as nothing short of hair-raising by text-book tacticians. Durnford-Slater had an impatience with needless paperwork. It was an attitude which was readily appreciated by Bob Laycock's brigade major, Brian Franks, and the camp commandant, Basil Bennett.

Durnford-Slater wrote later: 'Brian used to pull a few bits of paper out of his pocket occasionally and write something down. This was our filing system.'

Out of this haphazard staff work was hammered a Commando battle plan. About a mile to the west of Termoli a small bridgehead would be established by No 3 Commando. It would land from six assault craft, followed by brigade headquarters. Then would come No 40 (RM) Commando and the Special Raiding Squadron. They would land, pass through No 3 and seize the town and harbour. The squadron would grab a broad junction south-east of the town, the main link between Naples and Termoli.

Durnford-Slater had established a base at Manfredonia, up the eastern coast. From there the flotilla slipped anchor at 11.30 a.m. on 1 October.

Not for the first time in this war, Commandos were able

to snatch a few hours of relaxation in fine weather while hell-bent on raids where losses promised to be cruel. And the sun shone particularly brightly that day on the deceptively quiet beauty of the shimmering Italian coastline.

But, like a portent, the weather switched to showers as No 3 Commando and brigade headquarters transferred to their small assault craft.

To Durnford-Slater this was the highspot of every raid: the moment before the Commandos went in with the dark land looming ahead. It was at two in the morning that Durnford-Slater and Franks dashed from the craft. Four signallers carried a squat shape on a stretcher: not a wounded Commando but a heavy wireless set to transmit and receive a distance of at least thirty miles to General Dempsey's headquarters. Up the steep sandhills went the signallers, cursing under their heavy burden.

Brigade's base was a sand dune half a mile from the town; it seemed oddly remote and secure until Spandaus and Brens shattered the silence.

It was time to go in; the two men found most of the fighting centred near Termoli's railway station. Above the noise, Durnford-Slater heard the rattle and puff of a railway engine gearing up for a journey.

He and Brian Franks fanned out. Franks drew his pistol and leapt for the cab. The German driver swung round in surprise, but raised his arms in meek obedience.

German troops in the carriages slumbered and dreamt of the safe journey they were about to make north. They awoke still in Termoli station, looking down the barrels of Commando weapons.

But if these Germans were out of the war, there were plenty still in fighting mood. The same parachutists they had encountered at the Ponte dei Malati in Sicily were as belligerent as ever.

These were the stamp of German troops who fought with seeming indifference as to whether they lived or died. Durnford-Slater spotted one man in an olive grove behind a tree, his movements stiff with agony from severe wounds.

Although barely able to handle his weapon, he kept firing. The Commandos returned the compliment until he was dead.

The bag for the British was good : some seventy prisoners plus trucks and lorries swollen with a variety of loot, including precious cigarettes, which lay abandoned.

But the action was far from being over. Durnford-Slater was to face some of his most nail-biting moments of the entire war.

The opulent villa which overlooked the harbour of Termoli was a substantial stucco affair once occupied in considerable comfort by a notorious follower of Mussolini. The approach of the invading forces changed the man's life-style abruptly : he quit with his wife, leaving behind a manservant of pompous demeanour.

Durnford-Slater considered such facilities far too good to waste : the place was commandeered swiftly as Commando brigade headquarters.

The manservant, preserving his dignity, thought otherwise and promptly locked the best rooms. He was incarcerated in the cellar and told he would stay there until his mood changed.

Being without a butler had its drawbacks, of course. But as Durnford-Slater shaved in the sybaritic bathroom on the first morning of occupation, he reflected that life had its decidedly good moments.

But this good moment, it turned out, was not for long.

The noise of a dozen low-flying Messerschmitts over the villa shattered his sense of security.

The aircraft raked the town in wave after wave. In other circumstances, it might have been dismissed as little more than an annoying diversion, but this was Italy in 1943 with the Germans in retreat. They certainly did not have aircraft to waste on indulgence.

Durnford-Slater confessed later to a deep foreboding. Could it be that things had been too easy up to now?

And so it proved. To add to everything, the rain was coming down in torrents. Italian rains are among the most vicious in Europe. Within two hours an engineer's bridge over the Bifurno had been washed away, cutting the town off from the 8th Army.

The German barrage opened up. The entire artillery of the 16th Panzer Division, buttressed by heavy armour, threw itself at Termoli.

The 8th Argyll and Sutherland Highlanders had, until now, held the church, but the Panzers wrenched it away. In the olive grove, British anti-tank gunners opened up, but they had fired at too great a distance away. Their position was revealed as effectively as if someone had stood up and shouted. Now there was nothing for it but retreat.

A sergeant and three men stayed on, but now in defence was only 3 Commando, a troop of the Special Raiding Squadron and some other machine-gunners.

But the most dangerous enemy facing the Commandos that day was not the whole 16th Panzer Division. It was a single man, who came within an ace of scoring a great prize.

The German artilleryman groped his way gingerly up the staircase of the newly conquered church, his progress made slower by the weight of his radio. Soon he was steadying his field-glasses on the parapet and snaking the surrounding buildings for the tell-tale signs he sought.

After a few moments, he smiled grimly, turned away and reached for his radio. His instructions were concise and swift.

John Durnford-Slater was holding a routine briefing with Brian Franks. Suddenly a shell seemed to blow the house apart; it had landed next door, where many of the staff were hard at work.

Durnford-Slater was the first to recover. He dashed forward gasping : 'Let's hope they're all right.'

Somehow Franks got ahead of him and was able to crane his neck into the shattered remnants of the office. Then he turned round and said quietly : 'No, John, they're not.'

This was worse, far worse, than the battlefield, where a man worked more or less at even odds : kill or be killed.

There was a sort of awful logic in that. But this was slaughter.

There was the shattered body of Tim Leese, who had lost an eye at Ponte dei Malati and could have been out of the war with a clear conscience. Now he had been cut to pieces.

The other known occupant of the room, the intelligence officer Alan Piele, was at first nowhere to be seen. The blast had scooped him up and slung him way through the window. Several of the rest of the staff lay around in pools of blood.

There was no time for recriminations, no time for revenge. Termoli, so misleadingly peaceful but a short time before, was becoming an inferno. The explosions multiplied; the buildings were chipped, shattered and holed. Falling masonry killed a number of troops. At night, small fires made the whole area look like rows of blazing castles.

Durnford-Slater had to concede that things were decidedly not going his way.

The men in the olive groves had their problems, too. Some dozen German tanks loomed up a mere two hundred yards away. Behind them came a solid wall of infantry. The British were down to one infantry brigade and a badly sapped Commando brigade. To make things worse, the enemy had supply lines; the British had none.

What chance had the Royal Engineers of getting the all-important bridge rebuilt? They would take a dreadful pasting.

And they did. The sappers dangled over the roaring, churning, hungry waters; the shells showered in without mercy. But by nightfall the job was done and the tanks rolled across, zeroing in on Termoli as nick-of-time relief.

A new sense of purpose swept through the Commandos. There was a good chance that now the position could be reversed. Even the weather was smiling. Valuable air support was forthcoming.

Durnford-Slater stated: 'I now knew that we were sure to win, but that it might take a little time.'

Now at least there was a breather to bring to book one of the most dangerous threats to Termoli. Where was the man who held the clue to the headquarter's position and had tipped off its destroyers? It had to be someone in a good position to spot the tell-tale roof aerials. If such a man was still at liberty, the risk of a renewed attack remained.

The tower of the church was a strategic position; here was a hunch worth backing.

Cautiously, the party of Commandos edged its way up the twisting stairs of the church tower. For a while there was silence, then the sound of running. Up bounded the Commandos. A revolver shot crashed past them, a call for surrender was ignored. The firing party steadied the Bren. The roof was sprayed; there was total silence.

They found the German sprawled dead beside his set. The town's major menace had been removed.

No 3 Commando fought on that day. The tanks and the guns lashed them with fearsome fury. A unit had been forced to retreat. The remnants were exposed and bleeding on the left flank. But there was no thought of withdrawal. The Special Raiding Squadron and No 40 (RM) Commando refused to budge.

But reinforcements were there; sheer numbers made the retirement of the Germans inevitable. Mortar, tank, aircraft at long last lifted the curse of destruction from Termoli.

General Montgomery was at the top of his form. The action of the Commandos had acted as a kick forward for the 8th Army; Monty had not been held up by fighting on the Bifurno River.

Durnford-Slater, tactfully steering away all congratulations, risked being abrupt to the hero of the western desert.

'My men need a holiday.'

There was silence. Monty was by repute a Puritan; he was said not to care for the way in which soldiers traditionally enjoyed themselves.

Then he barked: 'Take them away to Bari, down the coast.'

There was another pause. Then Monty added with the

barest suspicion of a twinkle: 'I'm told there's everything down there.'

The victory of Termoli was yet another milestone on that bloody, tortuous trail from the western desert and Sicily to the very gates of Rome. There was general impatience to be done with this phase of the Italian campaign. Italy must be knocked out of the war and attention paid to the invasion of western Europe. That as nothing else would bring the war home to the borders of the Reich at last.

But Italy was not to be done with quite so easily. The fighting stretched into the months ahead.

On the morning of 20 January 1944, No 9 Commando and No 43 (RM) Commando had gone in on the flat, inhospitable plain of Anzio. After a series of engagements, the enemy broke through No 3 Troop of No 9 Commando and reached Commando headquarters.

The special forces retaliated, but the line held. Casualties were high, particularly among 1st and 3rd Rangers, who had taken on German tanks and mortars in the hills. The 3rd Rangers' commanding officer, Major Alvah Miller, was killed and Major Jack Dobson of 1st Rangers was severely wounded.

Darby had received their last radio messages. No taskmaster could have been so demanding as Bill Darby; on the other hand, no American officer could have cared more for his men. His grief was bitter as he reformed the units he had left.

The progress up the length of Mussolini's once-proud land was agonisingly slow. There had been soldiers who had cursed the western desert, but at least movement there had been more fluid. Many were the imprecations hurled at this terrain of mountains and sticky heat and its denizens of dubious loyalties. Indeed, it was not until April 1945 that, for Commandos and others, Italy was finally done for.

Elsewhere, great minds had other preoccupations: the concept of 'Overlord' – the 'D-Day' of legend – was rapidly becoming more than a planner's dream.

# 19

It might have been a gala festival from one of the long summer days cherished in memory from before the war.

Ships' hailers blasted tunes of jaunty optimism. Men on board a vast armada began to cheer; the nearest vessels started the hurrahs. The rest, in ships stretching away beyond human eye, came in on cue.

Spithead, off the Isle of Wight, was an exhilarating place that shimmering 5 June. An observer might well have imagined that this was a celebration for some home-coming hero.

Heroes were indeed there, but they were soon to sail away and make war anew.

Euphoria was understandable; D-Day was at hand. The Allies were returning to Europe, abandoned four long years before in defeat and shame under a jackboot advance. These were happy warriors, none more than the Commandos among them.

But 'D-Day' remains a misleading tag: in fact, it was to be 'D-plus-82' before the Commandos and the rest were to see the back of the last German.

The liberation of Europe – spearheaded by Operation Overlord – has its own niche in Commando history, but the blood was to flow even more cruelly than at Dieppe and St Nazaire.

Once again, men were to be spattered with the brains and entrails of comrades. They would lie in mud and filth and the stranglehold of their own blood. The blind would grope in vain for a helping hand from those catapulting up the beaches, weapons poised to gouge and maim.

Radio-listening in Britain had taken on a fresh urgency

throughout the early months of the summer of 1944. There had been the fall of Rome to raise the spirit, but it was one unemotional announcement from the BBC which made the pulse race.

It said: 'Under the command of General Eisenhower, Allied naval forces supported by strong air forces began landing Allied armies this morning on the coast of France.'

For four years, there had been radio accounts of victories and defeat. And there had been other sounds: the nights had been full of the beat of German bombers and the wail of sirens. Allied aircraft had left at dusk and returned at dawn.

Towns and villages in southern England awoke to the clatter of fast-moving open trucks crammed with troops and mounted with Brens against fighter attacks.

By contrast, other places were strangely quiet. Village pubs, whose landlords and customers had been used to friendly American twang, were now left with their elderly regulars. The skies were free of the familiar sight of mass drops in parachute exercises.

It was as if a single gigantic arsenal was on the move.

In fact, plans for something like it had existed for two years. Winston Churchill had told Lord Louis Mountbatten on his appointment as Chief of Combined Operations 'to plan for the offensive'. Then Russia and America had joined the war; the years of hard slog put such an adventure far into the future. It was not until 1943 that Churchill and President Roosevelt met at Casablanca and agreed to appoint a joint staff and make a definite invasion plan.

For six months that year, the coasts of Europe were studied minutely. The lessons of previous Commando raids were taken thoroughly to heart. Dieppe may have been needlessly wasteful of life but it had at least established beyond doubt the impossibility of holding a port in an opposed landing. Torch had demonstrated that many landing craft were needed not only to land assault troops, but to keep supplies moving during the vital build-up when troops struggled to establish a bridgehead.

In December, Roosevelt appointed General Eisenhower, then Supreme Commander of the Mediterranean, to take command of the invasion of France. Deputy Supreme Commander was Air Chief Marshal Tedder. Admiral Ramsey, General Montgomery (made a field marshal in 1944) and Air Chief Marshal Leigh-Mallory would command, respectively, the navies, armies and air forces.

The need for an invasion was beyond dispute. But *where*?

The Americans favoured Calais. Certainly, it was the most heavily defended part of the coast, but it offered the shortest route. Normandy, to the British, looked a far better bet. If the bridges of the Seine and Loire were blasted, the whole area might very well be cut off from Germany.

The shortest route argument, anyway, was considered irrelevant. All the ports from the Thames to the Bristol Channel would be needed to handle the vessels; the length of the crossings was the least of the problems.

In August 1943, Churchill, Roosevelt and the Combined Chiefs of Staff approved Normandy. But, it was suggested, there was no reason why the Germans should not be fed the illusion that the area of the Pas de Calais had in fact been chosen.

Armies and fleets assembled in the south-west of England, while dummy army camps and fleets were seen in feverish activity in the south-east. Reconnaissance flights in the area of Calais were stepped up; there were persistent bombing attacks. German radar screens showed up fleets of ships and aircraft; enemy agents sent back to Himmler and the German secret service reports of an undisputed build-up at Dover and elsewhere.

The lines of tiredness stretched taut across the scarred features of Field Marshal Gerd von Rundstedt, German Commander-in-Chief in the West. For thirty-five years he had served the German army without question : a steely professional with a healthy distrust of politicians, his Führer included.

Rundstedt's campaigns had been dazzling. His army group had destroyed Poland and performed with brilliance in

France. He was a survivor right from the days when he had approved the liquidation of Hitler's rivals in the early, brawling days of the brown shirt climb to power.

And now?

Losses in Russia had bled Germany dry of military talent; the material he was commanding these days was mediocre, the ranks swollen with a motley band of foreigners – as much as ten per cent of the strength of some divisions.

Rundstedt smiled grimly when he reflected that a few years ago such foreigners would have been regarded as 'animals' and shipped to extermination camps. Well, he was sixty-nine now and too old to be deceived : total victory for Germany had long been out of the question. He also reflected that nonsense was being talked with distressing frequency by the Führer these days.

Hitler was pinning an almost mystic faith in the much vaunted 'Atlantic Wall' at Calais, a network of fortifications built by slave labour and garrison troops.

Rundstedt had once remarked with contempt : 'Has he forgotten what we did to the Maginot Line? The Atlantic Wall is a propaganda structure. It fools no one.'

This criticism reached Hitler. The Führer exploded : 'I built the Atlantic Wall and the West Wall. I am the greatest builder of fortifications of all time.'

It was all proving remarkably tiring, and now Rundstedt faced the appalling task of defending the Atlantic coast.

What he needed above all was some really tangible officer talent. In this respect, Hitler did Rundstedt proud : he sent him the darling of the German people, Field Marshal Erwin Rommel.

The patina of desert glory still clung to the field marshal; he did not like the idea of a subordinate role but consoled himself with the thought that, at this stage of the war, a man was lucky to have anything.

His first appointment was to inspect such fortifications as there were. But Hitler gave his hero command of 7th and 15th Armies. Now Rommel could speak his mind to Rundstedt; the seeds were sown for a serious clash.

Rommel had respect for Allied air power. He was convinced it would cripple Rundstedt's plans to counter-attack by holding up movements of enemy troops and pushing them into the sea.

To Rommel, it was essential to prevent any landing force from achieving a bridgehead; the place to hammer it would be on the beaches.

The inevitable result was a compromise: the armour would be kept back and the infantry forward near the coast.

Neither man quite appreciated just what was coming from the other side of the channel: the greatest armada the world had ever seen.

But the Germans were soon to learn.

The years had wrought many changes in the structure of the Commandos.

Now there were plans to bring new marine Commandos into being, a mixture of volunteers and conscripts.

The traditional Commandos regarded such a move with suspicion and dislike. The whole Commando ideal had been built on the volunteer element. Many laid the blame squarely on Mountbatten's shoulders: what else could you expect from a navy man?

It was highly unlikely, many muttered, that units of conscripted marines could maintain the high Commando standards. The argument rages to this day, although time has blunted resentment into a good-humoured sparring at annual reunions.

The marine innovation was not the sole change at the time of Overlord. The Commandos had been reorganized into four self-contained Commando brigades. One was to remain in Italy, one to go to the Far East and two to operate in north-west Europe. Commando group headquarters was set up in control.

First Commando Brigade was commanded by Shimi Lovat, who had under his wing Nos 4 and 6 Army Commandos and was soon joined by No 3 Commando. The fourth unit was

No 45 (RM) Commando, which underwent the course at Achnacarry, concentrating on specialist and amphibious training for Overlord.

Fourth Commando Brigade, also due to operate on D-Day, was made up of Nos 46, 47 and 48 (RM) Commandos, all formed recently and buttressed by No 41 (RM) Commando, which had served with distinction at Sicily and Salerno.

Throughout the Normandy campaign, the brigade was under the command of 6th Airborne Division, which was to land in Normandy before dawn on D-Day and seize the vital ground on the eastern flank of the Allied seaborne invasion.

The strike area for Overlord covered an area roughly from Cherbourg in the west to Le Havre in the east. There were five clearly designated landing beaches; from west to east – Utah, Omaha, Gold, Juno and Sword.

Utah and Omaha were to be tackled by the Americans, Gold and Sword by the British and Juno by the Canadians.

The British were to land initially at five points, each about a mile wide and spaced across a twenty-four mile front.

On 5 June, the assault ships lay poised like greyhounds in the slips. Fixing D-Day was child's play compared with determining H-Hour, the moment of landing. Eisenhower had the unenviable task of trying to please a lot of people all at once.

Soldiers wanted to land under cover of darkness, the navy insisted that the navigation of landing craft and the preliminary bombardment made daylight necessary; besides, the beaches were known to be dotted with all sorts of delights dreamed up by Rommel: mines and 'hedgehog' barriers which could only be rendered harmless by men who could see what they were doing.

There *was* an ideal time, though: three to four hours before high water and about forty minutes following 'nautical twilight'.

On the other hand – and at this point the planners could scarcely be blamed for tearing their hair out at the roots – there was the need for moonlight for the passage of convoys and for the airborne paratroop landings to seize the flanks.

Satisfying everyone was not impossible, just difficult; anyway, the invasion was out of the question on more than three or four days of every month.

The favoured date was 5 June. On 24 May, the assault forces were formed.

A complete security blackout was imposed, but the longer it was necessary, the greater was the risk of the Germans learning something. A stand-down would mean movement, disorganization, rescheduling – all elements to attract attention. It was a nightmare time for Eisenhower.

Then came a new threat. Sunday, 4 June produced a wholly unacceptable weather report. Eisenhower took the gamble: D-Day was put off for twenty-four hours. But a large American convoy of one hundred and thirty-eight landing craft had already started out; it had almost reached German radar cover before it was recalled.

On the other side of the Channel, Rommel reflected that there had been a time when the Luftwaffe would have acted as Germany's eyes and told him what the enemy was up to. But the Luftwaffe was a sorry thing these days.

Radar? Early warning? With so much of the Reich shattered by British bombs, it was a wonder any ironmongery was at the disposal of the Germans at all. U-boats? So many of them had gone where they had once sent Allied shipping: to the bottom of the oceans.

At least there were *some* weather reports. Rommel studied those for 5 June. They gave him a perfect excuse to snatch a weekend with his family at Ulm on the Danube. Soon he was settled comfortably in his field marshal's car for the long drive ahead.

At fifteen minutes to ten o'clock on the night of 4 June, General Eisenhower made up his mind. D-Day would be on 6 June. H-Hours were 7.25 a.m. for Sword and Gold beaches, 7.35 to 7.45 a.m. for the two wings of Juno and 6.30 a.m. for Omaha and Utah.

British bombers began showering the skies above the Pas

de Calais with 'Window', tin foil strips to jam German radar. The deception was kept up even when paratroopers were landing at the river Orne, which flowed parallel with the Caen canal.

Aboard the *Princess Astrid*, the stomach muscles of Captain Murdoch C. McDougall, six-foot-plus section leader of F Troop, No 4 Commando, were tightening.

It was 3.30 in the morning; he was staring apprehensively at the cold dawn breaking over the sea. It was the moment of tenseness before 'boat stations'.

There was the bustle of men getting into equipment. Harness was being eased into as comfortable a position as possible and grenades checked, along with magazines and field dressings.

Then it was into the landing craft. Originally, Commandos were chosen from among men who were thought to be constitutionally incapable of seasickness. But now everyone was vomiting. Shells were screaming overhead; the whole coastline was under a thick pall of heavy black smoke.

McDougall got the feeling that their reception was far worse than had been intended originally. The first flight of assault troops, consisting of 8th Infantry Brigade, had been given the job of silencing the beach defences at La Brèche, about a mile to the west of Ouistreham. The casino there was a fortified point overlooking the flank of the British landings.

No 4 Commando was to repeat its success at Dieppe and take the battery that flanked the landing. But at 8.20, No 4 Commando had found the assault troops pinned down by deadly machine-gun and mortar fire from a strong point at the back of the beach. Some men had not got beyond the water's edge.

McDougall himself was thigh deep by this time, trying to remember his training advice that touching any obstacle for support could be tantamount to suicide : it was odds on that the enemy would have mined it.

He related : 'The water on my left seemed an odd colour; it was swirling around a threshing red stump, which was all that was left of an arm, the body attached to it was invisible under the churning water. I splashed forward into the shallower water and up on the smoke-laden beach. Through the wreaths of smoke I could see the hazy outline of the ridge of dunes.

'The air was full of peculiar whines and whizzing, while the clumping of the mortars and the tearing, searing rattle of machine-guns seemed to dominate everything.'

As McDougall splashed out of the water, he saw another man lying just above the water-line. A burst of machine-gun fire had caught him across his thighs; his legs were almost severed. McDougall tried to unfasten the harness of the man's rucksack. But its weight held it to the ground.

McDougall had to leave him to join the rest of the section which had stumbled on past him. Soon they were moving up the beach.

There was an open space to cross before reaching the start line for the attack on the Ouistreham battery. The leading section of F Troop made it, but McDougall's two leading riflemen were sent on their way with a burst of machine-gun fire. Both men dived for cover. Flakes of whitewash, stone and sand spattered around them.

Revenge was short and swift : the offending machine-gun stuck out of a window two hundred and fifty yards away. Bursts from the Bren enabled the riflemen of the sub-section to cross the eighty yards of open ground. Then they covered the crossing of the Bren gun team; the second sub-section followed the same drill. The battery could not be far off; there was no reason now why there should not be a clear path ahead.

McDougall tried to recall as many details as possible from the photographs of the area he had seen back in Britain. There had been a wide anti-tank ditch forming the outer perimeter of the battery itself. Then there had been wire and a short distance inside the battery proper was an important landmark. On the photographs it had shown up as a white square. One of the briefing teams had told McDougall : 'That's a solid building, maybe sixty feet high, built of white stone. It's been used as an observation tower to control the battery guns.'

Those who gave briefings were traditionally born optimists; after all, they themselves didn't have to risk all the filth and the danger. McDougall remembered one insufferably confident soul saying: 'By the time you get there, the building will probably have been destroyed. You'll have to use the white rubble as a check.'

Of course, it did not turn out like that at all. As they sped round the corner, the enormous Scotsman stopped in his track. The tower was completely undamaged. In other circumstances, it might have been possible to admire this tall, white, gleaming structure soaring in the morning sunlight. But now it looked merely sinister. From McDougall's side it presented a completely blank face: no door, no windows.

Whatever the danger, the troops could not stand gaping. Now there was another Commando section moving in extended order among the bomb-craters towards the gun emplacements at the far end of the battery enclosure.

The sudden small-arms fire was bewildering: no one could determine just where it came from. Speed of movement was impossible: the ground was too churned. But the craters did have one advantage: they were useful shelters. Two loomed ahead; McDougall and others dived for this welcome if dirty haven, sent on their way by a hail of bullets. Glancing back, McDougall noticed a slit in the white structure – a machine-gun could certainly be poked through it.

Sandy-haired Commando McDermott, notorious for a belligerence matching his courage, swore long and loud but made sure that his hands were busy at the same time. Up came the Bren; the stream of fire zipped towards the tower.

Then the party moved off, but for McDermott it was his last gasp. Like a paralytic drunk, he staggered from his crater, the Bren dragging heavily in his left hand. From his right shoulder to his right leg he was a single splash of crimson.

He gasped: 'Take ma Bren an' gie us a rifle.'

Brens and riflemen kept up a steady stream of fire at the seemingly unassailable white tower. A machine-gun post outside the battery received the same attention.

D Troop remained a solid wall. It hurled itself at the various battery defences, opening fire on numerous machine-gun crews, taking prisoner those it did not manage to hit. The object was to leave the battery nothing that would hold up the landing of following troops on D-plus-2.

Eventually, it fell to the Commandos. Then it was on to the next objective – holding the bridges across the river Orne and the Caen canal.

When brigade headquarters and No 6 Commando touched down at 8.40 a.m. in the second wave of the Commando landing, Lieutenant Geoffrey 'Tug' Wilson, Section Commander of No 2 Troop, No 6 Commando, experienced no tightening of the stomach muscles. His approach to Sword beach was the most exhilarating experience of his life.

He recalls: 'We arrived in a mood of complete defiance, green bereted heads high. The landing craft had begun sailing line ahead, then suddenly they fanned out, quickened speed and belted for the beach. It was the nearest thing to an old-style cavalry charge and did marvels for the adrenalin.'

'The seamanship was superb. Ahead of the LCs were Teller mines: round mines lashed to tripods sticking out of the water. The sailors snaked around them, dodging them like contestants in an obstacle race.

The feeling of being on cloud nine might easily have been fatal for Wilson. He remembers rather shamefacedly: 'I was lining up the blokes for the landing in such exhilaration that when it came to landing myself I was the only one without a weapon – I'd left my rifle in the LC and had to dash back for it.'

Wilson carried a sixty-eight pound pack; he lost his balance and was dragged ashore by his batman.

On they raced through the heavy gun and mortar fire. The beaches were eventually cleared, then their task was to get up on to the high ground beyond the river Orne and hold it. Ahead of them loomed buildings gaunt and gutted among tangled wire and shell craters.

But before these were fields and a sign familiar to Commandos, a notice inscribed 'ACHTUNG MINEN'.

The advance paused. Then came a remarkable distraction : the swirling of Highland bagpipes and the sudden dramatic appearance of Lord Lovat, the brigade commander, bellowing : 'Call yourselves Commandos ! Follow me !'

Into the minefield he strode, throwing the offending notice to one side. The rest of the Commandos stormed after him, all fear cast aside. The aerial photographs of the field had shown ominous little bumps, but not a single mine exploded.

Neither did the sight and sound of falling oil bombs – ugly weapons which make a man into a human torch – deflect the Commandos in their headlong rush.

Now their way was barred by apron fencing. Tug Wilson says : 'I was instantly suspicious because I knew that this sort of fencing could be hitched to a mine. Take a pair of cutters to it and you'd blow yourself and everyone else to glory.'

Wilson's cogitations were shattered by a yell of rage from a purple-faced Derek Mills-Roberts wanting to know why the Commandos had suddenly stopped.

Wilson continues : 'It was a toss up which was worse, being blown up by Mills-Roberts or a hidden mine. Anyway, there wasn't time to think. I took the cutters, snipped the fence and we streamed through.'

A rendezvous for the Commandos had been fixed with 13/18th Hussars whose tanks, their main guns waving up and down as a prearranged signal of friendship, would guide the men forward. One man from No 6 would wave a Union Flag by way of identification.

Wilson relates : 'It was one of the strangest sights in Normandy that day – Sergeant Whittaker sporting a green beret and wearing a Union Jack like an apron.'

On the other side of a hedge the troops heard the roar and rumble of a tank. British or German? There it was turning towards them, until they were looking down the barrel of the main gun. Sergeant Whittaker waved the Union Flag and the gun dipped in welcome. Now the Commandos had a useful escort : with the protection of the tank, snipers would find picking them off that much more difficult.

Progress was fast. The Commandos sped, pausing only for the occasional check. A crossroads lay in front, and beyond it rows of houses – from which the Germans suddenly poured.

They dropped to the ground, steadied their machine-guns on the road and fired pointblank at the approaching troops; a lad from the Cameron Highlanders fell down dead next to Tug Wilson. Amid the chaos one section was told to stay behind and mop up the enemy. The rest of the Commandos advanced firing. Soon the survivors were past the houses.

Major Bill Coade, second-in-command, tossed Mills grenades at the slits of a German-held pillbox. There was a swift riposte from a stick bomb. It bounced off Coade's head, flinging him to the ground and temporarily blinding him.

The path was now through small fields and thick banked hedges (the *bocage*). The men of No 6 Commando ran the gauntlet of snipers and brushed past Colleville sur Orne-half way to their objective of the Orne river.

Gliders with airborne troops had grabbed two bridges over the Orne; the Commandos had the job of securing the hold. The two bridges – one known as Pegasus Bridge – were crucial targets. Whoever held the bridges could secure the high ground beyond and command the entire Orne valley.

The tiny villages of Le Plein and Bréville loomed ahead. Tug Wilson and some of his men nosed forward gingerly towards the market square of Le Plein. They were beaten back by a ferocious bout of machine-gun fire. Bréville proved equally intractable.

No 6 Commando now felt isolated. No 3 Commando had crossed the bridges but had stopped to watch the right flank. No 4 Commando still had some unfinished business at Ouistreham. It was decided to dig in and fortify a position in a farm orchard some four hundred yards from Bréville.

Entrenching tools and shovels were part of the tools of a Commando's trade, and every man started digging a defensive perimeter. They whistled at their work as they learnt that No 4 Commando was now ranged with them on the left.

Inside brigade headquarters all was suddenly consternation. Corporal Ken Phillott, one of the earliest Commando volunteers, who had been in that first Lofoten raid, was now in the intelligence section of headquarters staff.

He remembers : 'Lord Lovat had a map unfolded and was expounding on the situation. Suddenly, there was a crack. A bullet cut into the table. It had evidently been fired by the Germans on the high ground around Le Plein. It had hit one of the farm buildings and ricocheted through the window. We had a bad case of nerves.'

Lord Lovat was the first to recover. He stared thoughtfully at a grey horse grazing peacefully in a nearby field.

He said smilingly : 'D'you know, Phillott, I don't think that horse has had any water today.'

With that, he strode into the field, a somewhat outlandish figure in corduroys and white pullover, with the inevitable rifle slung across his shoulders. The horse was gravely led out to a nearby pond, watered, and returned.

Phillott explains : 'The place was crawling with German snipers. He could have been shot a dozen times. You could say Lovat was the sort of man in whom you had confidence.'

German troops had been spotted in Bréville wood. Derek Mills-Roberts decided that a few shells from the sea would soften up the target. HMS *Ramillies* fired six gigantic shells from her fifteen-inch guns; another twenty rounds of supporting fire were provided by HMS *Serapis*.

Revenge would not be long in coming; it was obvious the Germans would make every effort to locate the Commandos. The orchard became a fortress with round-the-clock patrols. Snipers had to be stopped, not because they killed men, but because they encouraged retaliatory fire which gave away positions.

Shortly after dawn, machine-gun fire peppered farm and orchard. The hills were hit by 20mm shells and casualties were inevitable.

Blood was up. A medium battery pummelled Bréville wood. Then the Commandos, thankfully released from the war of nerves within the orchard, hurled themselves at the enemy like men possessed. Four field guns, two 20mm guns and five machine-guns were carted off triumphantly as booty, along with fifteen prisoners. The action at Bréville wood had cost one Commando life.

Attack and counter-attack wore on; reinforcements were pinned down and Lovat raged at the delay in bringing them up. He turned his full fury on Durnford-Slater, now headquarters second-in-command.

On 12 June, Lord Lovat was severely wounded by a large shell. The fragments lashed his back and side.

As he lay covered with blood he ordered Mills-Roberts calmly: 'Take over the brigade and whatever happens – not a foot back.'

The 12th Parachute battalion was among those that went in for the final push on Bréville. The battalion was badly mauled. The obscene oil bombs took a terrible toll: comrades desperately rolled blankets around blazing victims. The village was secured eventually; the blood-letting in that area at least was at an end.

After the fight for Bréville, which cost the Parachute Battalion one hundred and forty-two casualties out of one hundred and sixty men, Commandos moved into the Orne line with 48 (RM) Commandos digging in at the fashionable seaside resort of Sallenelles, north of Le Plein and Bréville. Its eastward slopes ran to the river Dives. The position was held grimly for two months, while forces were harassed mercilessly by snipers and mortar fire. Then there was a swing to the east, gathering momentum as the German armies fell back. Caen, eight miles from the coast, took a month to fall.

With its dry official terseness, the intelligence report of 1st Special Service Brigade stated: 'Information along the whole front indicated that the enemy had started to withdraw and the prearranged pursuit was put into operation.

'The brigade advanced through Le Bois de Bavent avoiding all roads where trouble was likely to be encountered. No 4 Commando led the advance, clearing and marking the route through the woods for the remainder of the units to follow ... The enemy was obviously conducting a carefully planned withdrawal ...'

The brigade had been in the fight for eighty-three days without being rested; the order came that they were to slow down.

Ken Phillott found himself billeted with his fellow Commandos at a hospital at Beuzeville which had been hastily evacuated. He stated: 'We were so bloody tired we just crawled into bed. It was only much later that we noticed that the wastepaper baskets were stuffed with amputated limbs.'

Of the one hundred and forty-six officers and two thousand two hundred and fifty-two other ranks who had landed on Sword on D-Day, seventy-seven officers and eight hundred and ninety ranks became casualties. And that was only one of the beaches.

# 20

It was as if a heavy curse lay over the forces on Omaha beach. Shambles and sheer hell greeted the American forces.

The softening-up process by aerial bombardment failed to subdue the defences; batteries had been sited well. The battleships *Texas* and *Arkansas*, the French cruisers *George Leygues* and *Montcalm*, and HMS *Glasgow* poured their fire at targets between Port en Bessin and the river Vire.

But the enemy was in good form that day. Murderously accurate fire poured down on the first assault waves, pinning down troops on the shore, and much of the artillery was lost on the way in.

Small craft had stayed the course in the churning seas only because the GIs had baled them out with their steel helmets.

Twenty-two-year-old Louis Lisko, of 2nd Rangers Battalion, was aboard the *Ben Machree*, a troop transport.

He relates : 'The waves were five foot high and the landing craft to which we transferred bobbed all over the place. We were scared and seasick.'

About sixty feet from the beach the ramps were lowered and the men jumped waist-high into the water. Ahead of them loomed a rocky, one hundred-foot cliff, Pointe du Hoc, jutting into the Seine Bay in the eighteen-mile gap between Utah and Omaha. It was a cliff-top battery bristling with the powerful one hundred and fifty-five French-made guns with a range of twenty-five thousand yards. They were capable of dominating Omaha's western half and the sea approaches to it.

The Rangers had been instructed to destroy the guns at once. Lisko goes on : 'So deadly were they that no big ships could come in close, which is why we'd got into our landing craft a full fifteen miles out to sea.'

Each Ranger at this point went over in his mind the very thorough briefing received back in the *Ben Machree*: a thorough study of the maps, the clay model of the eighty-five to one hundred-foot high cliffs.

Three companies of the 2nd Battalion were to scale Pointe du Hoc. One company of the same unit would land elsewhere on Omaha and assault the enemy at Pointe de la Perçée.

In charge was another Ranger hero in the sterling mould of Bill Darby: tough, leathery Texan rancher Lieutenant-Colonel James Earl Rudder.

Ranger Captain Ralph E. Goranson of Libertyville, Illinois, led sixty-eight men across the sand for the special mission at Pointe de la Perçée. The guns sprayed: the bodies of thirty-nine men lay on the surf and on the beach. What malignant fate decreed that one man should die, another live? Ralph Goranson told another Ranger officer some time later: 'I found nine slugs and bullet holes in my gear and clothing. Yet I didn't get a scratch.'

First Lieutenant William D. Moody, of 2nd Rangers Battalion, was in the thick of it at Vierville, near Pointe de la Perçée. Moody and sixty-three others from C Company had come in with the first wave of the assault boats.

They streaked in a short distance west of Vierville, where sands narrowed and bluffs became rocky cliffs. A German anti-tank gun opened up. Two shells crashed into the water near Goranson. There were thirty-two men in the section; twelve were killed and several wounded. But the landing craft kept going.

The machine-guns sustained the barrage. Many men never left the landing craft as bullets streaked across the ramps. Swimming was impossible; the Rangers had to hold their rifles high and keep them from getting wet. To move fast was difficult, but those who crouched down in the water were easy targets and most were hit.

Limbs were weighed down with unspeakable weariness. Those who survived spoke of taking an age to reach the shore. In fact it was no more than a few minutes. But the time allowed had been one minute and the delay proved disastrous.

It scarcely took great marksmanship for the Germans to pick off the Rangers. The dark, olive-grey uniforms of the Americans made them distinctive targets.

William Moody kept going but it soon became obvious that the survivors of C Company were unable to scale the sheer wall of rock.

He seized the initiative. Urgently, he barked out orders to two men near him to find an alternative place to scale. Soon all three men, with their ropes and stakes, were picking their way to the west, hugging the cliffs.

Moody had no idea what he would find. But soon he had spotted a crevasse snaking its way up the whole length of the cliff. It looked like a miracle; but what was waiting?

He jammed his bayonet into a handy crack. As a lever, it left much to be desired, but this was no time to be particular. It seemed to hold. Then he and his companions were scrambling up the cliff face – and dodging anti-personnel mines.

Now the cliff receded sharply. That would have made life easier, had it not been for the mines.

On level ground, there was a new diversion: a burst of fire near Vierville, where the three men had to go to contact the rest of C Company waiting below.

Moody yelled down to Goranson and the other Rangers, telling them the best point to make the ascent. Goranson led his men to the scaling point and all those left alive from C Company reached the top.

They reached an area well fortified by the enemy. Ranger fire then pummelled the enemy trenches, knocking out the more menacing of the gun emplacements. William Moody, courageous trail blazer, fell to a German bullet.

Below at Pointe du Hoc, American bombers had dropped their loads minutes before the Rangers hit the beach.

Lieutenant George F. Kirchner of Baltimore stared at the cliffs soaring up and away. He admitted later he had a stab of panic and muttered: 'The whole thing is a terrible mistake. We'll never make it. We can't possibly come out alive.'

But now men of D, E and F Companies were on their way up, using rocket-fired rope ladders anchored to the top of the cliff by grappling hooks. It had been intended to use amphibious trucks fitted with London Fire Brigade extension ladders, but the trucks could not make it across the cratered beaches.

The enemy fired from positions along the cliff edge; the US destroyer *Satterlee* edged in to give close support fire, sweeping the top of the cliff.

Inevitably, ropes severed. With long, thin screams, climbers crashed to their deaths. Survivors picked themselves up and began the whole process again. Men died as their heads were split open by grenades.

The first men reached the top in under five minutes. The scene that confronted them was out of a Jules Verne fantasy, some isolated lifeless planet fractured by craters from bombs and the big shells of the *Texas*.

Sergeant Hayward A. Robey threw himself in the direction of a knot of Germans lobbing their lethal loads. He sprayed them with up to fifty rounds of fast fire.

Now it was time to sort out the guns. To their astonishment, the Rangers found only ruined gun emplacements; no guns had been installed. Later, a patrol, led by D Company's 1st Sergeant Leonard G. Lomell of New Jersey found the 155s cleverly camouflaged in an apple orchard. They had been trained on both Utah and Omaha beaches. The patrol swiftly immobilized them, saving many lives below.

The medics were attending the wounded. Fatalities had been high. Colonel Rudder radioed desperately: 'Located Pointe du Hoc – mission accomplished. Need ammunition and reinforcements. Many casualties.'

Two hours later came a brief message from the commander of 1st Division: 'Sorry, no reinforcements available. All Ranger forces have landed.'

For Rudder's Rangers it was total isolation. Ground forces were only three or four miles away, but obviously tied down in bitter fighting.

There remained the destroyers off shore. A signal was

flashed to the *Satterlee*. When radio contact was established, signaller Lou Lisko queried: 'What's your call sign?'

Back came the cheerful reply: 'Just call us Slugger.'

And for the next forty-eight hours slug was precisely what the *Satterlee* did. Lisko says: 'She fired on every target we designated and a few of her own.'

From Pointe du Hoc a succession of shells crashed in the direction of the *Satterlee* but the destroyer stood firm.

The two Rangers groups involved carried out their missions. The force which had found and destroyed the missing guns advanced beyond and cut the coastal highway. The other stayed to form a defensive perimeter near the fortified area of the point itself. The naval bombardment helped both groups. But the need for defence forces from Omaha was still desperate; on D+1 the Rangers were in defensive positions. Still giving trouble was a German machine-gun position on the left flank.

Men from F Company went in yet again; still the Germans held. Numbers were down severely and another attempt was thought too risky. A desperate message was sent to the destroyer.

American fighter bombers streaked in low, strafing the machine-gun nest in attack after attack. Suddenly, the Rangers realized that the aircraft were not stopping; their objective had long been obliterated but the fire went on.

The men stood up and waved their arms, helmets and field jackets in desperate appeal. Someone spread out the American flag on the torn earth. The leader of the squadron had previously reported that all Rangers had been wiped out. Now he peeled off smartly with the rest and headed back for the Channel.

Rudder's men fought on for survival against enemy attack until D+2. Now there was a fresh disaster. Ammunition had run low; the men turned to the German weapons they had captured. Advancing American forces heard the distinctive sound of enemy machine-guns and opened up with mortar fire on the beleagured Rangers.

A wounded Rudder, above the noise of the explosions and

the gunfire, yelled : 'Stop firing.'

But it was useless. Radio contact, impossible when it was most desperately needed, was only achieved after four men were killed and six wounded.

The 5th Ranger Battalion and the 116th Infantry eventually mopped up resistance and relieved the men of Pointe du Hoc. The Germans retreated west towards Grandcamp-les-Bains, where there was to be another bitter battle.

Out of two hundred and twenty-five Rangers who had scaled the cliff, only ninety were now able to bear arms. In the D-Day assault as a whole, the 2nd Ranger Battalion landed some four hundred and fifty men on the beaches of Normandy. Seventy-seven were killed in action; one hundred and fifty-eight wounded and thirty-eight missing.

Today, it is only the waters of the English Channel which attack this coastline of France. On top of the cliffs are acres of grass dotted with small white crosses marking the graves of the Americans who died there.

The ravages of war have not been erased from Pointe du Hoc. The scars of battle – the bomb craters, the barbed wire and the bunkers – remain. As a tribute to the memory of the Rangers, the local people gave three and a half acres of French soil to America.

There is also a large stone monument erected by the French in tribute. In the summer, an American flag furls proudly in the wind.

The first to land of No 4 Special Service Brigade was No 48 (RM) Commando, due to come in at St Aubin, between Juno and Sword beaches. The plan was for No 48 to begin the advance at the village of Langrune.

The men of the marines were impatient for action. They had taken part in the Sicily landings, then had been designated Commandos with volunteers bundled off to Achnacarry. Just four months after touching down in the Clyde, No 48 Commando was landing again – on D-Day.

The progress of its commanding officer, Lieutenant-Colonel James Moulton, seemed set fair for St Aubin. But his wooden landing craft fouled one of the German beach obstacles nicknamed 'Rommel's asparagus'. A wave caught the stern of the boat and swung it round. Then the enemy let fly with mortars and machine-guns from the esplanade, a bare one hundred yards away.

Other craft were in the same predicament; it was some time before the Canadians on Juno screened the approach of the Commandos with smoke bombs.

Earlier Colonel Moulton had been puzzled by a long black line he had spotted through his binoculars. He recounted: 'Now I saw what this black line on the beach was – the human debris of the assault: some dead, many wounded, some bewildered, some, like the stretcher bearers, with work to do.'

The mortar barrage went on; through it a squadron of tank landing craft made an untidy beaching, hampered by the vertical tree trunks of the asparagus and the stranded Commando craft.

Moulton later recalled individual vignettes of horror: one tank running over some wounded men in its path, relentlessly pursuing its squash of slaughter until an anti-tank grenade was deliberately flung at one of its tracks by Moulton's adjutant, Captain Daniel Flunder. Afterwards, Moulton saw French women looting some of the stores and with them young children staring without emotion at the shattered dead.

Elsewhere, the carefully laid plans for this section of the beach had gone horribly wrong. The Commandos had been promised a sizeable pre-H-Hour bombardment, so why the reception committee on landing? St Aubin itself had been in the forefront for punishment but the Germans had proved alarmingly efficient.

At St Aubin, the task was to move into the houses at speed, seeking snipers. It was vintage Commando work: the sort of thing Durnford-Slater had done with No 3 Commando at Vaagso. But here was fearsome opposition.

Two Centaur tanks of the Royal Marine Support Regiment were reassuring shadows for Moulton's men attempting to get into houses beyond a crossroads. Then there was the shattering explosion of a mine; one Centaur, its half-track lost, swung round drunkenly and blocked the road and the other spent its ammunition. In vain, the Commandos crouched under a ten-foot wall for protection; a bunch of stick grenades was tossed over it by the Germans.

Miraculously, some survived and made the house. But the enemy had prepared another surprise; death came through strategically placed anti-personnel mines.

The houses had become a challenge for Moulton. He secured armoured reinforcements. A hole could be blown in the wall and a tank catapult through like a tiger with a paper hoop. The only trouble was the Centaur blocking the road.

On the far side was on open field – but mined. Nevertheless, a Bangalore torpedo was not just for cutting barbed wire; exploded over a mine it became a thoroughly respectable detonator.

Commandos, under smoke cover, darted behind the Centaur and into the field. Moulton sweated as he watched them place the torpedo, gingerly test its position and run back.

The explosion cut a pathway through the minefield. One of the tank reinforcements went forward. Moulton tensed again : one piece of wrong navigation and the tank would be torn apart in an eruption which would probably kill everyone within range.

For a moment, there was silence, broken with a vengeance by the M10 tank trundling round and sending its high-velocity projectiles into the thick concrete of the wall. Then it returned the way it came and everyone held their breath yet again.

Moulton sighed with relief, then gave the instruction for X Troop and a headquarters working party to blow down what was left. They got busy with explosives and shovels; debris was shovelled into trenches and fire positions around the wall so that a tank could get past.

A Sherman ground its noisy way through the remains of the wall towards the village promenade now being raked with German fire. One of the tracks edged into a trench and was ripped off. Now the main buffer between Commandos and enemy had seemingly been removed. What would happen under that intense German bombardment?

The Sherman struggled like a wounded animal. Then with a tremendous effort, it lurched forward, tilting ominously to one side.

Would the delay be fatal? Had the German fire penetrated? But the Sherman was soon spitting anew. The Commandos were in and out of the houses on the way to the promenade like men possessed. Grey figures emerged with their hands up and were hastily searched for arms.

The progress east went on, increasing in speed as town after town welcomed its liberators. The Commandos now faced no more alarming missiles than bunches of flowers thrown by ecstatic women. The Commandos also noticed women who were less happy : they were paraded with shame and shorn heads as collaborators.

Progress, though, was not just a victory parade. Ridge positions at Sallenelles, east of the Caen canal, were held for two months. As well as the Germans there was another enemy; the nightly curse of mosquitos, notorious pests in this part of Normandy in the summer.

One part of the training at Achnacarry suddenly had special relevance : food was getting short and pack rations running out. The Commandos scavenged.

The activity of one patrol might have made even the robust Charlie Vaughan blink : it commandeered a cart and relieved a local farmer of some of his sheep.

The role of the Commandos had steadily changed since the days of the high-spirited raids at Vaagso and St Nazaire. Often now they were fighting as infantry, but there were still traces of the old panache and offensive methods which were a tribute to special élite forces. Individual courage was as marked as ever.

On the east of the Dives, a penetration to Varaville was vital.

Troops of No 4 Commando which included in its ranks French marines, found themselves at the junction of two important roads. At around 2.30 p.m. on 19 June, Lieutenant Ross Littlejohn of No 4 Commando and a sergeant from No 3 Troop of No 10 (Inter-Allied) Commando crawled up in front of the enemy lines looking for the best point through. All day the line proved too formidable. The two men lay in a ditch, watching the enemy not fifty yards away. Towards evening, they decided on another try. Littlejohn crawled ahead to the road. He paused and raised his head. He was looking straight down the muzzle of a German rifle.

The mouth of the Wehrmacht soldier dropped open in astonishment. Littlejohn was the first to recover. He lobbed a grenade and dashed back to the safety of a ditch. The German recovered and red-hot pain coursed through Littlejohn's leg from enemy fire, but he dragged himself agonisingly towards the ditch.

Then there was silence. The pain calmed down, only to return with interest when Littlejohn attempted to move. For an hour, he lay helpless. Then he heard a sound he had feared : a German search party beating through the lines. Littlejohn reflected ruefully that he could be picked off at leisure. A shot crashed from a few yards' range, but it missed. Soon there would be others : the best thing would be to feign death. In a few minutes, pretence would be unnecessary, anyway. But it was worth a try.

Then the search party was standing over him. First they took his pistol and ammunition. With a supreme effort, he tensed every facial muscle as a bayonet picked and prodded. He knew he could not keep up the act for much longer : the pain was rushing back. But he made no move and eventually the Germans moved off, leaving him for dead.

It was very far from being the end. There were no more search parties, only retreating German troops out for what they could get. They dragged him roughly out of the ditch; his boots, compass, watch and field glasses were snatched from his pain-wracked body. But still he did not move. And again they left him.

At least now, there was the balm of rest. He awoke with renewed strength and crawled back over two thousand yards to the Allied lines, where he was picked up exhausted.

Both Rommel and Rundstedt now knew that the battle

had been lost once the Allies gained a foothold. On D-Day itself, the Allies had, some seventeen hours after H-Hour, one hundred and thirty-two thousand seven hundred and fifteen men ashore, together with some six thousand tanks and guns with four thousand three hundred tons of ammunition.

Rundstedt, who had favoured counter-attack on enemy troops by holding up their movements, had miscalculated badly the weight of the Allies' attack. And pre-invasion tactics had cut off much of the intelligence on which Rommel's plan depended: to annihilate the enemy on the beaches proved impossible with the rapid build-up ashore of troops and armour.

The D-Day landings were the start of the final phases of World War Two.

# 21

The North Sea lashes hungry for destruction at vulnerable stretches of the Netherlands coast. There is one particular point where waters churn and boil in impotent fury, their progress checked by one of the world's most impressive man-made barriers.

Nearly five centuries ago, Dutch engineers built the vast Westkapelle dyke to protect the low-lying island of Walcheren in the estuary of the Scheldt from inundation by the sea. Down the generations, farmers were able to live secure in the knowledge that their rich land was safe from destruction.

Then in 1864, the great dyke was reconstructed. Enormous wooden piles were sunk deep into the shifting sands, and on the core of the dyke there emerged a wall of massive unmortared bricks of basalt. One of the engineering wonders of the Netherlands, it attracted hundreds of tourists who came also to see the pretty villages of Westkapelle and Zouteland, nestling at the foot of the sand hills that piled into the basalt barrier.

In 1940, came less welcome visitors. The Germans mounted batteries. They tunnelled and bore into the sand dunes. Their defences were provided by a ring of concrete and barbed wire snaking around the innumerable minefields.

The area had become one of the strongest bastions of Adolf Hitler's much vaunted 'Fortress Europe'.

Night after night, the flak batteries opened up; the island had become an arsenal hurling destruction at RAF bombers on their numerous strikes against the Ruhr. And German radar stations quested the skies.

The humiliation of being a vassal of Hitler was visited on the Dutch for four long years. Then in 1944, the armies of liberation burst upon Europe.

But there was no sun or cloudless sky to herald the new dawn. Instead, there was a clammy desolation around the dunes of Walcheren that terrible winter. The menace of sea and floods reached biblical proportions, adding to the general misery.

The owners of the neat little houses with red-tiled roofs looked out at a soggy mess of fields. Waters of dirty brown spelt ruin and a new bitterness. The tragedy was that not all the danger was directed at the conqueror, for the floods were deliberate: they were unleashed by the British.

In late 1944, attention was focused on Antwerp. The opening of this vital port had been delayed because of the thrust on Arnhem, but now it was seized by the 11th Armoured Division, romping in triumph from the Seine. For the British and American armies it was an invaluable supply base, particularly for fuel.

But there was a formidable stumbling-block. Antwerp lay some forty miles from the mouth of the river Scheldt. Both banks were held in a vice by the Germans. Antwerp was unusable until the enemy was removed and that meant immobilizing Walcheren.

In four years of occupation, the Germans had turned the island quite literally into a fortress. It was not just a question of batteries, although these were formidable enough. The island was ringed with beach obstacles and wire-protected infantry devices. There were mortar positions, infantry pillboxes, machine-gun posts and minefields.

The coastal batteries would make mince-meat of the advancing armies; the river banks had to be cleared of enemy. For Eisenhower, that was the first priority. And very soon it became the main concern of the special forces. Picked for the job was No 4 Special Service Brigade, comprising No 4 Commando, and No 10 (Inter-Allied) Commando, together with Nos 41, 47 and 48 Commandos of the Royal Marines.

On the night of 2–3 October, the RAF launched a raid at the Westkapelle dyke and blew a hole in it. A few weeks later, the dyke was bombed yet again. The bombers also switched to Flushing in the extreme south of the island and pulverized that as well.

The island had to be softened up for the proposed assault on 1 November. In poured the sea; the south and west of Walcheren were submerged. Elsewhere, too, there was sodden devastation. But the Westkapelle dyke escaped; the batteries there were well above flood level.

The plan was for No 4 Commando to land at 4.45 in the morning at Flushing. At 10.00 at Westkapelle would come Nos 41, 47 and 48 (RM) Commandos. The marines would have twenty-seven landing craft to give close fire support. Marshalled ashore was an armoury : guns, rockets and pom-poms. There would be one battleship and two monitors for naval support. From the air, the Commandos could count on heavy bombing and low-level attacks. There was artillery on the southern shore of the estuary to cover the assault at various stages.

All this far from eclipsed the role of the special forces. Eisenhower wanted the island cleared quickly; the lightning raid had come back into its own.

The men of No 4 Commando received the news of their mission with mixed feelings. Not because there was a new fight in prospect, but because of the company they would be keeping. The Marines again!

There was resentment. But to do No 4 Commando justice, it had no idea of the job ahead : an amphibious landing to outdo them all.

In Belgium, between den Haan and Ostende, No 4 Commando trained. But their training had a new dimension : there was big emphasis on street fighting. An area of Ostende was set aside and troop by troop, the Commandos scaled walls with toggle ropes and edged their way gingerly between houses in narrow streets.

Then came news of the target at Flushing and a swift move to Breskens, the jumping-off point.

In his landing craft, Captain Murdoch McDougall remembered thankfully that a landing assault craft was almost invisible from the shore at night; only the white of the water caused by the blunt bows was likely to give the game away. Fire from the shore was doubtless being aimed above normal deck level in an attempt to knock out the navy personnel handling the craft. But McDougall's men were low in the water: the 20mm cannon's red streak of tracer cracked a few feet above them.

The Commandos scrambled up the wet stonework of a slipway in the sea wall. Ahead of them had gone another section whose job had been to find a landing place, establish a foothold and give the all-clear signal. Tapes were laid for the follow-up party.

Traditional Commando speed was essential now. McDougall's men threaded their way through the dim streets. The job of No 4 Troop was to attack the German barracks of fortified houses which overlooked the river half a mile west of the landing beach.

The section streaked down an alleyway towards the houses. Beyond them was the back of a garage, close to the barracks. A hole in the back wall of the garage was hastily enlarged. One by one, the leading group of men swung into the darkness of the building. The men in front reached a door but the Germans were beside the wall. Fire raked the garage. Murdoch McDougall lunged at the hole in the thin garage wall and yelled: 'Back out this way!'

If his command had been obeyed, the Germans would have fired into the Commandos' retreating backs.

If Private Donkin had been fighting in World War One they would have called him an 'old sweat'. He was an ex-miner and a father of nine, a bloody-minded, unsentimental professional soldier. At the grand old age of forty-one he was something of an uncle figure to his fellows. In the last few minutes of his life he became a hero. There was little chance of his surviving: the odds were fifteen to one. But he thrust his legs apart, brought up his tommy gun and emptied bullet after bullet into the ranks of the Germans. From left to right the weapon swung. It was at the right of the arc, when one man on the left, as yet unharmed, got in a swift shot. The bullet crashed straight into Donkin's throat; he died instantly.

Sergeant-Major McVeigh came up behind and shot the German, pausing only a moment to make sure that his sweet revenge was complete. Then he darted back through the empty garage and back to the alleyway.

It was an achievement of sorts, but far too noisy. Now the rest of the Germans knew exactly where the Commandos were.

McDougall realized they would have to punch on in double quick time. Between them and the barracks was a knot of sheds and outhouses.

The men scrambled on to the wall, darting across the shed roofs. There were several rotten tiles. McDougall's legs crashed through them a couple of times. For a moment he was as helpless as an insect on flypaper, but struggled through, finally reaching the lane on the other side.

One section stormed through the basement of the barracks. The rest darted throughout the building. One man crept in the door, sending his boot crashing through the woodwork. Another stood behind him in the passage, giving cover. Prisoners were ushered out.

McVeigh edged cat-like down a passage curving to the left; on the right, McDougall shadowed him. Suddenly, from in front, both men heard a strange scratching sound which for the moment had them puzzled. Both sensed that round the curve in the passage something sinister was about to appear. McVeigh's nerves, normally of iron, were now stretched to screaming point with fear of the unknown: the strange primitive instinct in every man which no amount of vigorous training can wholly eliminate.

It was McVeigh who saw the point of a bayonet. The German behind it was still invisible.

For the German to use the gun to any effect, he would have to jump out into the middle of the passage and let fly from there. McDougall would be the first to take the fire, then it would be the turn of the sergeant-major. The bayonet was inching still further forward. McVeigh tensed, then he smashed the German's weapon, which was forced away from the wall. McVeigh leapt and fired. His ears ringing, Murdoch McDougall ran across; both men gazed down at the body of the German.

In the town, the enemy had long since recovered. Under the heavy German counter-barrage, the 4th King's Own Scottish Borderers went in. But by now, further landings were out of the question. The whole offensive was slowing down a little. The Commandos carried on. They repeated their assault on the various buildings. They fought street by street.

The enemy was now concentrated at a strongpoint beyond the barracks. This was going to be the toughest nut of all to crack. Then rocket-firing Typhoons came in with a roar. They dived on the enemy positions in one continuous destructive wave. The strongpoint was knocked out and badly frightened Germans emerged with a white flag.

No 2 Troop on the other flank was now mopping up the far end of the town with its docks and harbour. In the landing area it was suddenly revealed how lucky the Commandos had been when they beached. A formidable array of booby traps and mines was uncovered: No 4 Commando had dodged the lot.

The Commandos next day left Flushing and worked their way to Domburg on the north-west coast, stopping off at Zouteland, which lay further south-west. Then it was on to Vrouwenpolder, the last place in the hands of the enemy.

Eighteen Commandos fanned out with bayonets raised high and advanced on the farm buildings where the last of the opposition was refusing to give up. There was deadly silence. The Brens stuttered; again an awesome nothingness. Then a white flag was poked hesitantly from one of the buildings.

McDougall later wrote: 'From the end of the building there appeared two of the oldest and scruffiest Germans I had ever seen and, although the section waited expectantly, no more appeared.'

McVeigh's reaction was characteristic: ' 'Ave I just gone

through all I 'ave for them old goats?'

There was no doubt he had.

The garrison in Vrouwenpolder itself had surrendered thankfully. Here was a bigger haul: one hundred and forty prisoners in one afternoon. No 4 Commando's role in the battle of Walcheren was over. It eventually linked up with the Marine Commandos.

The seas were calm, the wind minimal, for the Marine Commandos' attack at Westkapelle.

They planned to land over three beaches: Tare Red, an eight hundred yard-stretch north of the gap; Tare White, a three hundred and eighty-yard gap and Tare Green, near the dunes. Each Commando deployment was to have its platoon of Royal Engineers for vital mine-clearing.

The knowledge that objectives would be softened up by an advance bombing attack usually did the Commandos nothing but good. The RAF had promised this time to lay on something special. Then came the blow: fog wreathed the airfields of England and the attack was called off. Still, Bomber Command had done its stuff already by breaching the dyke. The Marines would have to try a little harder on their own.

The craft took up assault formation. No 41 (RM) Commando was on the left, No 48 behind and No 47 on the right. Behind them were the tank landing craft, packed with rocket dischargers.

Lieutenant-Colonel Moulton of No 48 (RM) Commandos saw a key target, the radar station, ahead. Oerlikon guns from the tank landing craft and the Posten 20mm guns of the amphibious Buffaloes swept the station.

A shell burst near the CO, throwing sand into his face. It was almost like cold water, a real bracer. Moulton reflected how hardened he had become; in past scraps, the experience would have scared him.

Major Derek de Stacpoole was a desperately handsome Irish rugger player from County Meath. For all his brogue and blarney, he was a cool leader men would follow into just about anything. Now to his Y Troop fell the job of attacking battery W-13 standing in the way of the advance.

For some of the beaching Buffaloes there was disaster. One provided a macabre spectacle : it lay shattered, shelled and drifting, its engines roaring away like a wounded animal. The driver had died with his foot jammed on a pedal.

Y Troop failed to get through. Moonlight was bathing the dunes when Jim Moulton went to look for the body of his friend, de Stacpoole.

He wrote : 'He was propped, half erect in a shallow German trench; it looked as if he had been shot trying to get a look forward or perhaps leading an attack. Ten yards in front of him was a dead German in a rather similar position; possibly they had shot each other simultaneously.'

The bid for W-13 had a fresh impetus now. Captain Dan Flunder was sent out with A Troop to a spit of sand running into the floodwater, where the troop could give covering fire for an attack on the battery. Mortar was heavy and so were the casualties, until a long-range burst from A Troop put paid to the German 88mm gun crew.

Moulton had appealed for air support as well as artillery bombardment. He now got both. At 4 p.m., the cannons of the Spitfires were providing their own brand of menace. For good measure, they each unleashed a five hundred-pound bomb. The dunes shook. Sullenly orchestrating the noise of the bombs and the spit of the cannon were the Brens of A Troop and the two-inch mortars of X Troop.

Drifting sand had rendered a minefield harmless. Across it belted the Commandos. Lieutenant P. H. Allbut, RN, found himself staring straight into the eyes of a German across the wire. Both men cursed as they wrestled with weapons made useless by clogged sand. In desperation, Allbut flung the sub-machine gun at the head of the German, and saw his enemy fall dead from another Commando's bullet.

After further skirmishes in failing light, the Commandos' strength began to ebb. The amphibious craft had not withstood the endless batterings so rations had to be manhandled over dunes. But the Commandos only had food that could be carried easily : tins of self-heating soup, chocolate, sweets.

No 41 (RM) Commandos had beached amid the enemy inferno. The Marines, doughty veterans of Sicily, Salerno and Normandy, poured out into the dyke.

One of the landing craft was hit at the moment of beaching and one section officer was killed. The initiative was seized swiftly by Sergeant Leslie Musgrove. He advanced towards the first objective: a pillbox now spraying its machine-gun along the length of the dyke. Pausing only to throw grenades, he advanced with his sub-machine-gun. He took the pillbox single-handed, killing or capturing its ten occupants and establishing a firm foothold on the dyke.

Major Peter Wood, in charge of the first wave, speedily directed his men into positions covering the ruined village of Westkapelle and facing W-15 battery just to the north. The rest of the Commando, under Lieutenant-Colonel Eric Palmer, roared ashore; the landing craft had beached in the very throat of the gap. Into the ruined village they all swept, covered by machine-guns and mortarmen.

The Commandos thrust down the village street, picking their way through piles of rubble and the bare stumps of trees. Their objective was a tall lighthouse tower which the Germans were using as an observation post.

A strong force of German infantry waited; the Commandos delivered a swift riposte.

Sergeant-Major C. L. Stockell led a PIAT mortar team over bullet-swept ground to a flank to support the attack. He opened on the enemy position from a range of twenty yards. He was heavily engaged by bullet and grenade, keeping his PIAT in action until the assault troops overwhelmed the defence.

No 41 (RM) Commando followed up the dazzling success at Westkapelle by storming the little town of Domburg, further up the coast. A badly shaken enemy was driven from the battery.

The balance sheet at the end of D-Day was highly satisfactory: three out of four batteries were in British hands. A patrol had pursued flying Germans to the edge of thick woods north of Domburg.

On the second day of the Walcheren attack, the brigade had developed its bridgeheads along the dykes and dunes right into Zouteland, which was transformed into a carnival riot of colour as Commandos were cheered lustily by the freed Dutch. Early bitterness over the flooding seemed to have vanished; the general view was that it was infinitely preferable to the prolonged presence of the Germans.

At Zouteland, No 47 (RM) Commando took over the battle from No 48 and pushed on until they reached a broad anti-tank ditch and the outer ring of minefields covering W-11, the remaining battery.

Lieutenant-Colonel C. F. Phillips, DSO, planned a double attack. One thrust aimed to cross the anti-tank ditch and capture a German position at Klein Valkenisse in the low-lying ground; the other was directed along the crest of the sand dunes against the battery.

The first wave got across the ditch, but was badly mauled. The attack along the dunes was master-minded by Captain Dick Flower. He led his men for nearly a mile across soft, steep sand hills covered with thick belts of wire and minefields. Heavy machine-gun and mortar fire were their constant companions. Dick Flower walked among his men, urging them on with a casual disregard for the inferno.

The advance turned into a nightmare. A strong, cold wind blew, whipping up a blinding spray of sand – so soft and loose that it was like struggling through freshly fallen snow in the teeth of a fierce blizzard. But this was sand that clogged automatic weapons, grittted between teeth and blinded the eyes.

Within thirty yards of the first line of defences, Flower was wounded in arm and chest. Under close fire he rushed the first German weapon pit and killed the three men in it. But there were plenty of other Germans and they counter-attacked, driving Flower and his men back.

Every troop commander was wounded. It was proving impossible to break the battery. Ammunition among the forward troops was getting desperately short. Communications broke down: wireless sets were casualties along with the signallers.

The tired but far from dispirited Commandos faced the enemy again after midnight. There were calls from the Germans for surrender, a suggestion that was greeted with ribald laughter and a hail of fire.

Colonel Phillips asked for the fiercest possible concentration of artillery fire and the whole weight of massed artillery from Breskins opened up. The guns flashed across a broad estuary. The Commandos advanced to the final assault across the bare slopes of sand.

German fire was desperate and again the enemy succeeded in checking the attack. The reply was a bayonet charge. Up the steep sand slopes the Commandos sped, breaking into one of the positions. Then they went through the maze of communications trenches and underground passages, driving the enemy before them. Under fire from a trench and a concrete pillbox called 'the Umbrella', the German machine-gunners were blinded with a smoke grenade and the trench attacked. Defenders were killed and captured in plenty.

In face of this giant attack and dazed by the shelling – many of the prisoners were half-crazed, the pupils of their eyes dilated – the German resistance cracked at long last and surrendered in droves. The advance swept irresistably forward till the Commandos reached the edges of the second gap. At dusk, they saw on the other side the Green Berets of No 4 Commando, which had fought its way up from Flushing.

Heroism throughout the battle had frequently been sublime. No 47 (RM) Commando had landed when the shelling was at its height. But there had been tragic chaos : three of the landing craft had beached on the north instead of the south, and one that had beached correctly received a direct hit, losing ammunition and explosives.

Casualties were grim. When one marine was blown into the sea with a broken leg, Marine F. M. Lanyon, not the strongest of swimmers, dived to the rescue. He dragged the wounded man two hundred yards to the beach, collapsing with exhaustion and all but choking on sea-water.

When he came round, Lanyon found that he had been put to bed by Canadian medical personnel. This suited him not at all. Pausing briefly to express himself volubly on the humiliation, he walked out of the dressing station, clad only in a blanket. Soon he was back with his troop, preparing for yet another gruelling battery assault.

The cost of Walcheren had been cruelly high. Allied casualties in the operation were about seven thousand seven hundred, including two out of every five Commando troop officers and one in four of the support craft's crews.

Montgomery stated that it had all been necessary 'to devote the whole of our resources into getting Antwerp working at once, and I had to shut down on other offensive operations . . . until this object was achieved.'

And achieved it was, with a path now open to the Meuse and the Rhine along which the British could hold positions in the last months of the war.

Hitler had given instructions three years before that 'German troops will destroy to the last man all enemy troops taking part in so-called Commando operations in Europe or in Africa . . . Even should these creatures when discovered show their readiness to surrender, they are no no account to be shown the slightest mercy.'

Surrender was not now in the mind of the creatures; indeed, it seldom had been. The Green Berets, their courage on the loose, were hell bent on the Reich itself.

# 22

When the Allied advance had reached the river Seine, there seemed no reason why it should not go on and cut speedily through to the Rhine and the very heart of Germany.

As for 1st Commando Brigade and 6th Airborne Division, the plans were that they should quit Europe for further training and eventual fighting in the Far East.

Such arrangements failed to take account of Hitler's astonishing staying power and his determination on a last desperate gamble to annihilate the armies in Europe and recapture the initiative he had lost so disastrously.

Eisenhower's armies had found the going harder than they had at first imagined. Progress had been slow. On 24 October 1944, Aachen surrendered to the First Army after a costly battle. It was the first German city to fall into Allied hands.

The achievement was a magnificent boost to morale, but as yet there had been no breakthrough to the Rhine. In many cases, actions were a weary grinding down on the weakening German army, which was on the defensive.

Throughout the war a defensive posture had been anathema to Adolf Hitler. Now he conceived a bold and imaginative plan in the Ardennes. There would be a gigantic hammer blow. The US Third and First Armies would be split in two. Then the German forces would penetrate to Antwerp, tearing from Eisenhower his major port of supply. Then would come the end of British and Canadian armies along the Belgian–Dutch border. After that, it would be the turn of the Americans.

The attack was launched by the German army under von Rundstedt on 16 December 1944. Two Panzer armies were flung into the fray: the 5th Panzer Army under General Manteuffel and 6th SS Panzer Army under General Sepp Dietrich.

Tactically, the offensive achieved maximum surprise. The Allied commanders experienced a stab of worry; the new threat called for drastic rethinking. The drive to Germany must be speeded up.

First Commando Brigade under the fiery Mills-Roberts was recalled to England; under his command he now had Nos 3 and 6 Commandos and Nos 45 and 46 (RM) Commandos.

Battles between the Meuse and the Rhine were carried out in the iron grip of this last winter of World War Two.

The final rout at the Meuse was followed by a new assignment for the brigade: the capture of the city of Wesel on the Rhine, an important communications centre for the Germans.

Success depended first on a sustained bombing raid by Lancasters of the Royal Air Force. The relevant stretch of river was over three hundred yards wide with a stream running at five knots. There were flood banks in the form of dykes or bund which soared to a height of fifteen or twenty feet.

Knowledge of likely enemy strength was sparse; those initial air strikes were going to be vital. Mills-Roberts realized that the Commandos would have to enter the town literally on the heels of the RAF. This meant crossing the river before the bombing started, then forming up ready for the rush while the defenders were still punch drunk.

Frontal assault would be too dangerous. Surprise and speed – tempered with caution – were essential. But they would have to come from the least likely place. Planners hit on Grav Insel, a mud flat practically an island some four thousand yards west of Wesel.

There would be preliminary consolidation in a tight compact area and that would include seizing a large factory dominating the northern exits. The counter-attack threat would have to be tackled; only then could the town be cleared.

Another part of the plan was that 17th Airborne Division was to drop in an area north of the town at 1.00 a.m., move south and contact the brigade in the northern part of the town. The airborne drop would continue for three and a half hours, during which time there was a complete ban on all artillery fire.

On 20 March 1945, the brigade moved to its concentration area a few miles back from the west bank of the Rhine opposite Wesel.

Reconnaissance was carried out over the next three days. The weather was excellent; at 4 p.m. on 23 March the message came through that the operation would take place that night.

Each man, as he made the final preparations to his equipment, kept his ears cocked. Then came the distant drone of the Lancasters, which were advancing across a clear sky in steady procession. At 5.30 the first bombs crashed on Wesel. A pall of dust hung over the town. Then the fearsome artillery concentration began.

The Commandos gulped down the last scalding mugs of tea before they clambered into the big-track amphibian Buffaloes. The craft roared and bumped over the uneven ground to the river. Then under the bund which hid them from the enemy, they turned parallel to the river to draw up around Husenhof, a small hamlet.

On the far bank, about two miles below Wesel, the Germans crouched in narrow trenches and listened to the screech of the shells.

It was ten minutes before 10 p.m. that the entire mighty force of four field regiments of Royal Artillery – ninety-six 25-pounder guns – crashed down upon the strip of trenches directly opposite the Commandos.

The Buffaloes were on the move again now, roaring up over the bund, down the steep bank and ploughing across the smooth surface of the water.

Captain Barry Pierce, RM, was the first Marine Commando ashore. This was war, 1914 vintage. Pierce leapt into a knot of Germans. Grenade, tommy gun and bayonet – all did their work – in five minutes the German defences at this point were annihilated.

Captain J. D. Gibbon of B Troop leapt ashore and made inland. Sub-sections of Y Troop swept right and left down to the flanks of the bridgehead.

B Troop's left-hand Buffalo burst into flames as it nosed into the bank. Lieutenant W. J. Allan leapt from the inferno, gritting his teeth against the pain of appalling burns and wounds. He caught up with the rest of the troop and finished the battle. An artillery observation officer from the 1st Mountain Regiment with some of his signallers also fled the burning vehicle. The rest were killed.

While the brigade crossed into the bridgehead and formed up, the leading RAF Pathfinder flew low over Wesel, dropping brilliant red flares.

In came the second wave of Lancasters; then the advance began. No 6 Commando led the way out of the bridgehead, and the white tape which marked the route was unfurled. By now the moon was up and nearly full. The long line of figures filed across the flood plain. By midnight, the head of the column had reached the outskirts of the town, sped on its way by enemy mortar fire which was spasmodic and largely inaccurate.

Behind it came No 45 (RM) Commando, feeling its way through deserted, shattered streets towards a big factory on the far side of the town. Buildings were mere mounds of rubble. Craters were everywhere; into them flowed water mains and sewers. There was the sweet-sour odour of escaping gas.

The Germans were far from giving in. They emerged from cellars to carry on the struggle. The Commandos pushed grimly on through the backs of houses, not at all deflected by bullets and bombs from *Panzerfaust*, the German version of the bazooka.

There was the odd prize for the Commandos – like the German colonel who was received in captivity at brigade headquarters, which Mills-Roberts had established in a cellar lit with captured enemy candles.

The German turned to one of his captors, asking loftily: Do you mind carrying my bag for me?'

The reply was frosty: 'As a member of the master race, you can surely deal with something as small as *that*.'

In high embarrassment, the prisoner let himself be led away.

The men of 45 (RM) Commando pushed on towards the factory. A *Panzerfaust* tore into the arm of Lieutenant-Colonel Gray. He had to relinquish his command temporarily. But soon he was back, for the next forty-eight hours fighting not only Germans but also appalling pain.

The various sections of the brigade joined up, securing firmly the northern and north-western suburbs of the town. Weasel-tracked amphibians were able to cross the vast craters and arrive safely with medical stores and wireless equipment.

House-to-house engagements went on all night and the headquarters of the German Commander, Major-General Deutsch, were located. A No 6 Commando patrol made its way gingerly to the building. It looked empty, which immediately suggested to the patrol that it was nothing of the kind.

The Commandos edged towards the cellar, inviting anyone lurking there to surrender. The result was an immediate fusillade of fire. Deutsch's resistance was brave but futile; he died from a blast of tommy-gun fire. The entire staff was captured, plus its maps.

A communication link across the Rhine was vital so another patrol was detailed to lay a telephone line. A bridge was found that had been imperfectly blown. The Commandos swung from girder to girder several feet above the Rhine. An MG42 opened up and was studiously ignored. Then the dangerous task was completed.

Mills-Roberts and his staff took a look at the maps of the dead general. Here was treasure trove indeed! All the flak positions for miles around were marked: well worth knowing because of the forthcoming Airborne landings.

With mixed feelings the brigade watched the Dakotas come in. They were welcome, of course, but strict instructions had been given that during the para landings not a single gun was to be fired. That was all very well, but what would happen if there was a major German assault?

The next couple of hours were distinctly unpleasant. Two separate enemy forces of company strength formed up to the east of the factory, and enemy guns were moved up to a cool three hundred yards of the buildings. All the Commandos could do was marshal their fire power. And wait.

Eventually the orders came to fire. The enemy was beaten back but the counter-attacks went on for another twenty-four hours until the link up with the paras.

The Germans, robbed of their commander, could not hold on for long. The sappers threw their bridges across the Rhine – north Germany lay open.

War correspondents now streamed into Wesel in strength. Mills-Roberts zestfully gave them a graphic account of the action. So did many other Commandos with remarkable garrulity. After all, examination of the house of the late General Deutsch had unearthed a large barrel of particularly excellent hock.

Heads had to be cleared soon, though, and the dust of Wesel forgotton.

Osnabruck was cleared for just twelve casualties. But crossing the broad-flowing Weser to the town of Leese, young recruits from the 12th SS Training Battalion – Germany's manpower problem was getting desperate – greeted the Commandos with small arms, grenades and *Panzerfausts*.

Mills-Roberts commented: 'Many of them showed fanatical courage and their sniping was really first-class. Anyone who raised his head above the bank was shot, nearly always through the eye.'

By midnight on 8 April, 1st Commando Brigade, now under the command of 11th Armoured Division, was across the river.

White tape once again marked the route, but the brigade making its way across uneven country in Indian file found the going tough.

Leese was soon just ahead and the path looked suspiciously trouble-free. Then came the discovery of a flak position just as the brigade moved to the rear of the town.

Captain Peter Cruden rushed it head on. Four 20mm dual-purpose guns were seized with two officers. The rest of the crew fled into the darkness.

Now No 3 Commando was in its element. Here it was, back in the good days when every order held out the prospect of a decent scrap. This time the Commandos were ordered to exploit to the north and capture a large factory in the woods a mile from Leese.

In vintage raiding style, Captain John Alderson, MC, led his troops across the open ground, only to fall dead from the opening assault. The men were suddenly dangerously exposed; Lieutenant-Colonel Peter Bartholomew ignored the vicious barrage snaking round him. He clambered on to a tank, moving at top speed up to the threatened point, then he personally directed close-range fire.

Snipers attempted to pick off the rest of the Commandos; the wounded were hastily evacuated under their fire.

Elsewhere the enemy was now giving ground. The Commandos pressed on to the factory and into the running fire.

The objective was seized – and with it a major surprise. For this was no ordinary factory : it contained a long train of low bogie wagons standing in a railway siding. On each wagon was a distinctive shape : here was a veritable arsenal of the notorious V-2s. On one of them someone had scrawled in German : 'To England. Victory at any price.'

This was something British Intelligence had not bargained for; maps had merely shown a series of small huts. The Commandos surveying the scene had to admit that here was a masterpiece of camouflage. An observer from the air would have seen only fir trees and vegetation, beneath which were concrete-roofed buildings. The Commandos had grabbed the entire establishment of the V-2 factory. Prisoners included technicians and research staff.

It had been a better day's work than anyone had dreamed.

Even while the Germans were being cleared from the factory area beyond the Weser, Commandos kept up their headlong dash. The route now lay across the river Aller, with the same determined resistance waiting.

The Germans made a stand at the village of Essel and stuck to it like glue. Mills-Roberts, consulting the map, realized that even if the enemy was dislodged from Essel, the problem would only get bigger.

The route – the *only* route – was across the river. The Germans, unless he misjudged them badly, would blow the bridge. The river bank would then be defended. There would be a vexing delay in getting across to the next key objective of Lüneburg. Furthermore, there was a shortage of boats.

Something dramatic was obviously called for. But what? Mills-Roberts decided on a dangerous gamble.

Snaffling the sentries on the particular bridge almost certainly primed for demolition might be well nigh impossible. However, further downstream was something else. Another bridge. If that could be captured by night, the brigade could be ferried across before the Germans realized what had happened.

Mills-Roberts told other officers: 'An alert will destroy the whole plan. But this is a railway bridge. In my experience, people forget about railway bridges once trains have ceased to run on them.'

The divisional commander decided to stake everything on Mills-Roberts' hunch. Twelve assault boats mounted on Weasels were kept at the ready.

It was the job of No 3 Commando to lead off, paying out white tape towards the bridge. They reached it just before midnight. Mills-Roberts followed in their wake, a patrol ahead of him.

There seemed to be only dark and silence. The silence was shattered all at once by a gigantic explosion.

The noise of the blast was terrifying enough but it was followed by a series of metallic crashes as the main span of the large railway bridge bounced into the air and fell back in a crumpled mass. Mills-Roberts swore with variety and colour; his whole plan had literally been torn apart.

Or had it? Maps do not always tell the whole story. Certainly the bridge had spanned the river. But seemingly only part of it. The main strut had in fact covered a meadow. The river lay some way beyond. Mills-Roberts and his men could just see the water glimmering ahead of them in the darkness. Was there a chance after all?

The Commandos streaked across the soggy grass. Soon they could see looming out of the murk a second span. It was apparently undamaged. His good humour restored, Mills-Roberts flashed a signal to the rest of the brigade to double up fast across the water meadow.

But what about the inevitable defenders on the other side? A section of Commandos speeding ahead, their boots muffled by stockings, soon found out. Machine-guns opened up and five of the attackers dropped in the onslaught. On sped twenty-five gallant men. The river bank was gained. Two machine-gun posts at the end of the bridge were knocked out.

Behind them, the men of No 3 Commando stormed up a shattered pier and across the bridge. There remained the explosives, skilfully dismantled by the Royal Marine Engineers.

The gamble had paid off.

Beyond the bridge lay a heavily defended village. That was an irritation the Commandos could well do without. The bridgehead must be seized and the advance carried on.

Mills-Roberts was also determined to have the best of both worlds. The other road bridge, which had been the original cause of all the trouble, must be seized as well. It was a tall order. The appalling racket caused by the explosion on the railway bridge would surely have alerted the Germans. Two bridges seized in a short space of time! It seemed highly unlikely. Nevertheless, a patrol raced towards the original objective.

Opposition was formidable: a solid road block. No 3 Troop, commanded by Captain Ellis, was in the lead. The first section rushed the block, killing and capturing all its defenders. But there still remained the opposition on the bridge itself.

The enemy came crawling from the woods which lay ahead. For the next three hours there was a shooting match of unrelenting ferocity. The Mountain Regiment of Royal Artillery attracted deadly fire from a range of seventy yards.

Reinforcements were soon needed amid the white heat of battle. By mid-morning, No 6 Commando had moved into position with its Vickers machine-guns and was impatient for the assault. For half-an-hour, the Commandos made their contribution to the general hell.

For a time, it was impossible to gauge who was getting the worst of it. Then all at once the men of No 6 Commando swept forward in one gigantic, victorious heave.

In the words of the intelligence report issued when all was over: 'Just before 11.30 hours, the hunting horns sounded, and with cries that must have curdled the blood of the Germans, 6 Commando went forward through the trees at a fast double with bayonets fixed.'

For over four hundred yards they raced. Any enemy that remained was slaughtered; those who fled were gunned down.

The bridge, which the Germans had blown, could not be captured intact. It was secured by No 6 Troop.

More than fifty enemy dead and two wounded were later counted in the path of the assault. Two German officers and seventy-five men were captured. Of No 6 Commando, nine other ranks were killed, and four officers and twenty-two other ranks wounded.

It was a great breakthrough. The Germans were now completely off their balance and never recovered.

For 1st Commando Brigade there was just one more task: 'Operation Enterprise', the storming of the river Elbe.

By 19 April, 11th Armoured Division reached Lüneburg, where Montgomery ultimately took the German surrender. The Commandos came in its wake.

The plan was for the brigade to cross the river in two squadrons of Buffaloes about two miles downstream from Lauenburg, to the north of Lüneburg. The attack would follow a similar pattern to the assaults on the other rivers, but this time the weather would prevent an advanced air assault.

A hail of fire from 20mm flak guns and machine-guns

accompanied the Buffaloes as they dipped into the water at 2.00 a.m. on 29 April.

Number 1 Troop under Captain John Clapton, MC, and No 2 Troop under Peter Cruden landed first, branching out to the right and left. Bundles of grenades hurtled down on the narrow beach from the steep cliff.

But nothing could stop the Commandos now; they had caught the scent of victory. Within an hour, men of No 45 (RM) Commando were lining the edge of a sandpit a little to the north of the town. All the high ground was seized.

The main bridge over the Elbe-Trave canal was secured intact by No 6 Commando. All opposition was overcome by the last day of April.

All that remained in this last action was to clear the streets of Lauenburg.

# 23

Field Marshal Kesselring kept up a long and stubborn defence in Italy. By the dawn of 1945, the Allies had been kept at bay in a long year of frustration. But with the coming of spring even Kesselring had been forced into gradual reluctant retreat to the line of the Po river.

At the extreme left of the line, the Germans held a spit of land separating the shallow lagoon of Lake Comacchio from the Adriatic.

Along this desolate, uninviting spit, were dug in a bizarre group of adversaries: mostly Turkomans, Russians from Soviet Asia Minor and the 142 Fusilier Battalion of the 42nd Jäger Division.

The 2nd Commando Brigade, under Brigadier Ronnie Tod, was given the job of rooting out a total of one thousand two hundred men in four enveloping drives.

Up till now Commando raids had involved a swift move in by landing craft dodging ferocious fire from the defenders. But at Lake Comacchio, disaster faced the raiders even before they came to grips with the enemy.

Intelligence about the condition of the lake was sparse, its shallowness barely appreciated. When the craft were launched, there was insufficient water for the outboard motors to be started. Many ran into shallows. The Commandos slipped and sweated to get them over a mile of glutinous mud.

Belfast-born Gunner Bill Cochrane of No 9 Commando remembers: 'Our instructions were to cross the lake and clear the south-west of the spit. It was stressed that we had to hit the top of the lake at first light because the opposition was so strong that, given good visibility, it could completely wipe us out.

'Things started badly because the craft were sited too far from the lake. The noise they made could have been heard in France, let alone on the other side. To make things even more difficult, at first all the boats did was bury themselves in the mud.

'Instructions were given to disembark. In place of the landing craft we were given rubber dinghies and ordered to load in our equipment and shove them across that mud-bogged lake. By now it was daylight and the thing was a shambles.'

The Commando plan was for an amphibious attack across the lake against the inland side of the coastal spit by Nos 2 and 9 Commandos. The Marines of 43 (RM) Commando would first clear the tongue at the mouth of the lake, then thrust up the spit to the Valletta canal, which bounded it on the north.

No 40 (RM) Commando was to make a feint across the Reno to the south to cover the crossing by Nos 2 and 9, then join in clearing the narrow area between the lake and the east-west channel of the river.

Confusion with the landing craft hit both army Commando units badly. They became entangled with one another, weakening the effectiveness of their separate assignments for a time.

Worse was to come. Bomb-carrying Spitfires intended to give the Commandos close support opened up drastically short of the German positions. Bill Cochrane recalls ruefully: 'The force of one explosion shattered my tommy-gun, making it completely useless.'

There arose the inevitable question: should the entire operation be abandoned? But by now at least some of the boats had got afloat – why should all the effort and loss of life and materials be set at naught?

For Ronnie Tod there could be only one answer. Soon the orders to press on were being shouted from craft to craft. In the first flush of dawn, the Marines waited anxiously for the news that the army Commandos were well on their way across the lake.

Then the men of No 40 (RM) Commandos were flung into the fray. The right-hand troop was pinned to the ground by intense machine-gun fire. A reserve troop moved up in armoured carriers. But once again the Commandos were unlucky in their hardware. The vehicles sank into the soft sand. The advance now had to be on foot; the troop ran straight into the German machine-guns. The troop on the left was luckier and broke through.

The right wing regained its confidence, swiftly reorganized and went back into the terrible path of the enemy guns. Two fresh troops formed up to force a crossing at the mouth of the river. The Commandos straightaway began to fight their way south along the left bank.

Further upstream, the crossing had to be made under fire in portable assault boats. Once on the other side, the troop held a bridgehead in ground that was flat and exposed. Reinforcements were ferried across, the heavy fire killing half the small party operating the ferry.

The next objective was an infantry position among scrubby sand dunes containing two anti-tank guns; the automatic weapons had a perfect field of fire across the flat meads of the riverside.

The artillery put down a heavy concentration of high explosive and a prolonged smokescreen to blanket the position while the marines moved up. Then the storm of shells ceased and the full force of the attack broke through on the bewildered Germans. They surrendered in droves.

The army Commandos by this time had landed further up the spit. Casualties had been heavy, but two bridges had been captured across the first of the canals linking the lake to the sea. Then they turned south. The Germans were sandwiched between them and the Marines and those in the southern half of the spit were eliminated.

One by one, the strong points were falling like ripe plums. No 43 (RM) Commando had pressed north to Scaglioca, clearing it of enemy. Beyond the small town was bare ground stretching to the enemy defences of the Valletta canal.

C Troop, leading the advance across the open spaces, was pinned down as half a dozen MG42s opened up.

Into the field of fire charged Corporal Tom Hunter, his only challenge a solitary Bren which he fired from the hip.

His progress towards a cluster of houses was swift and sure. He ran between them, routing out the opposition, emptying round after round into knots of Germans.

As if scarcely able to believe that one man would sacrifice himself in such an adventure, the enemy was so stunned that it turned and fled.

But soon they were back again, turning their machine-guns on the courageous tormentor. Hunter crouched on a heap of rubble, keeping up a solid wall of fire, barely noticing that he was completely exposed. Now he was drawing all the fire away from the troop.

Inevitably, the machine-guns got him; the single unlucky bullet did its work instantaneously. Tom Hunter was posthumously awarded the Victoria Cross.

On 2 April 1945, the brigade consolidated its position four hundred yards south of the Valletta canal.

The Commandos had acquitted themselves well, despite the bad start. A large, useful tract of land had been seized. Sixteen officers and nine hundred and thirty ranks of Germans had been taken prisoner. Losses among the enemy were even higher than had at first been supposed: three battalions, two troops of artillery and a machine-gun company had been wiped out.

Four islands in the centre of Lake Comacchio were the next objective, a task entrusted to the Special Boat Service, which was to produce its own outstanding hero in the two-day action.

Major Anders (Andy) Lassen led three patrols on a diversion raid from one of the islands, Caldirolo. The object was to make the Germans think that large forces were moving against Comacchio, to the north-east of the lake, by landing on an embankment road some three thousand yards from the town.

A breeze ruffled gently through the reeds as the two patrols approached. They had not gone five hundred yards before the challenge rang out. The troop had expected it; an answer was given confidently in Italian that they were fishermen. Then they moved slowly towards where they guessed the challenge had come.

Andy Lassen was out in front, throwing a couple of grenades towards a pillbox and clearing out the four Germans there. From further up the road came more enemy fire. No one knew its strength; there had been no time for reconnaissance. But it seemed to the Commandos that there were at least two more strong points and a firing position away to the left of the road.

Despite heavy casualties, Lassen reorganized and pressed forward.

Again a grenade was flung. There came the call 'Kamerad!' Was it surrender? Lassen went forward to discover. The MG42s erupted.

Sergeant-Major Leslie Stephenson was with the badly wounded Lassen when he died gasping: 'Steve ... try and get the others out!'

This outstandingly brave Dane was awarded the Victoria Cross posthumously, the first foreigner in the Commandos to be so honoured. Despite his wounds, he had thrown three grenades, enabling his men to get clear of the road. His body was found next day by Italian partisans.

The next order for the brigade was to divert the attention of the enemy on to the east side of the Argenta gap through which the armies were to pass to victory.

The job went to No 40 (RM) Commando. It had to seize a road bridge crossing the canal north of Menate, a village through which the Menate canal entered Lake Comacchio in the west. Then a pumping station was the key objective.

Although the Commandos were no strangers to speed, it was stressed that seldom had fast movement been more important. To be caught in daylight would very likely prove fatal; the men would be strung out upon an exposed bank in this hideously depressing country which consisted of little else but flood water and marshy lake.

River crossings so far in this campaign had not been exactly happy. Now the men learnt that they would have to traverse the Reno in those scarcely ideal rubber dinghies. It was not an encouraging prospect and there was trouble right from the start.

The lorry carrying the boats was hopelessly bogged down for one and a half hours; a gap in the dyke had to be bridged by joining together the boats and the 2nd Field Company of the Royal Engineers was fully occupied with lifting scores of mines.

The delay was serious; now the only way of securing that vital bridge was by frontal assault. The enemy had to be prevented from blowing it. But how?

Then came a piece of luck. A Marine had been keeping up steady fire with his Bren, then a single bullet crashed through the wires which connected the demolition charges with the firing mechanism. Blowing the bridge was now impossible.

But all was not well. The enemy was still in business and the Commandos now faced a self-propelling gun and a machine-gun.

The job of crossing the canal belonged to X Troop. Would it be able to complete the job under that withering fire?

Spitfires, doing the job properly this time, came in with immaculate timing to launch a prearranged assault. The rest was all the fruits of years of Commando training. X Troop swung by joined toggle ropes cross the canal and swarmed on to the pumping station; the garrison was overwhelmed and the bridge remained intact.

An advance guard of the 2nd/5th Queens Regiment arrived. The heart of the Germans was no longer in the defence. In a state of panic and indecision, they surrendered.

In the battle, the Commandos had suffered severely in order to draw off German troops from the road to Argenta. By mid-April, No 9 Commando and the Guards Brigade had forced the passage of the Fossa Maxima, north-east of Argenta. By 21 April, No 2 Commando and No 43 (RM) Commando had driven the Germans from the area south-west of the town.

The successes in the mud and water flats around Argenta had been decisive. The battle of Lake Comacchio was one of the last great actions in Europe of the Commandos. Yet it had carried all the seeds of disaster. Provision of the right sort of transport and equipment had been niggardly. Not for the first time, the Commandos had worked wonders with the tools they had.

But by now they were veterans.

# 24

The once seemingly impregnable German war machine was being crushed beyond repair in Europe. And Italy, shorn of the bragging, strutting Duce, had long lost the will to continue the fight.

But, on the other side of the world, there remained another enemy of single-minded purpose, for whom the very prospect of defeat was the ultimate dishonour.

The peasant armies of Imperial Japan were still fuelled for combat. Here was a force whose standards of discipline would have made even the most fanatical Teuton blench: troops who never knew the meaning of leave and whose officers ensured constant obedience with brute force.

They were quite happy to subsist on rice and vegetables. They tortured their prisoners without scruple. And their idea of paradise was to kill British troops in enormous numbers – dying themselves in the process.

But fortune turned eventually on even the Japanese. For many, their war was to end amid the paddy fields and mangrove trees and endless acres of the Burmese jungle.

Their opponents were 3rd Commando Brigade under its deputy commander, Colonel Peter Young.

Commandos had fought the Germans amid the cold of Lofoten and Vaagso, under the summer sun of the D-Day beaches and in the merciless torrential rain in Greece. They had fought Quisling Norwegians and turncoat French, as well as German stormtroopers and Italian infantry. But little prepared them for the sweat of Burma and a new sort of enemy.

Warrant-Officer Henry Brown from Stockport of No 1 Commando, formed in March 1941 for forays into France, recalls : 'We were all equipped for conventional amphibious raiding, but this time there was a special sort of uncomfortable dry heat. Often we were stripped to the waist in temperatures of 104° in the shade.'

The scene of the battle was the Arakan, a stretch of jungle hills standing between the centre of Burma and the Bay of Bengal.

On 11 March 1944, the Commandos went in three flights from their assault landing craft, running straight into expert Japanese snipers among the mangrove trees. Then it was on to the thick jungle, fractured by the muddy, stinking waterways (*chaungs*).

The enemy was everywhere, fighting with an array of tricks which knew nothing of the accepted rules of warfare. Snipers were tied to tree tops. The wounded were dumped in a field, and unwary Commandos were lured to destruction by going to the help of their comrades. The Japanese would shout in English, make a noise in one direction and come in from another. A favourite trick was to use British radio wavelengths.

In one respect the Commandos had good cause to be flattered : the enemy soon picked up the old trick of shouting to give an impression that a force consisted of more men than there really were.

This strange sort of warfare dragged on for months until the capture of Akyab on the north-west coast. Then it was on to the peninsula of Myebon. On the morning of 12 January 1945, No 42 (RM) Commando landed, followed by No 5 Commando, which was soon under fire after it reached a small hill beyond a patch of thick jungle.

No 1 Commando and No 44 (RM) Commando which tried to follow the same route were less lucky. The tide did not wait and the landing craft touched down some four hundred yards short of the beach in sheer slime. To cover the distance took a gruelling three hours. Once again, intelligence had been less than accurate about the sort of terrain.

Henry Brown remembers : 'The rule on this occasion was "land and then dig-in". But the mangrove roots in the swamps were like rubber : nothing gripped and everything slipped off. And then there was the murderous thick grey mud. We dragged each other ashore.

Tanks were put ashore on the other side of the peninsula and temporary roads built.

An early attack on the retreating Japanese was planned. No 5 Commando went in supported by the tanks. Around Myebon, No 42 (RM) Commando dug out enemy on three small hills, and Colonel Kenneth Trevor's No 1 Commando, buttressed by No 44 (RM) Commando, snatched a whole succession of other hills.

Tank support produced its own dramas. A Sherman rumbled forward at high speed, suddenly growled to a halt on the steep hillside and turned turtle, rolling over countless times. But there was a miracle that day in the remote Burma jungle : the crew emerged unscathed.

The brigade moved on into Kantha, yet another village abandoned by the Japanese but still shadowed by persistent snipers. The Commando brigade's tally was four killed and thirty-eight wounded. This had been but the overture; the assault on Kangaw, the big adventure, was about to begin.

Kangaw, a small village and supply point, lay only eight miles from Myebon by the Myebon river, but Japanese artillery held it in a ring of steel. Surprise was obviously called for so the approach was made up the twenty-seven-mile length of the Thegyan river and Daingbon *chaung*.

The 54th Japanese Division was falling back along the road through Kangaw. Peter Young put it succinctly : 'The aim of the operation was to cut off and exterminate as many Japs as possible before they could reach the An Pass.'

The plan was for No 1 Commando to land at noon and capture the long narrow-wooded ridge known as Hill 170 which was one and a half miles inland from the river. The landing place would be protected by No 42 Commando, which would put down on both sides of the Daingbon *chaung*. No 5 Commando was to reinforce the defenders of Hill 170, while No 44 (RM) Commando formed up in the beach area. It would lead the advance on Kangaw next day.

At 4 p.m. on 21 January, Peter Young and his chief, Brigadier Campbell Hardy, crammed with No 1 Commando and an Indian Field Ambulance aboard HMS *Narbada*, the headquarters sloop. Commandos scorned even steerage comfort; they kept their spirits high with endless mugs of tea.

By 10 o'clock, they had embarked in their landing craft, winding their way up the river in an endless procession.

The honour of seizing Hill 170 was given to No 1 Commando, the most experienced in the entire brigade.

The importance of speed had been emphasized time and again in the operations of special services : never was it more important than in this theatre of war.

In the mangrove swamps between Hill 170 and the river, digging proper trenches was out of the question. The Commandos surged forward. Three men were killed and nine wounded.

Henry Brown relates : 'The hill was a stiff slope knotted with jungle trees. The Japanese shells were hitting the trees and deflecting. But by nightfall the Commandos were more or less dug in on the centre of the ridge.'

The Japanese were to the north of No 1 Commando, while No 5 Commando and brigade headquarters were to the south. Nos 42 and 44 (RM) Commandos were down on the flat ground and a ridge east of Hill 170 was secured.

A couple of tanks had somehow been mustered and were in support. To the right Henry Brown saw a naked Japanese running along on the ridge and suddenly throwing himself at one of the tanks.

The incident was an indelible snapshot to Brown, who relates : 'It was a neat dive rather as if he had been in a swimming pool. He obviously had a charge strapped to him because the whole thing went up.

'More came in waves, killing themselves with grenades to avoid capture and inflicting quite serious damage in the process.

'Lieutenant Cotton of No 42 went down to nab a sword from one of the bodies, but as he secured it the Japanese opened fire and wounded him in the legs.'

The assault continued. Another Japanese came forward with a box of ammunition. He planted it on the edge of a slit trench: it was nothing but another suicide bid and the defenders shot him dead.

Yet another broke through to a hut. Fighting with the occupants was hand to hand. The Japanese were not above scorning conventional arms and strangling their opponents; the Commandos replied in kind.

There was a fierce clash at midnight. The Japanese were beaten off, leaving behind nine dead. For No 1 Commando, the loss was one man killed and an officer and ten others wounded.

The 3-inch mortar of the Commandos were ready for the next attack. They were emptied into targets only forty yards ahead of them. And 25-pounders were knocking off the opposition only one hundred yards away.

It was a bizarre enemy the brigade faced. The Japanese were armed with large clumsy rifles with long French-style bayonets resembling spears. Hatred glowered from beneath mediaeval helmets. Peter Young wrote of 'revolting faces, two of them with glasses, and many with gold teeth'.

The noise of battle rolled all day and another chapter was written into the annals of Commando heroism.

On 1 February, Lieutenant George Knowland of the Royal Norfolk Regiment and No 1 Commando, was in the forefront of the glorious defence.

With twenty-four men, he squared up to at least three hundred Japanese. He darted from trench to trench, carrying ammunition to where it was most needed. Like a man possessed, he kept up rifle fire and tossed grenades. It was more than enough action for one man, even a member of a crack Commando outfit. But Knowland did much more. The crew of one of his Brens had been wiped out. He kept it in action, awaiting the arrival of a fresh crew. So that he could get a better field of fire, he straddled a trench, firing from the hip.

The new Bren team was wiped out before it could get anywhere near. Right in the thick of a fresh attack, Knowland kept the gun in action, firing not only the Bren, but a 2-inch mortar as well. Six Japanese were annihilated.

Inevitably, his ammunition ran out. But still Knowland

was in there, this time with a rifle .The enemy charged full at him. Now he had a tommy gun : from ten yards the Japanese took its spray full in their faces. Then a bullet struck him and he was killed. But the advance had slowed up by now; the Japanese fell to tough counter-attacks. George Knowland was posthumously awarded the VC.

No 1 Commando was not dislodged but it had to go on fighting frenziedly to maintain the advantage. Next, the Japanese placed machine-guns on the spurs of the ridge. They beat back three separate attacks launched by No 6 Troop of No 1 Commando, half of which was lost.

A troop from No 42 (RM) Commando added its weight. Twelve men were hit in succession at one Bren position covering the assault. But one tank was left. The Sherman, its periscope shot away, rumbled into the hell. Its shell crashed fifty yards ahead of No 4 Troop, which was now in a state of near exhaustion.

In the tropical twilight, Thunderbolt fighter-bombers streaked in on the Japanese positions.

The next day, there were only the dead of both sides awaiting No 5 Commando, which had the job of clearing the hill. It was a grisly tableau; three hundred and forty Japanese covered an area not much more than one hundred yards square.

The fatalistic Japanese may have been happy enough ultimately to embrace death, but they had been in no hurry to reach their Valhalla. They had fought literally to the last man and they had taken many brave Commandos with them : in cold statistics, five officers and forty other ranks. Six officers and eighty-four other ranks had been wounded.

The faith that had been pinned on No 1 Commando had been more than justified. It took some of the world's toughest troops to subdue an enemy whose bravery nobody would deny. But it had been courage of a fanatical, brutal blend.

Peter Young on the hill gazed respectfully at another sort of courage : the serene, smiling face of the dead George Knowland, lying where he had fallen.

Young wrote : 'Further down the hill twenty paces from our forward trenches, two of our men lay side by side as if they had together made a private counter-attack. I saw one soldier dead in his slit-trench with three Japs. They were dead, too.'

Immediately following the battle, a special order of the day was issued by Lieutenant-General Christison, commanding the 15th Indian Corps, of which the 3rd Commando Brigade formed part.

The brigade's reputation, it said, 'for indifference to personal danger, for ruthless pursuit in success and for resourceful determination in adversity' had inspired their comrades.

For the victories at Myebon and Kangaw, Brigadier Campbell Hardy won a second bar to his Distinguished Service Order, an award gained three times in just six months. Colonel Kenneth Trevor, of No 1 Commando, won the Distinguished Service Order. There were also three Military Crosses and a bar to the Military Cross, one Distinguished Conduct Medal, twelve Military medals, six mentions in despatches and, of course, the Victoria Cross for George Knowland.

The bloody action of Hill 170 marked the last battle for 3rd Commando Brigade. The enemy had been routed. Happy warriors to the last, the men of the brigade were happy enough at the prospect of carrying on the war in Malaya.

But, early in August, two mushroom clouds at Hiroshima and Nagasaki ushered in the nuclear age. The heroic achievements of the Commandos had suddenly passed into history.

# 25

The men who wore the green beret during World War Two fought in every major theatre. They swam ashore on secret missions against enemy-held Atlantic, Mediterranean and Pacific coasts. The special forces slogged it out amid the desolate mountains and high hidden valleys of Yugoslavia as allies of partisans. There were fierce engagements on the islands of Solta, Brac and Vis, where Commandos had aided the partisan leader Marshal Tito.

And there had been the laurels for the victors: eight Victoria Crosses; thirty-five Distinguished Service Orders; one hundred and sixty-two Military Crosses, thirty-two Distinguished Conduct Medals and two hundred and eighteen Military Medals.

In his book *March Past*, Lord Lovat points out that in five years a force of five thousand volunteers had been reduced by a quarter of that number. The average age of Commandos who fell in France was twenty-three.

But that last action by 3 Commando Brigade on Hill 170 by no means ended the saga. Certainly, Commandos began their demobilization almost as soon as hostilities had ceased. Soon, however, the Commando legend was been triumphantly reborn.

Not in the army, though. The Royal Marine Commandos alone were retained – along with all the skills that had made the special forces such a formidable proposition during the war.

It might vex the veteran army Commandos, but there was no denying the pedigree of the Royal Marines. The other special forces could trace their origins essentially to World War Two; but the Royal Marines dated back to

1664, when the Duke of York and Albany's Maritime Regiment of Foot was raised to serve aboard the warships of the Royal Navy. Their versatility had been demonstrated time without number; in the wars with France between the 1790s and 1815 they had served as gun crews, as landing and boarding parties, and as sharpshooters.

The war against Germany and Japan was barely a five-year memory before Commandos were back in the Far East. In May 1950, they were deployed in Malaya, with Brigadier Campbell Hardy, DSO, who had led the Brigade at Kangaw in 1945, again holding the reins. Three Commandos, 45, 42 and 45 RM, spent two sweaty years in Malayan jungle patrols. Six years later, they participated in the ill-fated Suez adventure. Nos 40 and 42 landed in the van of the assault on Port Said, while 45 blazed a spectacular trail as the first British unit to land in a battle area.

Commandos went ashore with all the old style, springing from their assault landing craft and tracked landing vehicles, seizing the initial bridgehead through which 45 swept in Whirlwinds and tiny Sycamore helicopters. That in itself meant a tremendous hazard for the individual Commando. The Sycamores carried three Commandos; the outside two had their legs over the side of the chopper and each man held a 106mm anti-tank shell. Near the beach was the headquarters of Brigadier Rex Madoc, a veteran of the battle of Crete who was now Brigade Commander. The Marines fanned out in a two-mile radius within the hostile streets of Port Said.

But the coiled spring was destined never to be released; the British and French governments bowed to political pressure and no further advance was allowed on Suez. The Brigade was promptly withdrawn. But there was plenty of other work for it.

There were tours in Cyprus, training in Malta and North Africa as part of NATO's southern flank force. Many of the engagements may have been thought small beer by the veterans, but a new generation of Commandos found itself faced with fresh lessons. The traditional pattern of assault was changing; the helicopter Commando Ship was coming into its own, often superseding the old landing craft both in speed and efficiency.

The main menace was in the Far East. The first Commandos to land in Aden were sent in April 1960 to join the British garrison and its infinitely larger Protectorate, an area half the size of France, but with a population of 800,000.

Countless counter-terrorist actions took place on the Yemeni border at Dhala and in the vast mountain wastes of the Radfan. The Brigade, based in Singapore from April 1961, was deployed in Borneo. The Indonesians were confronting the newly formed Federation of Malaysian States which included three territories in North Borneo.

It was no mere internal squabble; British lives were threatened. Rebels had seized a number of towns, including the Sultan's capital, and ones in neighbouring Sarawak (surrounding Brunei) and Sabah to the east. Captain Jeremy Moore (later Major General Jeremy Moore, OBE, MC and Bar) flew into Brunei, which Gurkha troops had already secured for the Sultan. That was eminently satisfactory; elsewhere matters were less happy. At Limbang in Sarawak, the rebels were holding British hostages. Furthermore, they were threatening to kill them within twenty-four hours.

It was not merely a question of storming the town, much though that might have appealed to Moore. Many of the houses were built on stilts over the river. As for the jungle swamps near the water, there was no way of crossing them other than by boat. The river, therefore, gave the only practical approach to the threatened hostages.

The crews of two Royal Navy minesweepers in Brunei fitted out a couple of river barges and sailed for Limbang. Moore was only too conscious that speed was essential. Some 159 armed rebels were believed to be in the town and they would have to be dealt with before the hostages, thought to be held in a police station, could be released.

The journey to Limbang proved a nightmare. The barges had been assembled hastily; not surprisingly there were breakdowns. Negotiating the sometimes frighteningly narrow waterways was an added hazard, but despite this the barges were within shouting distance of the police station not long after the street lights had been turned off.

The Company's Intelligence Sergeant shouted into the loudhailer: 'Lay down your arms.'

The result was predictable: a vicious blast from machine guns, rifles and shotguns. It soon became obvious that some *three hundred* rebels were involved and all of them joined in the scrap. The Commandos held fast; the initiative was with the Vickers machine gun.

Now the first barge was forcing its bow ashore near the police station, but two Marines fell under fire before the craft could hit the bank. A sergeant led two sections ashore; within minutes the police station was cleared.

The cox'n of the second craft, meanwhile, had been hit. The vessel drifted past the landing point but mercifully made it ashore near the hospital further upstream. Happily, the principal hostages were found to be unharmed. The rebels, however, were ill-advised enough to keep up their fire within the Marines' perimeter. All were killed, and by the next day the town was calm.

Eleven years after the end of World War Two, the Commando spirit was alive and well.

The natural descendants of the wartime Commandos who endured the iron cold of Spitzbergen and Vaagso are these days to be found near Narvik in northern Norway. It is here that a vital part of the training of units takes place each year. And it is here, on NATO's northern flank, that the Commando forces would play their main role in any future war. Right out in front would be the operational units of Nos 40, 42 and 45 Commando Groups, together making up 3 Commando Brigade. Impressive muscle, but it does not end there. There are also 29 Commando Regiment, Royal Artillery; 59 Independent Commando

Squadron, Royal Engineers; and a Territorial Army unit, 131 Independent Commando Squadron, RE.

British Commandos train and exercise regularly with two companies of the Royal Netherlands Marine Corps, known with rough affection as 'cloggies'. The combined force trains for three months of every year, from January to March, in atrocious weather conditions where temperatures can fall as low as –46°C (–51°F). To live in the snow means to follow a 'decreasing curve' of comfort from the comparative luxury of a ten-man tent, through the tent-sheet, to the tent hole. This is an environment where the phrase 'fight to survive, and survive to fight' has its own special meaning.

It is essential that men work in pairs, so that they can watch each other for frostbite. As one Commando has put it: 'It's no crime to be cold in the Arctic – but not to tell anyone most certainly is.'

The bulk of 3 Commando Brigade is an ever-ready outfit, poised for instant deployment to Norway. Although Marine Commandos have trained with Norwegians since World War Two, their equipment is infinitely different from those days in 1941 when John Durnford-Slater and Peter Young battled it out on the streets of South Vaagso.

Here on a typical country patrol men may ski fifteen miles a day carrying sixty-pound loads, sleeping at night in two-men snowholes. Although ski-patrols can fire on the move, their ski-sticks can help them perform a much more useful function: skis can be converted into bipods on which self-loading rifles can rest.

But Commandos in the 1980s need other trappings appropriate to the nuclear age. An enemy would very likely use such refinements as Soman nerve gases or other chemical agents sprayed from aircraft. To combat these, Commandos would be kitted out with heavy protective suits into whose fabric would be built carbon-absorbent granules.

And there are the respirators. Without them, vapours or droplets would cause the collapse of the nervous system. The first effect would be the blurring of vision. Co-ordination of movement would then become impossible; in ten minutes at most, breathing would be stifled. Without protective clothing, a single drop on the skin would have a deadly effect in half an hour. True, there would be the reassuring back-up of the load-carrying helicopters – the choppers – but some things remain constant in the diabolical climate of north Norway. Not least there are the 'white-outs' – snowstorms which make ground and sky indistinguishable.

Lesser men may be forgiven if their stomachs sink to their boots at the very prospect of warfare in such conditions. Yet in *The Royal Marines 1956–84* (Osprey, 1984) William Fowler points out: 'Marines with experience of the two extremes of Norway and Brunei say that they prefer the cold of the former: at least in the Arctic a man may get warm, while in the sauna bath atmosphere of the jungle there is almost no way to get cooler.'

Not that life is exactly cushy for the fledgling Commando back in England. Set on a hillside above the estuary of the Exe, looking towards Dartmoor, is the Commando Training Centre at Lympstone in Devon. Every Marine comes to know Lympstone well, both as a recruit and later when he returns to take courses necessary for promotion to corporal and sergeant. Veterans of World War Two may be forgiven for blinking when they learn what is on offer here: a modern well-designed building with a sports complex consisting of gym, squash courts and Olympic-sized swimming-pool, reckoned to be one of the best equipped in the country.

If any recruit is ill-advised enough to think that he has fetched up in some superior holiday camp, it is not long before he is disabused. As the recruiting literature warns: 'It's a tough course, one of the toughest in the world, and there is no place for the inadequate or the half-hearted.'

A normal infantryman gets basic training of eight weeks; the Marine course lasts thirty. In the first month, the recruit stays up until midnight ironing uniforms, polishing boots and getting the kit ready for morning inspection. At this point, the pressure is only just beginning. Ahead is a gruelling mixture of parade-ground drills, night exercises and weapon training.

Refinements include an eight-hour thirty-mile march across the worst of Dartmoor, carrying full kit and rifle. There is an assault course – known as 'the Tarzan course' – along and over suspended ropes, netting, towers and walls. For light relief there are mud runs through the glutinous silt of the Exe estuary.

Then there are the night patrols – about one night in four is spent out in the open on heathland above Lympstone or on Dartmoor – when the recruit sleeps for just a few hours and there is a volley of invective from a grim-faced corporal should he lose so much as a combat cap. Anyone with rosy ideas of life as a Commando would be well advised to look at the figures. Out of more than 5,000 applicants each year, only 500 are selected for the Lympstone course, and by the twenty-fourth week one third of those will have been rejected.

Commando training includes learning the essential techniques of entering a hostile environment by boat, helicopter or submarine and of operating there with little more than what can be carried on the back. Failure in any of the tests means taking the entire course again; success on the other hand brings that most cherished of rewards: the Commando's green beret in place of the recruit's black.

The greatest comfort for any recruit is that the Royal Marines are as near to a democracy as anyone can get: officers train alongside the men they will command. Shared experience gives an egalitarian atmosphere to the Marine barracks; sergeants frequently call their officers 'boss' rather than 'sir' and NCOs can be on first-name terms with their units.

The ultimate test of all this training and discipline came in the spring and summer of 1982. Britain went to war in the South Atlantic.

# 26

It was a masterpiece of understatement deserving an honoured place in any respectable book of quotations.

The voice had said tersely: 'I think you should know that there is a problem in the Falklands.'

It could scarcely have come as a surprise to Brigadier Julian Thompson, senior fighting commander of the Royal Marines with 3 Commando Brigade.

On 2 April 1982, the military junta in Buenos Aires had carried out its long-standing plan to seize the islands by military force – an action which had been pre-sold to the Argentine people as a mere reclamation of their property, the return to Argentina of the so-called Malvinas.

Men of the Argentine special forces, the Buzzo Tactico, had landed by helicopter near the islands' capital, Stanley, on East Falkland. From there they had pressed on to Moody Brook, the small garrison accommodation of Naval Party 8901, a 'rotated' garrison of Royal Marines of roughly Troop strength.

The Argentine forces built up eventually to Brigade dimensions; after several hours of fighting, the Falklands Governor, Rex Hunt, invoked the 1939 Emergency Powers naming him commander-in-chief in the event of hostilities. Civilian casualties in a fight to the finish among the houses of Stanley would have been appalling; the order went out to the vastly outnumbered Royal Marine garrison to surrender.

The Falklands became a powder-keg. The occupation of South Georgia, a windswept mountainous speck lying 800 miles to the south-east of the Falklands, had been bad enough. Now a wave of British fury surged against the

Argentines on release of photographs of tired, camouflage-smeared Marines being disarmed, searched and generally humiliated. That fury was to contribute in no small measure to the buoyant spirit of the Task Force in its epic voyage south.

Initially, Thompson's problem was the disposition of his three operational infantry units: 45 Commando was at its base in Scotland, 42 Commando had gone on leave after exercises in Norway and 40 Commando was training in north-west England.

There could be only one immediate feasible course: the 600 men of No 40 were moved back to Plymouth. The rest soon followed. For the first time since World War Two, British railway stations were flooded with posters and announcements recalling troops from leave. RM Poole in Dorset was put on standby. Appointments and schedules that a mere day before had seemed vital and immovable were cancelled out of hand.

In Whitehall, politicians and civil servants were wandering about like chickens with no heads. By contrast, back in the Falklands, Rex Hunt had come to terms with the situation. With elaborate British politeness, he had invited the commander of the Argentine forces, Admiral Busser, to leave the island. Busser declined with equal politeness – but not before pointing out that he had 2,800 men ashore and a back-up force of another 2,000 on the ships lying off the coast.

Hunt confided to his aides: 'It looks as if the buggers mean it.'

They did.

The bulk of 42 Commando, together with 40 Commando, a company of 45 Commando and 3 Parachute Brigade, embarked on 9 April aboard the liner *Canberra,* the 45,000-ton cruise vessel which, with her white paint-scheme, had been quickly re-christened the Great White Whale by the troops of the Task Force. The remainder of 45 Commando shipped aboard the Royal Fleet Auxiliary *Stromness* and the carrier *Hermes.*

If the untried conscripts of the Argentine army – the village boys and young men from the poorer quarters of the country – had been given any inkling of the calibre of the Commandos steaming south with the Task Force, they might well have refused to fight and thus averted their own tragedy. For aboard all three ships a rigorous training programme was instituted immediately. It was designed to bring the Marines to the peak of physical and mental preparedness. On the *Canberra* the troops exercised around the promenade deck, six circuits of which approximated to one mile, while lectures on the geography of the Falklands and the known capabilities and resources of the enemy were given daily.

Anyone who nursed the idea that all this was simply macho-building did not appreciate that a Commando at war in the 1980s would be carrying up to 120 pounds of equipment on his shoulders – personal equipment, rifle and ammunition and the firing post for a Franco-German-designed Milan anti-tank missile or launcher or one of the other support weapons.

There was no let-up in training even when the *Canberra* reached Ascension Island on 22 April. A string of firing ranges had already been constructed on the island; the Marines practised intensively for the two weeks they were there. This did not mean walking up to the ranges and simply firing. First came a helicopter drop at Wideaway airfield and a march – more often a run – to the ranges. In combat equipment, naturally.

May was ushered in by vast delta-winged Avro Vulcan bombers strafing the airfield at Port Stanley with the intention of damaging the runway just enough to inhibit Argentine air movements. Royal Navy Sea Harriers streaked from the two British carriers *Hermes* and *Invincible*. On 2 May, the Argentine cruiser *General Belgrano* was torpedoed and sunk by the submarine *Conqueror*. Two days later, the British destroyer *Sheffield*, 3,500 tons with her Sea Dart air defence missiles, was hit and mortally damaged by an AM39 Exocet missile.

Back in England, plans for reinforcing the Task Force grew apace; the liner *QE2* would become a troopship for 5 Infantry Brigade and the Gurkhas. As for the men of 3 Commando Brigade and 2 and 3 Para, they embarked at Ascension on the amphibious assault ships *Fearless* and *Intrepid*.

On 19 May came the day of decision for Task Force Commander Rear Admiral 'Sandy' Woodward: the main attack would go in at San Carlos, chosen because it was both sheltered and dominated by high ground, giving good positions for observation posts. To send the entire Brigade to San Carlos in the *Canberra* was unthinkable. The risk would have to be spread by dispersing units between the two ships. The weather was grim; it looked as if the only way to transfer the men to the vessels was one at a time by jackstay. It seemed almost ludicrously cumbersome, but helicopters could not be tied down to so lengthy an operation.

Miracles can happen, even in war. The weather changed, and the South Atlantic relapsed into a mild swell; the snail's-pace rate of transfer became unnecessary. The assault ships launched their giant LCUs (Landing Craft, Utility). From the *Canberra*, long files of arms-laden Marines moved through the liner's dining-rooms. Then they leapt heavily between ship and pitching and bumping landing craft. This in itself was perilous; one man missed, crashing into the sea between the liner and the LCU and smashing his pelvis. The huge, difficult cross-decking operation took till noon and then the landing force was at the ready. The order eventually went out to sail for a landing at San Carlos in the early hours of Friday, 21 May.

HMS *Plymouth* bombarded Argentine positions at Goose Green and there were diversionary attacks elsewhere. If the men of 40 Commando, flanked on their right by 2 Para, were aware of these, they did not deflect them from their own tasks. The job was to wade ashore from the landing craft across the gravel beach and head up to the hillside for the dig-in. It was a familiar special services role; all the Commando traditions and expertise had prepared them for it, as they had their forebears in enemy-occupied France, Norway and Greece barely two generations previously.

At first, it seemed something of an anti-climax and a relief. Of the enemy there seemed no sign at all; there were only Special Boat Squadron (SBS) Marines who stood around leisurely watching the landing craft draw closer and who gave directions for moving off the beach.

But this was just the lull before the storm.

Back went the landing craft to bring in the second wave – 45 Commando on the right of 2 Para in Ajax Bay and 3 Para on the left of 40 Commando on Fanning Head. Then came the back-up ironmongery; helicopters ferried in the 105mm guns, the Rapier anti-aircraft missiles. It was not before time. In swept a military Argentine Puccara ground attack aircraft, only removed from the scene by a pair of Mirage supersonic fighters after it had made a bid to fire at the *Canberra* and the *Broadsword*. The Puccara had been a one-plane advance party; soon there were more and they dived straight for the boats.

Recalled one Marine: 'We opened in a fury with everything we had. We pumped in Gimpys [General Purpose Machine Guns] to pistols and SLRs [rifles]. The result was total confusion because we were firing towards the ships and they were firing back, wondering what the hell was going on.' Rapier missiles were slow to close with the menace; at first only three hits were scored out of ten. Then the figures mounted; fourteen Argentine aircraft were removed in this particular engagement and there were six 'probables'.

As it turned out, the Argentines had delayed too long before sending in their first air strikes. The Task Force had been allowed to establish itself ashore; the Argentines had effectively lost the campaign.

Success was inevitably spelt out in blood. That Britain should lose the Falklands war was unthinkable; now it was brought home to television viewers and newspaper readers at home that if victory was to be achieved there was a price to pay. And it was heavy. On 21 May, HMS *Ardent* was sunk. Two days later, it was the turn of the *Antelope*, then of the *Coventry*, together with the *Atlantic Conveyor*. Other ships were damaged, including the *Broadsword* and the *Glasgow*.

The three Commando and two Para battalions, dug into the peaty soil, had established their beachhead. Now there was only boredom; they could do nothing but wait for reinforcements before beginning the long uncomfortable slog to Port Stanley. That had not been the original intention. Brigadier Thompson had wanted to leapfrog his units across East Falkland. The job would have been done by the heavy-lift Chinook helicopters, but these had been lost. Now there was a complete change in strategy. On 26–27 May, while 2 Para headed towards the epic battle at Goose Green, 42 and 45 Commando and 3 Para flexed their muscles for the long cross-country march to the other side of the island. The scene was set for the final act at Port Stanley itself.

The men of 45 Commando have their own special memories of that forced march, of hauling one hundred pounds of gear per man across treacherous rocks fractured by bogs, streams and ravines. It was terrain where leather boots were speedily soaked and the weight of the equipment appeared to treble. And there was the pain – the agony of turned ankles, sprained muscles. What these men bequeathed was not just their contribution to ultimate victory, but a hitherto strictly regional word to the general English language: the west country verb 'to yomp', beloved of headline writers depicting the epic march of Commandos manpacking all that equipment over the hills from the other side of East Falkland.

It was an excusable opportunity for some jingoistic purple prose back home, the most lurid examples of which later drew cynical smiles and caustic comments from the yompers themselves. For a decidedly irreverent assessment, one should perhaps turn to Colour Sergeant Bill Eades, who, surveying the grimed faces, the twisted ankles and the struggles of tired men, proclaimed: 'It looks to me more bloody like the retreat from Moscow.'

As for 42 Commando, Lieutenant-Colonel Nick Vaux was tasked with an attack on Mount Harriet, one of the Argentine defence positions in front of Stanley. A frontal assault was too dangerous; Vaux led K Company on a dangerously exposed march around the south of the hill, through an Argentine minefield which an earlier patrol had scouted and in which two Marines had lost their legs by detonating anti-personnel mines. Then K Company wheeled in an 180-degree turn to ram the Argentines from the rear. L Company remained in reserve to secure the position.

The vicious battle for Mount Harriet was fought without quarter. The steel power of the Marines slammed into the Argentine bunkers, devastating the enemy with 66mm and 84mm anti-tank missiles. Came the riposte and it was lethal: 0.50 calibre machine guns, 7.62mm assault rifles and a mix of 7.62mm and 0.45 calibre sub-machine guns. The din was terrifying, the crunch of explosions and the hammer of automatic weapons blending with the screams of the wounded and the dying and the hoarsely shouted orders of officers and NCOs.

But eventually Nick Vaux stood with his headquarters group surveying the abandoned Argentine weapons, clothing and supplies on the summit of Harriet. Marines and Paras herded away demoralized groups of prisoners. The air was fractured with the sound of helicopters shuttling wounded across the hill.

The yomping 45 Commando, assigned the capture of the ridge of Two Sisters, had penetrated the Argentine positions; cold, frightened but still defiant defenders had thrown down their arms. After Two Sisters was secure, the weary Marines had wrapped themselves in captured Argentine sleeping bags and ponchos to snatch blissful sleep in drifting snow.

By 14 June, the Argentines had been pushed back into Port Stanley itself; there was no further room to manoeuvre. The hills in front of the enemy were covered with the triumphant movement of British troops streaking towards them. With the ceasefire, Marines and Paras removed their steel helmets and replaced them with the proud berets of green and maroon. The Argentine surrender was graphically described in the House of Commons by the Prime Minister, Margaret Thatcher, at 22.32 on 14 June: 'Large numbers of Argentine soldiers threw down their weapons. They are reported to be flying white flags over Port Stanley.'

After their operation in the South Atlantic, the Commandos came home to a delirious reception as the *Canberra* docked in Southampton. There was a period of leave. But ahead lay plenty of work. A Marine detachment was destined for Diego Garcia, 3 Commando Brigade was earmarked for exercises in Norway and for operations in Northern Ireland. United Nations forces in Cyprus would be buttressed by 40 Commando.

The Royal Marine Commandos have been in action almost continuously since 1946. There is no reason to suppose that the need for their particular grit and resource will ever cease. Neither are the achievements of World War Two forgotten; practically every part of the world in which Commandos fought can jog the memory.

A plain squat structure in Amfreville, Normandy, pays tribute to 1st Commando Brigade; No. 6 Commando is remembered close by. At Flushing in Holland, No 4 Commando is commemorated by a magnificent figure of a grim-faced raider crouched for take-off. There is a Commando memorial in the cloisters of Westminster Abbey, and the Commando Association battle honours flag in green and gold and recording thirty-eight campaigns is laid up in St George's Chapel.

In a remote part of the Scottish Highlands, commanding the valley of the river Spean, Ben Nevis and the western end of the Great Glen, rises the Commando memorial – sited next to Achnacarry. With a backdrop of snow-capped mountains, its three stark figures stand for all time among the swirling mists. They are cast in bronze and set high on a single plinth. Yet glimpsed suddenly through a break in rain and reek they appear sharply lifelike.

Here are champion troops, poised in raiding order. Their gaze is towards the dawn.

# BIBLIOGRAPHY

Altieri, James, *The Spearheaders* (Bobbs-Merrill, 1960)
Bliven, Bruce Jnr., *The Story of D-Day* (Landmark Books, New York)
Clarke, Dudley, Brigadier, *Seven Assignments* (Jonathan Cape, 1948).
*Combined Operations: the official story of the Commandos* (Macmillan, 1943)
Cook, Graeme, *Commandos in Action* (Hart-Davis, MacGibbon, 1973)
Cowles, Virginia, *The Phantom Major* (Collins, 1958)
Devins, Joseph H. Jnr., *The Vaagso Raid* (Robert Hale, 1967)
Durnford-Slater, Brigadier, *Commando* (William Kimber, 1953)
Fowler, William, *The Royal Marines 1956–84* (Osprey, 1984)
Gilchrist, Donald, *Castle Commando* (Oliver and Boyd, 1960)
Howarth, David, *Dawn of D-Day* (Collins, 1959)
Ladd, James, *Commandos and Rangers of World War II* (Macdonald and Jane's, 1978)
Lovat, Lord, *March Past* (Weidenfeld & Nicolson, 1978)
McDougall, Murdoch C., *Swiftly They Struck* (Odhams, 1954)
Maguire, Eric, *Dieppe August 19* (Jonathan Cape, 1963)
Mason, David, *Raid on St Nazaire* (Macdonald, 1970)
Mason, David, *Salerno: Foothold in Europe* (Pan/Ballantine, 1971)
Mills-Roberts, Derek, Brigadier, *Clash by Night* (William Kimber, 1956)
Moulton, J. L., *Haste to the Battle* (Cassell, 1963)
Phillips, C. E. Lucas, *The Greatest Raid of All: St Nazaire 1942* (Heinemann, 1958)
Quarrie, Bruce, *The World's Elite Forces* (Octopus Books, 1985)
Robertson, Terence, *Dieppe: the Shame and the Glory* (Hutchinson, 1963)
Ryan, Cornelius, *The Longest Day* (Gollancz, 1960)
Saunders, Hilary St George, *The Green Beret* (Michael Joseph, 1949)
Swinson, Arthur, *Mountbatten* (Pan/Ballantine, 1971)
Young, Peter, Brigadier, *Storm from the Sea* (William Kimber, 1968)